LAN
AND

This fror
literacy i
ethnogra
sociolog
offers an
language

More th
interacti
sections:

- Bri
- Lan
- Wo

The aut
with ri
approac
yield fr
to more

Micha
College

David
at the (

Cheryl Hardy is Principal Lecturer and Head of Work-related Learning at Liverpool John Moores University, UK.

Kate Pahl is Senior Lecturer in Education at the Department of Educational Studies, University of Sheffield, UK.

Jennifer Rowsell is Associate Professor of Literacy Education and a Canada Research Chair in Multiliteracies at Brock University Canada

Brian Street is Prof ge, London
University, UK, and e School of
Education, University

LANGUAGE, ETHNOGRAPHY, AND EDUCATION

Bridging New Literacy Studies and Bourdieu

*Michael Grenfell, David Bloome, Cheryl Hardy,
Kate Pahl, Jennifer Rowsell, and Brian Street*

Routledge
Taylor & Francis Group

NEW YORK AND LONDON

First published 2012
by Routledge
711 Third Avenue, New York, NY 10017

Simultaneously published in the UK
by Routledge
2 Park Square, Milton Park, Abingdon, Oxon OX14 4RN

Routledge is an imprint of the Taylor & Francis Group, an informa business

Library of Congress Cataloging in Publication Data
Language, ethnography, and education : bridging new literacy studies and Bourdieu / Michael Grenfell ... [et al.].
    p. cm.
    1. Literacy–Social aspects. 2. Literacy–Research. 3. Language and education. 4. Educational sociology. 5. Ethnology. 6. Bourdieu, Pierre, 1930–2002.
    I. Grenfell, Michael, 1953–
    LC149.L235 2011   2011003273
    379.2´4–dc22

ISBN: 978-0-415-87248-5 (hbk)
ISBN: 978-0-415-87249-2 (pbk)
ISBN: 978-0-203-83605-7 (ebk)

Typeset in Bembo
by HWA Text and Data Management, London

CONTENTS

1 Introduction   1
MICHAEL GRENFELL

PART I
Bridging New Literacy Studies and Bourdieu – Principles   **5**

2 Classroom Ethnography   7
DAVID BLOOME

3 New Literacy Studies   27
BRIAN STREET

4 Bourdieu, Language, and Education   50
MICHAEL GRENFELL

PART II
Language, Ethnography, and Education –
Practical Studies   **71**

5 LETTER: Learning for Empowerment Through Training in
Ethnographic-style Research   73
BRIAN STREET

6 Seeing with a Different Eye   89
KATE PAHL

7 Artifactual English 110
JENNIFER ROWSELL

8 "All that Jazz": Classroom Reading as Intertextual Practice 132
DAVID BLOOME AND AYANNA BROWN

PART III
Working at the Intersections – In Theory and Practice 149

9 New Literacy Studies and Bourdieu: Working at the
Intersections of Theory and Practice 151
CHERYL HARDY

10 A Future Synthesis: Bourdieu, Ethnography, and
New Literacy Studies 174
MICHAEL GRENFELL

11 Conclusion 197
MICHAEL GRENFELL

Bibliography 202
Index 218

1

INTRODUCTION

MICHAEL GRENFELL

No one could deny the interest and attention that language in education has attracted in recent decades. That interest itself arose from a century wide preoccupation with language and the part it played in human systems of interaction and communication. But, the study of language in education has its own history and traditions. This history can, of course, be traced back for centuries well before the last one and would involve the philosophy of human thought. However, language in education as we currently know it has, however, only come about in the last fifty years or so, and is intimately bound up with the growth and development of research and scholarship over this period.

For the first half of the twentieth century, research in language and education was mostly characterised by a model which mirrored that of the physical sciences. Here, a psychological paradigm was dominant, and with it, a focus on psychometric testing, statistics, and a broadly positivistic approach to scientific enquiry. For language, structuralism was still influential, a tradition which looked for the meaning of language processes in the structure and form of language itself. The behaviourist perspectives emerging from the 1930s did nothing to attenuate the centrality of linguistic form as the established object of academic research. Education took a similar approach, and was preoccupied with intelligence tests and empirical methods of analysis to measure the psychological processes of learning. Theory formation itself was developed and tested in ways analogous to the normative sciences in search of the rules of human behaviour. However, all of that changed from the mid-century point.

Linguistics, the 'science' of language, was first rocked by the Chomskyan revolution, with its claim that language was an innate characteristic of the human brain, of a Language Acquisition Device (LAD), and consisting of 'deep' structural properties which generated speech. Differences between languages – individual 'tongues' – were simply the 'surface' phenomena of these structures. This discovery subsequently founded an entire new paradigm, one which studied the 'universal grammar' apparent in all languages. The core of such an approach was, however, no less analytical, with a focus on the predictable transformations of grammar in their universal forms. However, another perspective entirely was about to explode onto the scene, one which took an altogether different track.

In retrospect, it is easy to see how the 1960s represented an 'opening out' of human relations. The age of communications was born and, with it, easier access to other peoples and cultures, and a growing curiosity to raise horizons beyond conventional boundaries. These boundaries need to be understood as social, cultural, and psychological. In educational research, the new epistemological zeitgeist turned its back on the psychometric methods of the past, and instead adopted more so-called 'qualitative', approaches. Disciplines such as philosophy, sociology and history – as applied to education – challenged the established dominance of psychology. All of these fields encouraged more naturalistic approaches to the study of education and, increasingly, researchers became interested in the 'culture of classrooms' and the socio-historic factors impinging on the processes of teaching and learning. The discipline of language in education itself was born as a new focus within such a changing perspective: the speech event became a unit of analysis, as did the study of 'the rules of use without which the rules of grammar would be useless' (Hymes: 1972/67).

These are the roots of our book – language, ethnography, and education – and it seeks to bring the three traditions together in a new way. Of course, and from what is stated above, it is clear that language and education have existed side by side for some time; and also that ethnographic approaches, with their anthropological heritage, have long since been one option for researchers wishing to study education from a naturalistic perspective. From the 1970s, with the birth of the 'new' sociology of education (see Young, 1971), there developed a preoccupation with classroom discourse, the way it was constructed, and the individual and contextual factors at stake in the teaching/learning environment. And, borrowing from anthropologists, there grew up, side by side with this focus, a group of researchers intent on providing 'thick descriptions' of the cultures of learning they saw during their 'participant observations' of schools, classrooms, teachers and pupils. The key central focus of the book is, however, literacy.

Until the 1980s, literacy was seen mostly in instrumental terms; that is, as a prescribed set of skills, techniques, and know-how required to be 'literate'. However, one realisation emerging from the new socio-cultural mood was that such prescriptions were at best arbitrary, and at worst ideological. Street (one of the contributors to this volume) announced a major shift in our perceptions of literacy in work stemming from the 1980s (see 1984, for example) when he contrasted what he termed an 'autonomous' view of literacy, one which saw it in the kind of absolutionist terms described above, with a more 'socially constructivist' perspective. The latter version of literacy is more sensitive to the notion of a range of literacies possible in any one context – as many, in fact, as represented by those present in it. It probably goes without saying that the study of such literacy events from this more socio-culturally sensitive perspective necessarily involves naturalistic or ethnographic approaches to some extent. But, what exactly is ethnography, and what does it bring to literacy that other perspectives do not? This book sets out to answer these questions and to show the possibilities of an ethnographic understanding of literacy.

So-called 'New Literacy Studies' (NLS), themselves over twenty years old now, have evolved considerably from their early founding principles. Ethnography also has been somewhat eclipsed as the most popular research paradigm in educational studies by a new focus on school improvement and achievement, and therefore a preoccupation with evidence-based practice and impact. Both ethnographic and NLS researchers have consequently developed new tools and methods. Within the field of ethnography, the work of the French social theorist Pierre Bourdieu has become extremely influential in a range of disciplines. It is probably therefore no surprise if educational researchers working in a qualitative framework should embrace many of his ideas and concepts. Similarly, NLS and language in education research have increasingly made use of his methodology. This volume brings together these three traditions – literacy, ethnography, and Bourdieu – and takes the reader on a journey.

Part I of that journey is entitled 'Bridging New Literacy Studies and Bourdieu – Principles'. Here, the authors set out the building blocks for the book. This part is intended to provide basic theoretical parameters. It does this in a developmental narrative. Chapter 2 establishes the context of classroom ethnography. It shows conventional approaches and gives an account of its evolution over recent decades. Various theoretical perspectives are contrasted, and there is discussion of the principles of practice advocated by a range of practitioners. The idea here is for a standard history of ethnography in general and classroom ethnography in particular to be presented as a way of providing a contrastive base-line for what is to follow.

Chapter 3 then gives an account of New Literacy Studies – its history and current state of the art. This is an enormous field, but the core idea here is to indicate how NLS emerged and how its concerns and practice have developed over the past decades. A range of NLS issues are contrasted with conventional approaches to literacy and classroom ethnography.

Chapter 4 considers Bourdieu, language, and education. Bourdieu wrote extensively about education, language, and academic discourse. This chapter sets out what he had to say about each; and does so in terms of his own ethnographies. Key concepts are presented and their relevance to the themes under discussion addressed.

Part II, titled 'Language, Ethnography and Education – Practical Studies', includes a series of practical examples of NLS and Bourdieu used in ethnographic studies of language in educational settings. Individual contributors present, discuss and reflect on their use of these approaches in teaching, learning and teacher training contexts whilst highlighting a range of methodological issues.

Finally, Part III, 'Working at the Intersections – In Theory and Practice', offers a synthesis of Parts I and II from a theoretical and practical point of view. It also draws out a number of features concerning the use of classroom language ethnography incorporating NLS and Bourdieusian sociology.

Chapter 9 considers the practical examples in terms of the range of issues of theory and method. Questions of theory and practice are raised in terms of their inter-relationship in trans-cultural settings. The usefulness of both NLS and Bourdieu is addressed.

Finally, Chapter 10 extends and develops many of the questions and issues raised in the previous chapter in terms of a future practical research approach, and the principles and perspectives that might guide it. Issues of theory, methodology and policy are again salient in offering a framework for future research practice.

A book such as this can be read in various ways. Those well versed in NLS and Bourdieu may begin with Part II and the further exemplification to be found there of their applications in practice, and read out to the methodological synthesis of Part III. Those with mostly theoretical concerns might start with Part III and then consult Part II for examples exploring the perspective in practice. Whilst those wishing to extend their own language in education research in new directions will need to read through from Parts I to III in order to see the sequential development of theory and practice. Any one person's reading of the book will therefore be determined by their own particular background and intent; a principle which goes to the heart of the literacy event itself.

Of course, the literacy word itself has also developed a life of its own and, with it, a polysemic character; it is not uncommon to come across a whole battery of 'literacies' besides the original focus on reading and writing, for example, 'emotional literacy', 'media literacy', 'physical literacy', 'computer literacy', 'aesthetic literacy', 'cultural literacy', etc. The individual chapters in Part II touch on some of these literacies to a greater or lesser extent. However, our central concerns are both pedagogic and methodological. The authors of this volume believe that 'classroom language ethnography' is a new emerging field; one that is distinct from conventional approaches to literacy and education. It takes literacy in its broader sense and sets it within a socio-constructivist framework, and consequently takes an ethnographic approach to its study. However, that ethnography itself is informed by the principles of NLS, themselves extended within a Bourdieusian paradigm. What emerges is a genuinely new perspective. It is one with rich and developed traditions behind it, but is nevertheless quite new. By their synthesis, we believe a bridge can be built between those traditions, one that offers fresh and more fruitful insights on literacy in all its manifestations, therefore providing the foundations for a more robust science of language in education.

PART I

Bridging New Literacy Studies and Bourdieu – Principles

As stated in the Introduction to this book, the intention lying behind its conceptualization and realization has been to develop our thinking and research practice about literacy in the classroom. We also noted the way that, over the past 50 years of so, naturalistic approaches to literacy have superseded more traditional perspectives which saw it as little more than a let of technical skills. This book is about taking such naturalistic approaches to a next stage. In Chapter 2, we therefore show how ethnography is an important methodological practice in studying language in educational contexts. Ethnography itself has its own theory and practice, the principles and techniques of which are highlighted in this chapter. Chapter 3 follows this account by setting out the case for New Literacy Studies, its concerns, history and developments. Key texts and arguments are considered. Here, we begin to see what happens to the traditional view of literacy when it is regarded from a more qualitative, socio-cultural perspective. Chapter 4 offers an account of one particular socio-cultural theorist, Pierre Bourdieu. This chapter includes details of his own intellectual provenance by way of demonstrating the practical demands which necessitated the development of his conceptual tools. The suggestion is that language in education needs New Literacy Studies, and the latter in turn need Bourdieu – each as a way of extending thinking and providing a range of insights and understandings opened up by such a methodological advance. At this stage in the book our aim has been to offer a fairly bounded account of these three traditions – ethnography, NLS and Bourdieu – with little cross comparison or integration; as a way of providing theoretical and practical building blocks on which the rest of the book can be constructed. Part II will then show their elucidation in practical settings and research projects; whilst Part III will return to issues of theory and practice in developing the methodology of classroom language ethnographies.

2

CLASSROOM ETHNOGRAPHY[1]

DAVID BLOOME

Introduction

Classroom ethnography is a research practice for generating "thick descriptions" (cf., Geertz, 1973) of what is happening in a classroom with an emphasis on social and cultural processes. At its best, classroom ethnography contributes to reconceptualizing what a classroom is and what happens there: it illuminates a subset of a society's socialization and enculturation efforts; it articulates the relationship of dominant social, cultural, and linguistic groups to non-dominant groups; it generates new directions in curriculum and instruction that address long-standing inequities; and it challenges extant educational theories of learning and knowledge. This chapter addresses ethnography through a series of questions about the classroom, its participants, its language and its broader socio-political environment. Particular emphasis is given in this discussion to issues of literacy, particularly to the language experiences of non-dominant ethnic groups in North American schools.

Any individual's perspective and location influences how they see a history of classroom ethnography. From the current author's perspective – broadly speaking an educational one based in the United States – classroom ethnography emerged there in the 1960s and 1970s as researchers sought to use the insights, theories, and logics of inquiry from anthropology, sociolinguistics, and sociology to address the ethnic, racial, and linguistic diversity of classrooms and the corresponding inequality of educational achievement and outcomes (Hammersley,1990, provides a different history, briefly discussed later). In the United States, desegregation of schools and classrooms was promulgated as a consequence of court cases (e.g. *Brown v. Board of Education; King v. Ann Arbor; Lau v. Nichols*) which focused attention on the educational conditions and learning needs of students of color, native students, students who were not speakers of Standard English, and English language learners. At the same time, a broad range of social scientists began to challenge deficit theories of educational achievement that had posited lower intelligence, deficient cultural backgrounds, and impoverished language as explanations for the lower educational achievement of African-American, Latino, Native American and students from low-income backgrounds (for discussion of deficit theories and challenges to them see Valencia, 1997). Classroom ethnography was one way to generate alternatives to these deficit theories (e.g., Cazden, John, and Hymes, 1972; Trueba, 1994; Trueba et al., 1981).

Classroom ethnography provided an alternative to the then emerging paradigm of process-product studies (see Dunkin and Biddle, 1974). Process–product classroom studies identified either an input factor (such as teacher education) or a classroom factor (e.g., teacher questioning), quantified it, and then statistically related it to a classroom outcome (e.g., an achievement test scores). Although process–product studies were guided by cognitive theories of learning and social psychological theories concerned with motivation and other affective factors, their inherent design, their reductionism and their linear nature obscured cultural and social processes that are an integral part of classroom life. Classroom ethnographies provided a vehicle for capturing those cultural and social processes.

Classroom ethnographies also provided insights into cross-cultural issues and miscommunication issues in classrooms (discussed later in this chapter), and generated a series of curricular and pedagogical approaches (also discussed later). Educational researchers, interested in how teachers and students constructed learning opportunities in the classroom, used classroom ethnography to generate theoretical constructs about learning as a social and cultural process (building on cultural psychology, cultural historical activity theory, and related theories derived from the work of Vygotsky, 1987).

Although some educational researchers equate classroom ethnography, and ethnography more generally, with a set of methods, that definition of classroom ethnography is not taken up here. Rather, the focus is on the theoretical stance, logic of inquiry, and epistemological locations of classroom ethnography and not on the particular methods and techniques typically associated with it (e.g., participant observation, field notes, open-ended interviewing, long-term field-work, detailed descriptions). Classroom ethnography is not simply a method. The meaningfulness of any set of research methods and techniques must, after all, be derived from the principles in which they are embedded (see Zaharlick and Green, 1991).

Classroom ethnography can equally be viewed as a political stance concerned with the nature of what it is to be human and the role and nature of education in the production of personhood. Recounting his own history of involvement with classroom ethnography, Hammersley (1990) writes:

> Like many others at this time [the 1970s], I believed that the previous sociological work on education had failed for both theoretical and methodological reasons. Theoretically, it had placed too much emphasis on the social determination of human behavior and not enough on the ability of individuals and groups to

transform the social world. This not only misrepresented the nature of human social life but also served to preserve the political status quo.

(p. vii)

Hammersley goes on to note that, at the time, researchers took three different directions with classroom ethnography.

[First] collaborative work with teachers to help them put progressive educational ideas into practice ... Second, there were researchers who were concerned with bringing about radical educational and social change, and who became increasingly concerned to analyze the constraints placed upon teachers by wider social structures. Finally, there were those who were strongly influenced by symbolic interactionism, and who placed primary emphasis on exploring and documenting the world of school life largely for its own sake.

(1990: viii)

(Chapter 9 will readdress these directions in the light of Bourdieu's work).

Although much has changed since the 1970s, and although there have been other intellectual and philosophical influences on classroom ethnography (see Eisenhart, 2001), Hammersley's description of the political motivation behind the conduct of classroom ethnography and the three directions pursued are still valid. After discussing what makes a classroom ethnography "ethnographic," the rest of the chapter problematizes two key theoretical constructs refracted by classroom ethnography: the concept of the classroom itself, and language; and culture in the classroom. The chapter ends with a brief discussion of the nature of knowledge in classroom ethnographies. Throughout, there is recurrent discussion of the three approaches to classroom ethnography outlined by Hammersley.

Ethnography and the Classroom

At the core of our discussion of classroom ethnography is a definition of "ethnography" itself: a principled effort to describe the everyday, cultural life of a social group. Grounded in cultural, social, and psychological anthropology, ethnography seeks a holistic, cultural description of the multiple dimensions, aspects, domains, institutions, activities, practices, and settings of a social group. It seeks to understand what is happening, what it means, and its significance to the social group from an *emic* (native, insider) perspective rather than from an *etic* (external, outsider) perspective. Its focus is on what is learned, public, and shared (cf. Hammersley and Atkinson, 1983; Heath, 1982a; Heath and Street, 2008; Hymes, 1982; Spindler and Spindler, 1987b).

Given this definition of classroom ethnography (and by analogy to ethnography more generally), a distinction needs to be made between classroom ethnography and qualitative methods. The phrase "qualitative methods" refers to a broad category of research techniques that allow researchers to focus on the quality of human experience including interactions, thinking, emotions, imaginations, views, etc. of an individual or group within the contexts in which the experiences occurs. The use and interpretation of qualitative methods may also be influenced by phenomenological philosophies, theories associated with life history or naturalistic inquiry, grounded theory, or even positivist research perspectives. What distinguishes classroom ethnography from qualitative methods is: first, that the former is not a set of methods; and, second, that classroom ethnography builds on a set of epistemological principles from anthropology and sociology concerned with the cultural nature of social groups including an emphasis on seeking an *emic* perspective.

Ethnographers vary in the definitions of culture they bring to their studies, and such differences influence what is studied and how. The debate about how to define culture is long-standing and extensive (see Baldwin *et al.*, 2006; Kroeber and Kluckhorn, 1952). Among the dozens, if not hundreds, of definitions, culture has been defined as a set of traditions and rituals; particular human ecologies, a homeostasis of institutions and social structures that function to meet the basic needs of a social group; a set of themes that structure social life and its meanings; a set of shared and learned standards (expectations) for acting, feeling, believing, using language, and valuing; a set of shared and situated "models" of how the world works and how things mean; shared cultural models; a set of shared semiotic resources held not so much by individuals but in their social interactions, practices, institutions, art, law, and rituals. Street (1993) has argued that culture should be viewed as a verb (see also Heath and Street, 2008); it is what people do (the events and practices in which they engage) in making their social lives and in making meaning. But, whatever the definition of culture taken, for us, a classroom ethnography (indeed any ethnography) is derivative of the (explicit or implicit) definition(s) of culture driving its logics of inquiry, interpretive framework, and construction of meaning.

If taken literally, the term "classroom ethnography" is a misnomer because the extent of the object studied – a classroom – is not sufficiently broad to provide a holistic understanding of the "culture" of a social group, an ethnography of that group. Although a classroom may be "cultural," and although some educators and researchers do refer to a "classroom culture," classrooms are embedded in broader social groups and structures. Classrooms exist within schools, one institution among many within a community and the broader cultural contexts in which the people in a classroom participate. At its best, classroom ethnography acknowledges such embedding. For example, Foley (1994) describes how the community and school context in a small, south Texas town, at a particular time in American history in which issues in civil rights were fore-grounded, influenced the dynamics of the high school classrooms including race relations, class divisions and social status, the negotiation of student workload, grades, and the centrality of "making out" games: A "making out game is simply the way that workers collaborate with each other to make the work task easier, thereby achieving the same or higher pay rates for less work, or the same work in less time" (p. 112). The many classroom "making out games" which Foley describes, provide ways for the students and teachers to get through classroom lessons with more fun and entertainment, less strain and stress, and less confrontation and controversy while nonetheless looking like they are accomplishing the school agenda of differentially preparing students for the world of work or higher education.

Isolating a classroom and the people in a classroom from the broader social and cultural contexts in which they exist potentially distorts descriptions of what they do and what it means; narrows the dimensions of their personhood (shared understandings of what it means to be human); and makes opaque the power relations among various social institutions (e.g., the influence of the business community on what happens in schools and classrooms).

As a practical matter, it is often difficult for a researcher or a small research team to fully research a classroom and the school, community, and society in which it is embedded. Thus, a classroom ethnography can be viewed as a matter of foregrounding the classroom and back-grounding the broader contexts; but such do not and should not obviate the inherent relationship between a classroom and broader social and cultural contexts.

Furthermore, as a heuristic process for focusing on classrooms, it is important to make a distinction between *ethnography* and *ethnographic*. "Ethnographic" refers to the use of theoretical principles and logics of inquiry derived from ethnography grounded in social and cultural anthropology. Thus, although we may call a study a classroom ethnography, it is a classroom *ethnographic* study. When done well, a classroom ethnography not only seeks to understand what is happening in the classroom but also how the interactions of the people in the classroom both reflect and refract the multiple social and historical contexts in which they are embedded; in part, through their interactions with each other people construct definitions of what they do, what it means, and who they are while at the same time, the social and cultural contexts define and influence what they do and its meaningfulness.

As noted earlier, classroom ethnography is not simply a set of methods. A similar distinction also needs to be made between an ethnographic perspective and ethnographic tools. Ethnographic tools consist of participant observation, taking field notes, open-ended interviewing, the collection of artifacts, and other qualitative research techniques typically associated with an ethnography. Studies of classrooms may involve ethnographic tools but, in our view, if it does not employ an ethnographic perspective, it is not a classroom ethnography. It is simply a qualitative study. What is at stake here is not merely whether to define a classroom study in terms of its research tools, but rather whether the concept and practice of classroom ethnography is embedded within the debate between qualitative and quantitative educational research. In our view, that dualism does not apply to classroom ethnography. As many scholars have noted, ethnography may involve a broad range of research tools including tools associated with both qualitative and quantitative studies (Agar, 1980; Hammersley and Atkinson, 1983; Pelto and Pelto, 1978).

The Classroom and Ethnography

What is a classroom? What is in a classroom? Who is in a classroom? What happens in a classroom? For many educational researchers, these questions have obvious, if non-reflected answers. Based on their own experiences in classrooms or on widespread, mass media representations of classrooms, the questions above would seem easy to answer. A classroom is a room in a school, with desks, blackboards, books, and writing utensils, with a teacher and students who are engaged in the learning of academic knowledge. As such, the dimensions of classroom life are easy to frame as a series of moral dualisms: if what is happening in a classroom involves academic learning, then it is good, if not, then it is bad; if the people in a classroom are acting like teachers and students, then it is good, if not, then it is bad; if the classroom has the materials the teachers and students need for academic learning, it is good, if not, then it is bad; and, if the classroom is a defined space for teaching and learning separate from the rest of the world, it is good, if not, then it is bad. The work of the classroom researcher, like that of the teacher, is to increase the good and diminish the bad: diminish the behavior of children that is not consistent with being a student, increase their academic motivation and dispositions; diminish time off from academic tasks and increase academic engaged time; increase the presence and use of classroom supplies and materials that increase academic learning, diminish the presence and use of less effective ones.

However, for researchers taking an ethnographic perspective to the study of classrooms such answers and the moralistic dualisms implied will not do. To paraphrase Robinson (1987: 329):

> it will no longer do to think of [classrooms] as solitary places in which a mainly passive student responds to a teacher and acquires academic knowledge; it will no longer do to think of [classroom research] as leading to the mechanical manipulation of instruction leading to perfectible learning schemes; [classrooms] are not reducible to [sets of instructional components falling under discrete categories of effective or non-effective; rather, classrooms are locations of and constituted by] complex human activities taking place in complex human relationships.

Classroom ethnography involves the study of those complex human activities and relationships in their fullness. The answers to the questions posed at the head of this section often involve contradictions and complexities no less than those of people's everyday lives outside classrooms. They require the acknowledgment and exploration of multiple (and sometimes competing) social and historical contexts that are themselves constantly evolving and shifting. Indeed, one could argue that a goal of classroom ethnography is to problematize the concept of "classroom education" and its ancillary concepts including "learning," "knowledge," "achievement," "student," "instruction," etc. (see Bloome, 2003). This point also connects with Bourdieu's concern to be explicit about the "construction of the research object" discussed elsewhere in the book.

Classroom Ethnography and the Question "What is a Classroom?"

Spindler and Spindler (1987a) define education as "*calculated interventions* in the learning process" (p. 6) and make a distinction between education and the learning that occurs as an ongoing process of living everyday life. Another distinction is often made between formal education and informal education; the former referring to education occurring in social institutions such as schools where students are removed from the flow of the everyday life of the rest of the community in workplaces, families, government, religion, etc. Informal education referring to that education which occurs in the authentic doing of the practices of everyday life, such as occurs through internships. By definition, formal education requires classrooms, spaces apart from the rest of everyday life that are explicitly dedicated to calculated interventions in the learning process. As such, classrooms are not defined by their architecture (e.g., walls and doors) but by their separation and purpose.

Some scholars, including anthropologists (e.g., Goody, 1968) and psychologists (e.g., Olson, 1977) have linked classroom education and its separation with shifts in the nature of knowledge and knowing. They argue that classroom education is a response to and facilitator of the abstraction and decontextualization of knowledge (its separation from a specific place and situation and its potential application to other places and situations) and to the accumulation of knowledge beyond that which any one person could hold and then share. This accumulation of knowledge requires knowledge to be stored in schools and libraries and to be stored in written texts; and as such reading and literacy becomes the center piece of classroom education. It is a particular kind of reading, a reading focused on the acquisition of decontextualized skills and knowledge that can be applied to a broad range of extant and new situations. As such, knowledge and knowing can be described as linear, cumulative, and emphasizing abstraction and related higher order thinking skills. Olson has labeled such knowing and knowledge as "literate" thought (1977).

But, such characterizations of the essential nature of classroom education, reading, and knowledge have been challenged by other scholars, including anthropologists (e.g. Street, 1984, 1995) and psychologists (e.g., Scribner and Cole, 1979). They argue that although classrooms are separated from the rest of everyday life, that claims about the effect of separation on the inherent nature of knowledge, knowing, and reading, are not warranted by the empirical evidence. With or without schooling, people are capable of engaging in abstract thinking, learning to read in diverse ways, and can make use of a society's accumulation of knowledge across various social contexts. They argue that knowledge, knowing, and reading are not decontextualized skills but rather are intellectual practices often contextualized in a particular manner in schools in which emphasis is placed on the display of metalinguistic skills and on classroom-specific tasks (e.g. answering multiple choice test questions about a specific paragraph) (Street and Street, 1991). The application of the knowledge acquired in a classroom to situations outside the classroom is not viewed as a matter of the application of learned abstract knowledge and skills but rather is a matter of recontextualiztion (cf., Bernstein, 1990; van Leeuwen, 2008), adaptation (Banquedano-Lopez *et al.*, 2005), and improvisation (Becker, 2000; Erickson, 1982). The argument here is that although classrooms may be physically separated from the rest of everyday life; they are social and cultural spaces and are socially and culturally connected to the rest of everyday life; they are explicitly and implicitly charged with the acculturation of students to fit in with and contribute to the extant society, so that they can find an appropriate place within its social life and order.

From the perspective of classroom ethnography, what is at issue, then, in answering the question "What is a classroom?" is not a set of moral dualisms or the assumption of an inherent effect on knowledge and knowing, but rather the identification and the description of the social and cultural nature of the classroom and the functions, meanings, and import of the separation (and of the connections) between the classroom and the rest of everyday life. Such a description is historical since both the classroom itself and the separations and connections between the classroom and the rest of everyday life are not static but constantly evolving, and may even be the site of contesting groups and institutions.

Classroom Ethnography and the Question "Who And What Are In a Classroom?"

The most obvious answers to these two questions are: teachers and students, and, desks, chairs, blackboards, books, and other learning tools, respectively. Although these people and objects are indeed materially present in most traditionally conceived classrooms, from an ethnographic perspective answering the question is problematic, because of the variety of responses possible to the question – "What is a classroom?" When one further asks what does it mean to be "in" the classroom, "who" influenced "what" is in the classroom (and thus, these influencers have a presence although not physically so), and "who" and "what" are notably absent (such absences also have a material presence much like the space once held by a book removed from a shelf), there are further issues concerning conceptualizing this social space.

"Who" is materially present in a classroom is not an unmotivated[2] process. In classrooms in the US, who the students are in any classroom is a reflection of a history of race relations, immigration policies, economic class boundaries, gender politics, and debates about the social, cultural, and economic purposes of schooling (e.g. debates related to tracking). Although factors such as race, gender, and socio-economic status are referred to in non-ethnographic studies of classrooms, they are primarily noted for their potential statistical contribution to correlations between a set of classroom processes and outcomes (e.g. the statistical contribution of students' race to the effectiveness of a classroom discussion technique in raising test scores). Within a classroom ethnography, who the students are is not defined by demographic variables per se but by the meaningfulness and histories of their social identities (including their racial, ethnic, linguistic, gender, and economic identities) as they play out and have import in and through that classroom. For example, it will not do to merely label the students as "African-American"; rather, when done well a classroom ethnography will demonstrate what this means for students and the teacher in that classroom, and how that meaning has significance. For example, Heath (1983) in her study of Trackton (a small, rural, working-class African-American community) and the classroom education of its children provided an extensive history of the region and of the everyday life of the various communities in the region. Through that history and community background, and by comparison with the histories and backgrounds of nearby communities, she was able to illustrate the meaningfulness of race and class as cultural (and cross-cultural) processes with import in the classroom. Carter (2007) in her classroom ethnographic study of two African-American high school students in a classroom that was mostly white similarly provides a thick description of how race was played out in the classroom and its meaningfulness for the two students, for the white teacher and the other students. In brief, the two students found themselves isolated, while their historical experiences as African-American were ignored and their personhood undermined. Yet, such meanings and import were not articulated or visible in the classroom itself, except through subtle, non-verbal communication that the two young women used to support each other and build solidarity. Descriptions of how race was played out, its significance, and the meaning constructed, were different in studies by Heath and Carter, which emphasizes that, within a classroom ethnography, it is not enough simply to label students in terms of broad demographic variables as if the implication of such labels can be known a priori. At one level, while ethnographic descriptions may suggest similarities across classrooms at one level (e.g. in each classroom race was a meaningful issue and social maker), at other levels there were significant differences in how its meanings and their practical consequences were socially constructed.

Questions can also be asked about what it means to be *in* the classroom. For example, in many classrooms in the US, an intercom allows the principal to make announcements from a distant office and to talk with the teacher and students. Increasingly, nowadays, some classrooms provide computers as a means to connect to the internet and to interact with others. A teacher may give a lecture that is shown in multiple classrooms in different places and respond to questions from each of those classrooms, visible to all. Does the whole body have to be encompassed by the classroom walls or is it enough to have the voice or image there to be defined as "in" the classroom? Online classrooms provide similar challenges to traditional notions of what and who are in a classroom. "Who" – and their occupation – is in the classroom would seem to depend on how a person's presence in a space is defined, where and how the boundaries of the classroom are drawn, and on who gets to draw those boundaries – considered from an *emic* perspective. In other words, the classroom is equally defined by what and who.

Also, there needs to be consideration of who is *not* in the classroom. Perhaps the most significant factor is that there are no adults other than the teacher, and no children other than those from a particular, narrow age band. In many countries, the organization of classrooms by age (and grade) is ubiquitous, taken-for-granted, and never questioned. Such cohorting both reflects and constructs a system of meanings related to learning and achievement, social identity, definitions of growth and development, social relationships including competition and comparison, the relationship of the family to the state, etc. Questions can be asked similarly about the significance of classrooms that have neither rich children nor poor children, Black children or white children, children with special needs, etc. Each of these segmentations and separations is more than simply demographic, but it is an enacted history that is intentional. Although it can be difficult to trace the people who originated such policies, decisions are constantly made by school officials and politically motivated agencies to maintain the original decisions. Such continued support and maintenance are no less intentional than the original decision. Thus, in response to the question, "Who is in a classroom?" part of the answer involves the people who made (or maintained) decisions about who is not there. They are also "gatekeepers."

Asking of "who" and "what" are not in the classroom can involve naturalized[3] absences: so taken for granted that they are not even missed. For example, in a classroom ethnography of an urban fifth grade classroom in the US, Morris (2003) asks about the absence of "Africa" in "African-American." In this classroom, the students were studying sub-Sahara Africa – its geography, cultures, economies, histories, etc. Approximately, two-thirds of the students in the classroom were African-American. Morris notes than nowhere in their study of Africa was a connection made between Africa and the African-American students themselves. Nor did the teacher or the students explicitly make the connection. They may have all assumed it, but it was not made public nor a part of what they were studying. Indeed, during a classroom activity in which the teacher invited a student from another classroom who was from Nigeria to join their classroom, the discussion among the students focused on the differences between themselves as Americans and the Nigerian girl as African with no indication that the African-American students recognized a historical connection to Africa. Morris contextualizes the absence by noting the complex, historical relationship between African-Americans and Africa and how the latter has been represented in American mass media (e.g. Tarzan movies) as well as the history of European colonialism in Africa and the slave trade. What is at issue is the naturalized absence of this socio-political history, and of the historical connections between the African-American students and the Nigerian student, and with the study of sub-Saharan Africa. Within a classroom ethnography, it is not only important to identify and describe naturalized absences, but to inquire about the meaning and significance of such absences in that classroom. Such inquiry, although grounded in an *emic* perspective, does not remain within a single layer of context (e.g. the enactment of the instructional activities of the classroom) but extends across contexts both historically and in scope (e.g. the relationship of the classroom to the students' overall schooling, to the local community, to the broader African-American community, to the nation-state, etc.). The key question for study here is whether personal dilemmas, contradictions, and conflicts are seen as *emic* or *etic*; that is, historic or ahistoric, separate from socio-cultural contexts or embedded and defined within them. And, what language can we use to describe such a study?

Decisions are also made about *what* is or is not in a classroom. For example, let us use the seemingly mundane issue of decisions about desks and chairs. Although this is often a hot topic among teachers, for almost everyone else, it appears to have little significance. Classrooms have desks and chairs, the inquiry goes no further. Yet, some teachers can get quite upset when they find that their classroom has individual desks and chairs rather than work tables and chairs. What is at issue is not the practicalities of using desks versus tables but rather what the furniture says about the instructional philosophy held by the teacher and the classroom; tables and chairs suggest more group work, cooperative learning, active student engagement in project-based learning, and a sense of community. Although individual desks and chairs can be arranged in circles or grouped together similarly to tables, to some teachers they still suggest an instructional philosophy of individual work and learning. At another level, whether the furniture is desks and chairs or tables, there is a nearly invisible issue concerned with the discipline of student bodies. Both desks and tables mean sitting often for long hours without break. Students may squirm and slouch in their chairs and occasionally teachers may give students a "break" and let them stretch or send them out to recess. Students' readiness for learning may be, in part, determined by their ability to sit for long periods of time; and student attitudes toward schooling may be inferred by teachers based on how they sit, how they discipline their bodies. The significance of furniture is therefore in how it can actually shape both teacher and classroom identities, and influence the process of learning itself.

Johnson (1980) has argued that "environments [what is in the classroom, its material culture] are not passive wrappings, but active mechanisms for socialization and enculturation" (p. 174). He goes on to argue that the material culture of the classrooms across grades in a public elementary school he studied in the United States were oriented toward national society and culture. What is at stake in Johnson's argument is not whether a specific set of classrooms are oriented to national society and culture versus local society and culture, but rather that the material culture of the classroom suggests the symbolic integration of individual local classrooms into national schools and societies. Part of what is at stake here is that although each classroom is organized locally by who is there and what is in the classroom, they are often influenced in ways that connect with other classrooms and with the national society and culture. The nesting of classrooms within such a national culture is not so much a *top-down* process as a *two-way* process. Such a national orientation is promulgated top-down in part by the production of commercially available standardized items that can be found in classrooms across the nation (e.g. clocks, calendars, flags, posters, and alphabet signs, maps, globes), and partly by legislation requiring common practicalities, traditions (e.g. holidays, pledges, anthems) and curriculum (e.g. national tests and standards). Complementarily, it is constructed bottom-up by teachers and students as they interact with each and their environment: for example, when they design their classrooms; "as teachers are not told exactly how they are to, say, decorate their rooms, material culture variation is expected. Consistency in visual displays is also expected. Teachers are under both state and federal mandate to ritualistically observe particular holidays, as well as to include particular activities within the curriculum. ... Most teachers were aware of the socialization and enculturation implications ..." (Johnson, 1980: 185).

Classroom ethnography is not then just about noting what furniture and material objects are in the classroom and the way they influence classroom practices versus others, but rather what meanings they have for teachers and students and how those material objects connect the classroom to spaces and institutions outside the classroom. In sum, the questions, "Who and what are in a classroom?" can never be fully or completely answered, but rather they serve as a heuristic problematizing of the classroom and its relationships to other people, places, and social institutions.

Classroom Ethnography and the Question "What Happens in a Classroom?"

The description of "What is happening and how?" is a central question to any classroom ethnography. The result is what Geertz (1973) has called a "thick description"; and is one that addresses multiple levels of social and cultural meaning and the significance of *what* is happening and *how* from an insider's view – that is an *emic* perspective (also see McDermott *et al.*, 1978). Although a thick description must be grounded in the interpretations of the people involved in social events, its meaning is not so much what they individually think and believe but lies in the culturally and historically available, shared and public significance, practices, and understandings present.

Consider an event in a US classroom in which the teacher is reading a story aloud to the 4- and 5-year-old children who are seated on a rug in the early afternoon just before nap time. The event is likely to have been given a label by the teacher and the students, for example "story time," but such labeling is at best a brief functional, but surface level, description of what is happening. The teacher has deliberately scheduled "story time" as a prelude to nap time to provide an opportunity for the students to become calm and quiet, a way to ease them into this nap time. So, it might be more accurate to describe the event as "prelude to nap time." Yet, within this classroom event, some of the children compete to see who can sit closest to the teacher as such spatial arrangements have come to have a meaning for them as being "most liked by the teacher." Such a meaning is not strictly logical as it is not the teacher who arranges the students' seating; nonetheless, such seating arrangements have significance for them. Indeed, on occasion a student will deliberately misbehave in a carefully modulated way provoking the teacher to punish the student by having him/her sit right next to her during story time so she can carefully watch her/him. The teacher may not be explicitly aware of the significance of the seating arrangements for the children, or of how misbehavior is orchestrated within the context or why. Given these seating dynamics, perhaps the event should be described as "competing for being most liked by the teacher." However, there are a few students who always seat themselves on the periphery of the group. None of the other children make room for them in the crowded center front of the group. Who sits by whom, and where, has significance for how the children are constructing a social structure within their peer group. The teacher picks books to read from the selection provided by the school librarian who has carefully chosen what she considers high-quality children's literature: decisions based on a university course she took. All of the books have what the teacher and librarian view as happy and morally appropriate endings. As such, story time could be described as an event inculcating particular literary and moral values and interpretative frameworks. In effect, the school administration, other educators in the building, parents, and the classroom teacher herself are, by expressing approval for these events, implicitly actualizing their belief that reading to young children will motivate them to learn to read, and that 4- and 5-year-old children need an afternoon nap (views they do not hold or express about 15- and 16-year-old students). The event might thus be described as the shared promulgation of cultural models of young children and childhood.

In brief, it will not do simply to describe the event as "story time," nor will it do to refer to it simply in terms given by the teacher; neither should the event be described from or in the terms of an outsider, regardless of how insightful that outsider is, since the meaningfulness of the event is generated by the interplay of all of those *in* the classroom and *what* is found there. A thick description needs to follow, not only how the people in the classroom build and share meaning, interpretations and the significance of practice at multiple levels, with all of their complexities, contradictions, and incoherencies, but must also take account of how these meanings and practices evolve over time and are recontextualized across situations. They can, after all, only be studied and understood in terms of other events both inside and outside the classroom.

This effort to describe how the people in the classroom build and share meaning from an *emic* perspective distinguishes a classroom ethnography from a Critical Ethnography. A Critical Ethnographer brings to bear and foregrounds Critical Theories about the structuring of society and inequitable power relations in the description and analysis of classroom life (see for example, Anderson, 1989; Carspecken, 1996). Street (2003) makes a distinction between Critical perspectives (with an uppercase "C") that is an a priori foregrounding of power relations and critical perspectives (with a lowercase "c") that acknowledge and describe such relations without necessarily prioritizing them. A classroom ethnography may be critical (lower case "c"), and may gain insight from Critical Ethnographies and Critical Theory, but they are not the same research endeavor. This distinction between classroom ethnography and Critical Ethnography should not be taken as suggesting that one is "better" than the other (and similarly so with earlier distinctions between classroom ethnography and qualitative methods). Rather differing research perspectives have different agendas and each provides a set of distinct insights and understandings that, at a particular moment, may be more or less useful in better understanding the human condition in and through classrooms.

Framed in epistemological terms, ethnographic descriptions of what happens in a classroom, therefore, need to be grounded in a theoretical understanding of how people act and react to each other (cf. Bloome *et al.*, 2005; Erickson and Shultz, 1977). As Bloome *et al.* (2005) note, although seemingly a simple notion, unpacking what occurs in the classroom shows it to be complex and multi-layered. First, we do need to see it in terms of the *people* who are acting and reacting with respect to each other. That is, the basic analytic unit is not the individual but a group of people, since people are the context for each other (cf. Erickson and Shultz, 1977). Of course, people are sometimes by themselves and two or more people do not have to be co-present in order for there to be a social event. However, whether with others or alone, a person is acting and reacting in response to other people – present or absent – what they have done and what they will do. The task, in part, for the ethnographer interested in understanding the meaning of a person's social behavior (whether that person is alone or in a group) is precisely to identify the *people* context and the *action* context within which that person is acting and reacting (cf., Erickson and Shultz, 1977). Second, moreover, when people *act*, they do so in a strategic way. Furthermore, when they *react*, it is in relation to actions immediately previous and to actions that occurred sometime earlier, as well as to specific sets, groups and patterns of action. Similarly, people react to future actions: and any action, including a reaction, inherently includes within it a concept of consequence. Time and timing is therefore an important element in classroom ethnographies. Consequences must also presume future outcomes and actions, either by others or by oneself. Indeed, even a "non-action" needs to be understood as a certain form of reaction. Third, the actions and reactions people take to each other are not necessarily linear. People may act together, and actions and reactions may occur simultaneously. Finally, people may respond and react to each other not simply in separate actions but through sequences of events.

Language and Culture in the Classroom: Ethnographic Perspectives

How people use language is derivative of their culture while simultaneously constituting it, including both their social identities and social relationships. By looking closely at the language people use, and how they use it, researchers can explore and describe cultural practices and events, shared meanings and cultural models (Agar, 1995; Hymes, 1974; Quinn, 2005). In classrooms, language is both the primary object and the means of instruction; students are taught to read, write, calculate, and use language consistent with disciplinary communities. They are taught through classroom discussions, lectures, recitations, reading, writing, and other uses of language. In other words, teachers and students build knowledge and learning through language (Green and Dixon, 1993; Heras, 1993). Thus, it is not surprising that classroom ethnographers have focused on the uses of language in the classroom (see, for example, Bloome *et al.*, 2005; Cazden, John and Hymes, 1972; Green and Wallat, 1981; Wilkinson, 1982).

We can identify salient related directions of such classroom ethnographies: and heuristically these fall into two distinct groups. The first has focused on what it means to be a competent student, and the communicative competence needed to participate in the various events of the classroom. The second has concentrated on cross-cultural issues; on miscommunication between teachers and students who bring different ways of using language to the classroom.

Classroom Ethnography and the Competent Student

What does it mean to be competent in a classroom? What does a student need to do in order to be viewed by others as competent? From a traditional educational perspective, competence refers to academic ability and achievement. However, classroom ethnographies show that teacher judgments of competency are more complex, and involve both how students participate in the classroom and indeed how they use language to establish their interactional competence. As Mehan (1980) notes, students need to behave appropriately to the context, and they are interpreted by the "rules" of the classroom. Students then need to learn rules for appropriate participation in a variety of classroom events, including the *what*, *when*, and *how* to talk: how to take a turn at talking, how to sit, what should and should not be said, the appropriate tone and register to use, what intertextual references are appropriate, how to configure one's body, how to direct eye gaze, etc. This socialization to the classroom "rules" is mutually constituted by teachers and students: it is not unidirectional, teacher to student.

Classroom ethnographies of preschool and early elementary classrooms have shown that most children learn how to display appropriate participation in classroom events very quickly (see Kantor *et al.*, 1992, 1993). However, what constitutes appropriate participation may vary across different types of events (e.g. deskwork, whole class discussion, getting ready for lunch) and also for different groups in the same type of event. For example, Borko and Eisenhart (1989) have shown that what constitutes appropriate talk and reading in high and low reading groups can vary dramatically within the same classroom; so much so that students socialized to the appropriate participation in the low reading group may have difficulties appropriately participating in the high group even when assessments of their reading achievement indicate that this is an appropriate placement. As important, the interactional and participatory behaviors they displayed within the reading groups in this study were taken by the teacher and other students as identifying them as members of that reading group and as not belonging to another reading group (see also Eder, 1982). In brief, appropriate participation within classroom events is not just a matter of being competent but has consequences for social identity, social status, and social position.

There is tendency in classroom ethnographies to frame any lack of participatory competency as misassessment by the teacher or other educators. However, the issue may be more complex than it seems. In a description of the interaction of a teacher and student in a first-grade reading group, McDermott (1977) describes what appears to be a failure for everyone (here, the student is removed from the reading group, the teacher loses an opportunity to teach, and the reading group is disrupted). However, he shows that, viewed differently at another level, the same incident could be understood as being a successful interaction aimed at avoiding embarrassment, frustration, and threats to social identity. In brief, what appeared to be a pedagogic failure may be judged to have been an interactional "success." Bloome, Puro, and Theordorou (1987), in their classroom ethnography of seventh-grade social studies classroom found similar dynamics. They described classroom interaction as often involving *procedural* display: the display by teachers and students to each other of the interactional procedures that count as "doing lesson," getting through the time and space of the lesson in an interactionally appropriate manner, etc. They argue, however, that procedural display is not the same as substantive engagement in the academic subject manner and, in their classroom ethnography, show how the students failed to acquire the academic knowledge taught despite a "successful" lesson at the level of procedure and interaction. What these and similar classroom ethnographies do is problematize what counts as "competent," the effective uses of language and, consequently, how "success" and "failure" in lessons may be judged. Cultural and cross-cultural features of the classroom are central to an understanding of the relationship between issues of competence, language, and the outcome of lessons.

Classroom Ethnography and Cross-cultural (Mis)Communication

The emergence of sociolinguistic ethnography (also known as the ethnography of communication) in the 1960s and 1970s (Gumperz and Hymes, 1972; Hymes, 1974; Gumperz, 1986), has provided a theoretical framework for studies of cross-cultural communication (for example see Cazaden *et al.*, 1972). Cultural differences in the ways languages are used were often negatively interpreted by people in gatekeeping positions and positions of authority and power. These differences frequently reinforced stereotypical conceptions of students from other cultures as less competent.

Archetypical of cross-cultural miscommunication studies is Phillips' classroom ethnography of Native American students on the Warms Springs Indian Reservation (see Phillips, 1972, 1983). She found that the students were silent and did not respond to the teacher in some instructional events. The white teacher from outside the Reservation was frustrated with what appeared to be the students' lack of participation. What Phillips showed was that students in fact had different expectations for appropriate communicative behavior in such situations. She labeled these "participant structures." She argued that the participant structures the students had learned for such situations in their families and community differed from that which the teacher expected. Thus, the students were engaged in what they considered as appropriate and respectful behavior, while the teacher, who was unfamiliar with the students' culture, ways of using language, and ways of participation in various events, interpreted their interactional behavior as indicative of lack of ability or lack of interest in academic learning.

Such cross-cultural miscommunication extends beyond mismatched participation structures. Classroom ethnographies and related studies have shown cross-cultural miscommunication in students' ways of signaling coherence in their spoken narratives (e.g. Champion, 2002; Heath, 1982; Michaels, 1981, 1986), in organizing turns at talk (e.g. Au, 1980; McCollum, 1989), in how to interpret written text (e.g. Heath, 1983), and in how to display emotion and attitude (Gilmore, 1987). Studies of cross-cultural miscommunication have covered a broad range of cultural groups who have not traditionally been served well by schools, including indigenous students (e.g. Erickson and Mohatt, 1982; Phillips, 1972, 1983; Guilmet, 1979; McCarty *et al.*, 1991), African-American students (e.g. Foster, 1995; Gilmore, 1987), Latino students in US schools (e.g. Delgado-Gaitan and Trueba, 1985; McCollum, 1989), and students of Chinese heritage in US schools (e.g., Schoenhals, 1994).

The significance of classroom ethnographies in showing cross-cultural miscommunication is not just in provoking educators to become more sensitive to cultural differences, but in promulgating approaches to instruction and curriculum that conceive of classrooms as cultural spaces (see, for example, Frank and Bird, 2000; Jordan, 1985), and approaches that build on students' culturally derived ways of using language and participating in social events. The curricular implications of cross-cultural miscommunication can be divided into four related approaches.

The first approach has been to incorporate students' ways of using language in their home and community cultures in classroom instruction. In her study of a teacher who was successful with Native Hawaiian students, Au (1980) described how the teacher orchestrated turn-taking (the participation structure) in ways that were similar to narrative and storytelling events in the students' homes and community. The students were highly engaged in the reading instruction tasks and were successful in learning to read. The study by Au provides additional validation that cross-cultural miscommunication affects students' participation in and academic success with classroom instruction. It also validates the notion that the organization of instruction conversations is culturally-based, even when the teacher and students do not themselves identify it as being cultural.

A second related approach is exemplified by Ladson-Billings' (1994) study of a series of teachers in a low-income, urban community who were successful with African-American students. Although Ladson-Billings' study generated findings that also showed the importance of instructional practices built on the cultural and communicative practices of students' families and community, she also found that connecting the culture of the classroom with the students' cultural lives outside the classroom involved a series of additional dimensions, including a caring ethic, a focus on academics, high academic expectations, a sense of "family" in the classroom, curriculum related to the students' history and culture, as well as incorporation of classroom practices consistent with family and community cultural practices. Ladson-Billings labeled the set of practices as culturally relevant pedagogy. As a set of principles, this pedagogy was applicable across cultural groups who were also at risk of cross-cultural miscommunication and potential "misinstruction" and "misassessment."

A third approach is highlighted by Gutiérrez and others who focus on classrooms where teachers and students construct a "third space." Gutiérrez (2008) writes:

> [W]e proposed the idea of a Third Space where teacher and student scripts
> – the formal and informal, the official and unofficial spaces of the learning
> environment – intersect, creating the potential for authentic interaction and
> a shift in the social organization of learning and what counts as knowledge
> (Gutiérrez *et al.*, 1995) ... our use of the Third Space construct ... has
> always been more than a celebration of the local literacies of students from
> non-dominant groups; and certainly more than what students can do with
> assistance or scaffolding; and also more than ahistorical accounts of individual
> discrete events, literacy practices, and the social interaction within. Instead, it
> is a transformative space where the potential for an expanded form of learning
> and the development of new knowledge are heightened.
>
> (p. 152)

The construct of "third space" provides a way to view the meeting of different
cultures (different ethnic cultures, different institutional cultures, etc.), as having
the potential to redefine academic learning and development. Of course, not all
classroom spaces involving the meeting of different cultures are "third spaces."
Thus, what classroom ethnographies of third spaces provide is a way to imagine and
conceptualize classroom learning grounded in anthropological theories of culture
and thinking and, as such, they shift the learning theories underlying classroom
instruction.

A fourth direction in the use of classroom ethnography for promulgating
curriculum and instruction has been in teaching students to become ethnographers
of their own communities. The students are taught the methods, concepts, principles
and language of ethnographic research, and the traditional skills of reading, writing,
calculating, drawing and other traditional classroom learning practices are redefined
by the students' engagement in ethnographic research. In some of these teaching-
learners-to-be-ethnographer programs the students gain awareness and appreciation
for their own and others' cultures and communities (see Curry and Bloome, 1998;
Egan-Robertson, 1998; Mercado, 1998; Torres, 1998). In other cases, students
developed an understanding of how to approach academic learning through the
inquiry processes of ethnography (Yeager, Floriani, and Green, 1998). In still other
cases, students examined how social and political problems in their communities
affected their lives and the lives of their families and other community members.
Students in such programs became active agents who used the knowledge they
gained to reframe academic learning, to make the cultures of their communities
visible, and to engage in action-oriented service projects. In effect, they redefined
what it meant to be a student.

Part of what these curricular and instructional uses of ethnographic research is
developing is an understanding of teaching, learning, and the curriculum as complex
cultural processes conducted in varied cultural settings among people of diverse
cultural backgrounds and histories; as features of the classroom which operate in
political contexts marked by struggles over what counts as knowledge (and whose
knowledge counts) and over personhood (what does it mean to be human and who

counts as being human). It is also acknowledging the importance of recognizing the legitimacy of students' community cultures, histories and funds of knowledge, and using such legitimatization as a basis for education itself (e.g., Moll and Diaz, 1987; Trueba, 1994). From this point of view, what is at stake in classroom ethnography is not just a redefinition of classroom processes but the very way to address and redress the inequities, pain, and trauma suffered by many young people, especially those from non-dominant social, cultural, racial, linguistic, and economic communities.

In Conclusion: On the Nature of Knowledge in Classroom Ethnographies

Any classroom ethnography is inherently incomplete (not everything that happens in a classroom can be studied). Furthermore, although the classroom ethnographer is trained to seek an *emic* perspective, it is impossible to entirely do away with one's own social position in the conduct of research. As such, classroom ethnography must always involve a reflexive component. As McDermott and Varenne (2006) argue:

> A strict cultural approach is necessarily reflexive. We have no choice but to study that which we also make. There is no privileged position from which to escape culture ..."Knowledge" is not disembodied from the texts that codify it, from those who author and authorize it, or from the audiences that support the activities that produce and establish it.
>
> (p. 23)

In later chapters, we shall see how central a reflexive approach is to Bourdieusian perspectives on the classroom. The acknowledgment that the knowledge generated from a classroom ethnography is not "disembodied" from its authors should not necessarily invalidate it. As Atkinson (1990) points out, acknowledging the construction of an ethnography (or any research effort) does not negate its usefulness but rather should only raise a level of awareness and caution for the authors and consumers of the research.

The knowledge generated through classroom ethnography differs from the knowledge generated in psychological studies (those derivative from experimental psychology) of classroom processes. Rather than seeking the identification of processes of learning and instruction that are decontextualized and that can be utilized in any classroom, classroom ethnography emphasizes a knowledge base that is inherently contextualized and that might not be simply "scaled up." Rather, the knowledge base is defined as a series of cases which challenge taken-for-granted definitions of classroom and educational processes and that calls for abduction. Knowledge from a classroom ethnography must therefore be "recontextualized" (cf. van Leeuwen, 2008) in order to be of use in other classroom and situations. As such, the consumer of classroom ethnographies must engage in a dialectical relationship in which the classroom ethnography is placed in tension with other classroom ethnographies as well as to the situation to which it is being applied (cf.

Bloome *et al.*, 2005). To return, finally, to a theme used at the outset of this chapter, there is a further tension in the way that an *emic* perspective might consequently be seen as focusing on the classroom itself, as a microcosm of a culture, rather than the relationship between the classroom and the broader culture and society. We shall further explore the consequences of this tension in the next and later chapters of the book.

Notes

1 I want to acknowledge the contributions of Marlene Beierle, Julia Averill, Margaret Grigorenko, and Huili Hong to the writing of this chapter. Whatever flaws remain are my sole responsibility.

2 In this section we use "motivated" to indicate a choice (conscious or unconscious) to pursue one social agenda versus another or one set of meanings versus another (see Kress, 1993, for a detailed discussion of signs as motivated).

3 Our use of "naturalized" derives from Fairclough's (1992) discussion of naturalization as part of critical discourse analysis.

3

NEW LITERACY STUDIES

BRIAN STREET

Introduction

This chapter deals with the topic of New Literacy Studies. As such, it forms
the second ingredient of our background perspective to classroom language
ethnography. The research area of New Literacy Studies emerged in the 1980s.
The chapter begins by addressing its inception, issues of definition, and the context
for early studies. A number of works and studies are cited throughout. The chapter
then deals with the key concepts of New Literacy Studies and their rationale. A
range of theoretical concerns and critiques are also included, as well as further case
examples to illustrate a range of methodological issues. Finally, the chapter addresses
the implications that New Literacy Studies may have for policy and practice. The
intention is to give an explicit account of the provenance and state-of-the-art of
this approach to literacy.

The Context and Background

What has come to be termed the 'New Literacy Studies' (hereafter NLS) (Gee,
1991; Street, 1996) represents a new tradition in considering the nature of literacy;
one which focuses not so much on acquisition of skills, as in dominant approaches,
but rather on what it means to think of literacy as a *social practice* (Street, 1984).
This approach entails the recognition of 'multiple literacies', varying according to
time and space but also contested in relations of power. NLS, then, takes nothing
for granted with respect to literacy and the social practices with which it becomes
associated, problematising what counts as literacy at any time and place and asking
'whose literacies' are dominant and whose marginalised or resistant. A key issue in
approaching NLS is to clarify what the term 'new' refers to. For many researchers
and practitioners, especially those in the field of education, it is often assumed that

what is 'new' is the 'literacy' that is being described. So-called 'new' technologies are increasingly being brought into schools, for instance, and with them 'new' online forms of reading and writing – sometimes described as 'second life'. The uses of reading and writing associated with novel access to visual images may well justify the epithet 'new'. However, the debate is still unresolved as to how far the features of such activities are really different from more 'traditional' uses of reading and writing. We will consider these issues further below, as we engage with discussion of multimodality and its association with literacy. But, in the 'New Literacy Studies', the term 'new' refers not so much to these *forms* but rather to the *studies* themselves; that is, it is the ways in which literacy is conceptualised and researched that is 'new' in the 'New Literacy Studies'. In this chapter we consider just what exactly is 'New' in NLS and lay the ground for then linking our theoretical take on literacy to the theoretical perspectives offered by social theory and the implications of such for our understandings of language and education, literacy, and classroom ethnography.

One of the key ways in which literacy studies of the kind we are considering can be described as 'new' is in their methodological perspective. Whereas dominant approaches to literacy in education tend to conceptualise literacy as a set of skills and study it through cognitive based theories of learning and activity, New Literacy Studies adopts an ethnographic approach to the study of reading and writing in varied social contexts, both in and out of education systems. In addressing the issues associated with understanding literacy ethnographically, literacy researchers have developed a conceptual apparatus that both coins some new terms and gives new meanings to some old ones. My own work, for example, begins with the notion of multiple literacies, makes a distinction between 'autonomous' and 'ideological' models of literacy (Street, 1985), and develops a distinction between literacy 'events' and literacy 'practices' (Street, 1988); concepts we will explore further below and that will carry through to discussions in later chapters with further links and explorations in connection to Bourdieu's theory of practice.

The standard view of literacy in many fields, from schooling to development programmes, works with the assumption that it is, in itself, independent and will consequently have effects on other social and cognitive practices. Introducing literacy to poor, 'illiterate' people, villagers, urban youth, etc., will, therefore, have the effect of enhancing their cognitive skills, improving their economic prospects, making them better citizens, regardless of the social and economic conditions that accounted for their 'illiteracy' in the first place. This as the *autonomous* model of literacy, and I have argued (Street, 1984) that one of its consequences is that it disguises the cultural and ideological assumptions that underpin it; so that it can then be presented as though such are neutral and universal and that literacy will have benign effects. Research in NLS, as we will see, challenges this view and suggests that, in practice, literacy varies from one context to another and from one culture to another, as do the effects of the different literacies in different conditions. The autonomous approach is simply one approach amongst many, but it presents itself as though it is 'natural' and, indeed, many who adopt it often tend not even to indicate the grounds for their treatment of literacy, assuming these are known and obvious. When made explicit, this unselfconscious use of the autonomous model can be seen as the imposition of the views of one sub-group on another; whether within a country, where the version of one class or cultural group are imposed onto others, or more generally, between countries, where 'western' conceptions of literacy imposed on to other cultures.

The alternative, *ideological*, model of literacy offers a more culturally-sensitive view of literacy practices as they vary from one context to another. This model starts from different premises from the autonomous model: it posits instead that literacy is a social practice, not simply a technical and neutral skill; and that it is always embedded in socially constructed epistemological principles. It is about knowledge: the ways in which people address reading and writing are themselves rooted in conceptions of knowledge, identity and being. It is also always embedded in social practices, such as those of a particular job market or a particular educational context, and the effects on learning of that particular literacy will be dependent on those contexts. Literacy, in this sense, is always contested, both in its meanings and its practices. Hence, although it might seem sufficient to many to refer to such variations as 'cultural' models of literacy, I want to suggest that this is not enough and that what we need is indeed better described as an 'ideological' model of literacy: particular versions of literacy are always 'ideological', in the sense that they are always rooted in a particular world-view and a desire for that view of literacy to dominate and to marginalise others (Gee 1990; Besnier and Street, 1994). The argument about social literacies (Street, 1995) then suggests that engaging with literacy is always a social act imbued with power relations from the outset. As such, the ways in which teachers or facilitators and their students interact is already a social practice that affects the nature of the literacy being learnt and the ideas about literacy held by participants, especially the new learners and their position in relations of power. It is not valid to suggest that 'literacy' can be 'given' neutrally as a set of 'skills' 'available to all', and its 'social' effects only experienced afterwards.

These ideas were first laid out in a book called *Literacy in Theory and Practice* (Street, 1984) in which I challenged the outstanding examples of the 'autonomous' model at that time, many of them rooted in cognitive theories of learning and development and often focused on how children learn to read, and how educationalists should address acquisition. In this book, I drew upon my own field work in Iran, focusing on the everyday uses and meanings of literacy 'outside' of school, as well as 'inside', to propose a more social practice view of literacy and show what happened when this view came into contact with the dominant theoretical and policy perspectives of the time. An issue here was the shift from a more cognitive view of literacy – as skills embedded in mental procedures – towards a more social constructivist view – as practices embedded in different social environments and cultures. Before giving more detail of this work, I am going to briefly recall the history of debates about literacy as reading, cognition and early learning, and to look at how a social practice view of literacy has been developed in recent years.

Earlier Views of Literacy and Cognition

Many of the earlier theories of literacy and of learning that the ideological model has taken to task rest on deeper assumptions about cognition and in particular regarding the 'cognitive consequences' of learning/acquiring literacy. It is these that I questioned in the 1984 book. A dominant position, for instance, was to apply the idea of a 'great divide' – originally used to distinguish 'primitive/modern' or 'underdeveloped/developed' – to 'literates' and 'non-literates', a distinction that implicitly or explicitly still underpins much work in and justifications for international literacy programmes. I showed how anthropologists, such as Goody (1977) and psychologists such as Olson (1977, 1994) linked the more precise cognitive argument to broader historical and cultural patterns, regarding the significance of the acquisition of literacy for a society's functioning. These claims often remain part of popular assumptions about literacy and have fed policy debates and media representations of the significance of the 'technology' of literacy.

Whilst rejecting an extreme technological determinist position, Goody (1977) for instance did appear to associate the development of writing with key cognitive advances in human society – the distinction of myth from history; the development of logic and syllogistic forms of reasoning; the ability of writing to help overcome a tendency of oral cultures towards cultural homeostasis; the development of certain mathematical procedures, such as multiplication and division; and – perhaps the key claim for educational purposes – that 'literacy and the accompanying process of classroom education brings a shift towards greater "abstractedness"'. Whilst he is careful to avoid claiming an absolute dichotomy between orality and literacy, it is partly on the grounds that his ideas do lend credence to technological determinism that he was challenged, through the experimental data provided by Scribner and Cole (Scribner and Cole 1978; Cole and Scribner 1981) and the ethnographic data and arguments by myself (Street, 1984), Heath (1983) and others (see Finnegan, 1988; Maddox, 2001). Goody himself has criticised many of these counter arguments as 'relativist', a term that might be applied to much contemporary thinking about literacy (and social differences in general) as we shall see below.

During the 1970s the social psychologists Sylvia Scribner and Michael Cole conducted a major research project amongst the Vai peoples of Liberia in order to test out the claims of Goody and others about the cognitive consequences of literacy in a 'real life' setting, and I drew extensively on their work in the 1984 book. Their accounts of the outcomes of this research (Scribner and Cole, 1978; Cole and Scribner 1981) represented a major landmark in our understanding of the issues regarding literacy and cognition that we are considering here. They quote Farrell, as a classic example of such claims (1977: 451): 'the cognitive restructuring caused by reading and writing develop the higher reasoning processes involved in extended abstract thinking' and they argue, 'Our research speaks to several serious limitations in developing this proposition as a ground for educational and social policy decisions'. They address the limitations of these claims in both empirical and theoretical terms. For instance, many of the claims derive from abstract hypotheses not based in evidence, or the evidence used is of a very specific form of written text, such as use of western scientific 'essay text' literacy as a model for accounts of literacy in general (cf. Olson, 1977; Street, 1984). Many of the assumptions about literacy in general, then, are 'tied up with school-based writing'. This, they believe, leads to serious limitations in the accounts of literacy: 'The assumption that logicality is in the text and the text is in school can lead to a serious underestimation of the cognitive skills involved in non-school, non-essay writing'. The writing crisis, to which many of the reports and commissions in recent years refer (cf. Adams, etc.), 'presents itself as purely a pedagogical problem' and arises in the first place from these limited assumptions and data.

Scribner and Cole, instead, tested out these claims through intensive psychological and anthropological research of actual practice, taking as a case study the Vai peoples of Liberia, who have three scripts – Vai (an invented phonetic script); Arabic; and Roman – each used for different purposes.

> We examined activities engaged in by those knowing each of the indigenous scripts to determine some of the component skills involved. On the basis of these analyses, we designed tasks with different content but with hypothetically similar skills to determine if prior practice in learning and use of the script enhanced performance.
>
> (Scribner and Cole 1978: 13)

The tests were divided into three areas: communication skills; memory; and language analysis. On the basis of the results, they argue that all we can claim is that 'specific practices promote specific skills': the grand claims of the literacy thesis are untenable:

> there is no evidence that writing promotes "general mental abilities". We did not find "superior memory in general" among Qur'anic students nor better language integration skills "in general" among Vai literates. … There is nothing in our findings that would lead us to speak of cognitive consequences of literacy with the notion in mind that such consequences affect intellectual performance in all tasks to which the human mind is put.
>
> (Scribner and Cole 1978: 16)

This outcome suggests that the metaphor of a 'great divide' may not be appropriate 'for specifying differences among literates and non-literates under contemporary conditions. The monolithic model of what writing is and what it leads to … appears in the light of comparative data to fail to give full justice to the multiplicity of values, uses and consequences which characterise writing as social practice'.

Scribner and Cole, then, were amongst the first to attempt to re-theorise what counts as literacy and to look outside school for empirical data on which to base sound generalisations (cf. Hull and Schultz, 2002 on literacy in and out of school). One of the main proponents of the 'strong' thesis regarding the consequences of literacy has been David Olson (1977), who has been, and is, one of the sources for claims about the 'autonomous' model of literacy (cf. Street, 1984) and was indeed cited by Scribner and Cole in their account. But, in a later book (1994) he tries, like them, to modify the inferences that can be drawn from his own earlier pronouncements and to set out what is myth and what is reality in our understanding of literacy. He draws an analogy with Christian theologians trying to put the faith on a firmer basis by getting rid of unsustainable myths that only weakened the case. As he describes the unsustainable myths of literacy, he seems to be challenging those put forward in his own earlier accounts (1977) and by Goody, Farrell and others. In arriving at 'the new understanding of literacy' he describes six 'beliefs' and the 'doubts' that have been expressed about them as a helpful framework for reviewing the literature on literacy (Olson, 1994):

1   Writing is the transcription of speech.
2   The superiority of writing to speech.
3   The technological superiority of the alphabetic writing system.
4   Literacy as the organ of social progress.
5   Literacy as an instrument of cultural and scientific development.
6   Literacy as an instrument of cognitive development.

He then outlines the 'doubts' that modern scholarship has thrown on all of these assumptions. For instance, with respect to (4) literacy and social development, he cites counter arguments from such anthropologists as Lévi-Strauss (1961) who argued that literacy not only is not the royal route to liberation, but is as often a means of enslavement:

> It seems to favour rather the exploitation than the enlightenment of mankind. … The use of writing for disinterested ends, and with a view to satisfactions of the mind in the fields either of science or the arts, is a secondary result of its invention – and may even be no more than a way of reinforcing, justifying, or dissimulating its primary function.
>
> (Lévi-Strauss (1961: 291–2) cited in Olson, 1977)

With respect to (5) cultural development, Olson cites the work of cultural historians and anthropologists (cf. Finnegan, 1999) who 'have made us aware of the sophistication of "oral" cultures', and from whose work it appears: 'No direct causal links have been established between literacy and cultural development'.

Like Scribner and Cole, Olson's conclusion challenges the dominant claims for literacy for adults as well as for children:

> the use of literacy skills as a metric against which personal and social competence can be assessed is vastly oversimplified. Functional literacy, the form of competence required for one's daily life, far from being a universalizable commodity turns out on analysis to depend critically on the

particular activities of the individual for whom literacy is to be functional. What is functional for an automated-factory worker may not be for a parent who wants to read to a child. The focus on literacy skills seriously underestimates the significance of both the implicit understandings that children bring to school and the importance of oral discourse in bringing those understandings into consciousness in turning them into objects of knowledge. The vast amounts of time some children spend on remedial reading exercises may be more appropriately spent acquiring scientific and philosophical information'.

(Olson, 1977: 12)

He concludes: 'For the first time, many scholars are thinking the unthinkable: is it possible that literacy is over-rated?'

As we shall see below, for many researchers the rejection of the 'literacy thesis' does not necessarily mean that we should abandon or reduce work in literacy programmes: but it does force us to be clearer as to what justifications we use for such work and how we should conduct it. The next section shows how new theoretical perspectives, themselves growing from the debates outlined above, can provide a way of pursuing work in the field of learning and teaching literacy without the 'myths', over statements and doubtful bases for action of the earlier positions.

Learning and Literacy

The issue of how children learn to read has been highly contested in recent years and has tended to lay the ground for approaches to literacy more generally. In many circles, still, the term 'literacy' is interpreted to refer to 'reading' and more particularly to the learning of reading by young children. Adams (1993), for instance, herself a key figure in US National Commissions on Literacy, begins an overview of the literature on 'literacy' with the claim:

> The most fundamental and important issues in the field of reading education are those of how children learn to read and write and how best to help them.

The piece from which this comes was included in a book entitled *Teaching Literacy Balancing Perspectives* and offers an introduction to some of the key terms in the field of reading; for example, 'phonics', 'whole language', phonemic awareness', etc. It also makes claims about what 'scientific' research now tells us about learning to read. There is now a requirement in some countries for 'scientific-based' approaches that can provide sound evidence of which methods and approach is superior and that can claim to 'soundly refute' some hypotheses in favour of others (Slavin, 2002). Adams' response to these requirements, based on a year reviewing the literature on the 'reading wars' and looking for alternatives, was that there has been a coming together of different disciplinary strands, that different perspectives are beginning to agree on what counts: the whole language view of learners engaging in a 'guessing game' (Goodman (1967) or that the spellings of words are minimally relevant to reading (Smith, 1971) have been rejected in favour of attention to 'phonics'. The key to improvement in literacy, especially amongst the 'economically disadvantaged', is 'phonic instruction ... word recognition, spelling, and vocabulary'.

If one were only to read such accounts, then the picture would seem clear enough and the task of increasing literacy – not only within the US as in this case, and in the UK as in recent years but across the world, for adults as well as children (cf. Street, Baker, and Rogers 2006) – would be simply a matter of putting these principles into practice. However, once we take into account the theoretical debates outlined above and we read recent authors writing about the learning of literacy, then the apparent security and certainty of the dominant policy and educational positions comes into question. Goodman, for instance, who is largely seen as the leading international figure in 'whole language' approaches, refers like Adams, to 'what we have learnt' and to 'scientific knowledge' – but in this case that requires a different 'knowledge', namely 'of language development, of learning theories, and of teaching and curriculum' (Goodman, 1996), not just of 'spelling-sound relations'. For him learning literacy is a more 'natural' process than described in the phonics approach and he likens it to the way in which humans learn language: 'Written language is learnt a little later in the life of individuals and societies, but it is no less natural than oral language in the personal and social development of human beings' (Goodman, 1996).

Whether language and, by analogy, literacy are 'taught' or 'learnt naturally' represent extreme poles of what, for most educators is a 'continuum'. As Goodman states, 'while I separate *learning* reading and writing from *teaching* reading and writing, I can't do so absolutely'. What is evident from these accounts, then, is that underpinning approaches to literacy are theories of learning. What the ideological model of literacy addresses is that such learning does not take place only in the formal context of schools, but is also a key aspect of everyday life – as Rogers argues, we need to distinguish 'acquisition' and 'learning'. Rogers refers to 'task-conscious learning' and 'learning-conscious learning' and for him, these forms of learning are to be distinguished by their methods of evaluation (task-conscious by the task fulfilment, learning-conscious by measurements of learning). Whilst this may at times appear to differentiate adults strongly from children, Rogers and others argue that both children and adults do both – that in fact they form a continuum rather than two categories. Whilst adults do much less of formal learning than children, the difference, he suggests, really lies in the *teaching* of adults (i.e. the formal learning) and in the power relationships, the identities built up through experience, and the experiences adults bring to their formal learning, issues we will address more closely later in the book where we look at example of the application of new theories of literacy and of learning to development programmes around the world. Much of learning theory in the discipline of psychology, then, is rooted in the 'autonomous' model of literacy and has failed to address these features. Aspects of the more traditional literacy learning of children (including 'assembly-line preparation' and 'test learning') have consequently been used for adults, as is evident in many adult literacy programmes: adults are encouraged to join younger age groups, to take tests, to decontextualise learning and ignore their own previous knowledge, etc. The cognitive theories of great divide were combined with learning theories to generate formal approaches to the teaching of literacy, to children and to adults. In the second and third Parts of this book we address a number of contexts where these older theories of literacy and of learning have been challenged and the concepts embedded in New Literacy Studies and extended through the ideas of the social theorist, Pierre Bourdieu.

Further NLS Concepts: Multiple Literacies; Events and Practices

It follows from the distinction between models of literacy that researchers in NLS employing an 'ideological' model of literacy would find it problematic simply to use the singular term 'literacy' as their unit or object of study. Literacy comes already loaded with ideological and policy pre-suppositions that make it hard to simply ground ethnographic studies of the variety of literacies across contexts in a single underpinning concept – Literacy (with a capital 'L' and a single 'y'). Researchers in the field have addressed this methodological complexity in describing and comparing the object of study by developing alternative terms. This acknowledgement itself connects with issues of the construction of the research object and the need for a reflexive approach addressed later on in this book. We must begin with the recognition that there are 'multiple literacies'; not a single uniform phenomenon we can term 'literacy', and then simply compare across contexts. Indeed, the tendency often has been to see one context, the researcher's or educator's own, as setting the standard, and other literacies as being somehow 'less', inferior. Educational practice, from this perspective, has tended to assume that the educator is filling an empty space in the learner's knowledge, and must therefore bring 'light' into 'darkness' as it were – a phrase common in international statements about literacy. In a recent account of work in international settings concerned with adult literacy, a group of practitioners and researchers, adopting a 'New Literacy Studies' approach, contextualised their work in relation to these traditional views:

> Traditionally, however … the world is divided into two, the literate and the illiterate; and by definition, it is thought that illiterates know nothing about and have no experience of literacy. In this case, the adult learners (so it is assumed) do not bring any existing experience and knowledge with them. It is taken for granted that 'starting where they are' means starting without any perception of what literacy and numeracy mean, without any existing skills or practices.
>
> (Gebre *et al.*, 2009)

In contrast to this position, as we will see in our account of the LETTER Programme in Chapter 5, new approaches to literacy – both research and pedagogy – recognise that this view:

does not tally with life. We know that all adults (including so-called 'illiterates') can and do count, that they can and do measure and calculate (for example, in the market, in cooking or in farming) – in other words, they engage in numeracy activities. We know that they can and do negotiate literacy tasks such as money, bills, letters, election notices etc. And in any case, so-called 'illiterates' have experience, often deep experience, of being excluded from literacy activities – they see texts and many think, 'That is not for me'.

So adults do bring to adult literacy learning programmes experience and knowledge, perceptions and some practices relating to both literacy and numeracy. So, if the facilitator is to 'start where they are', is to build on their existing knowledge and experience, how can we and the facilitators find out what they know and do?

(Gebre *et al.*, 2009)

We will later describe some literacy and numeracy programmes that have attempted to answer these questions and to develop new ways of engaging with adult learners. These approaches build upon the conceptual frame being outlined here, starting with the recognition of 'multiple literacies', but then also recognising that it is not very appropriate or helpful to simply rank these different 'literacies' in ways that emphasise the deficit of some learners at the expense of the supposedly 'fuller' knowledge of others. Rather, we begin by attempting to understand the different uses and meanings of literacy in different contexts and to compare in a more ethnographic sense rather than a dominant or judgemental sense. In adopting such a framework, I argue, we need some further 'new' concepts to help us *see* what is going on and to understand and appreciate the engagement with reading and writing of people from other groups than ourselves, whether these include learners in educational programmes, villagers in 'development' contexts, urban poor in western societies or, as in my own work context, PhD students struggling with the discourse and genre features of 'academic literacies' (see Street, 2009). We address these issues later as we look at the implications of New Literacy Studies for work in education.

As noted, in attempting to develop a conceptual framework for handling these complex issues, I have both drawn upon the notion of 'multiple literacies' and also developed a working distinction between 'literacy events' and 'literacy practices' (Street, 1988) that I suggest is helpful both for research and in teaching situations. The term *literacy events* is derived from the sociolinguistic idea of speech events. It was first used in relation to literacy by A.B. Anderson *et al.* (1980) who defined it as an occasion during which a person 'attempted to comprehend graphic signs' (1980: 59–65). Shirley Brice Heath, further characterised a 'literacy event' as 'any occasion in which a piece of writing is integral to the nature of the participants' interactions and their interpretative processes' (Heath, 1982b: 93). I employ the phrase 'literacy practices' (Street, 1984: 1) as a means of focusing upon, 'social practices and conceptions of reading and writing'; although later elaborating the term to take account both of 'events' in Heath's sense and of the social models of literacy that participants bring to bear upon those events and that give meaning to them (see Street, 1988; 2000). David Barton, in an Introduction to his edited volume on *Writing in the Community* (Barton and Ivanic, 1991: 1) attempted to clarify these debates about literacy *events* and literacy *practices* and, in a later collaborative study of everyday literacies in Lancaster, England, Barton and Hamilton begin their account with further refinements of the two phrases (1998: 6). Baynham (1995) entitled his book *Literacy Practices: Investigating Literacy in Social Contexts*. Similarly Prinsloo and Breier's volume on *The Social Uses of Literacy* (1996), which is a series of case studies of literacy in South Africa, used the concept of 'events' but then extended it to 'practices', describing the everyday uses and meanings of literacy amongst, for instance, urban taxi drivers, struggle activists in settlements, rural workers using diagrams to build carts and those involved in providing election materials for mainly non-literate voters. The concept of literacy practices in these and other contexts attempts to handle the events and the patterns of activity around literacy events but also to *link* them to something broader of a cultural and social kind.

More recently, I have further elaborated the distinction with respect to work on literacies and multilingualism in an edited volume on *Multilingual Literacies* by Martin-Jones and Jones (2000). As part of that broadening, for instance, I noted that we bring to a literacy event concepts, social models regarding what the nature of the event is and that make it work and give it meaning. Participants not only 'do' reading and writing, they also have ideas about what they are doing – whether this means, as we noted briefly above, not counting their own activities as 'literacy' at all or, on the other hand, considering their own 'literacy' to be the norm against which other practices should be judged – as in many contemporary policy documents and in the kind of pedagogy identified in national government strategies, such as *No Child Left Behind* in the US and the *National Literacy Strategy* in the UK. Literacy practices, therefore, refer to both the activities of reading and/or writing in which people are involved in specific contexts and also to the ideas that such people have of literacy, involving the particular ways of thinking about and doing reading and writing in cultural contexts.

Methodological Issues – Applying Ethnographic Perspectives to Research on Literacy

A key issue, at both a methodological and an empirical level, is how we can characterise the shift from observing literacy events to conceptualising literacy practices. How can we get beyond the temptation to describe what we *think* is going on as we watch people engage with reading and writing, and to put thoughts into their head about what they are doing, without actually asking them. Or, further, since their own views might also be tainted by their exposure to 'our' views, by engaging in longer term ethnographic-style enquiry into 'what's going on'. What does an 'ethnographic' perspective bring to the understanding of multiple literacies and of literacy events and practices? I will briefly describe my own 'field' experience in Iran as an example of the link between adopting an ethnographic perspective and the study of literacy.

Iran: A Case Example

When I went to Iran in the 1970s to undertake anthropological field research, I did not go to study 'literacy', but I found myself living in a mountain village where a great deal of literacy activity was going on. Maybe part of my interest derived from having done my first degree in English literature. I had moved into anthropology, because of dissatisfaction with looking only at 'texts'. I wanted to locate them with respect to 'practices'. I attempted to bring English literature together with anthropology through a PhD on European Representations of Non-European Society in Popular Fiction. I looked at popular stories of adventure in exotic places: the Tarzan stories, Rider Haggard, and John Buchan as popular authors and Rudyard Kipling, D.H. Lawrence, and Joseph Conrad as more established authors. I arrived in Iran at my field site already excited by the ways that writing and anthropology could be brought together. Perhaps it was this sense that led me to focus closely on the literacy practices of the villages I lived amongst and even more on the 'representations' of these practices by different parties.

I was drawn then to the conceptual and rhetorical issues involved in representing the variety and complexity of literacy activity at a time when my encounter with people outside of the village suggested the dominant representation was of 'illiterate' backward villagers. Looking more closely at village life in light of these characterisations, I saw not only a lot of literacy going on but several quite different 'practices' associated with literacy – those in a traditional 'Quranic school', those taking place in the new State schools, and the inscribed means that traders used in their buying and selling of fruit to urban markets. Versions of literacy by outside agencies (e.g., State education, UNESCO, and national literacy campaigns) did not capture these complex variations in literacy happening in one small locale where the people were generally characterised as 'illiterate'. These external 'representations' seemed as much out of line with the ethnographic reality as earlier representations of non-European society had been. Just as theories of race, evolution and hierarchy used by 19th century writers, academics and policy makers have proved inadequate to making sense of human diversity, so the academic writing and policy pronouncements concerning literacy did not usefully describe or explain what was going on in this Iranian village and – as I discovered later – in many other parts of the world on which literacy policy and theory have been brought to bear.

(from *On Ethnography*, Heath and Street, 2008)

What happened in this case is repeated in certain ways for every ethnographer: a host of questions emerge from initial curiosity about patterns of symbolic structures and their uses; the prior questions arise perhaps from other domains and the ethnographer is struck by contrasts between 'common sense' views of what was going on and what they are learning from longer, more intense engagement with local practices. But, in later discussions in the present volume on the links between

Bourdieu's theory on the one hand and classroom engagement with literacy on the other, we are aware that not everyone is likely to engage in such long term fieldwork as they struggle with the meanings of literacy we outline here. David Bloome and Judith Greene have provided a helpful way of characterising the features of an ethnographic approach that everyone can draw upon, particularly in the present case as we consider literacy events and practices in different cultural contexts. They make a distinction between conducting ethnography, adopting an ethnographic *perspective,* and adopting ethnographic *tools. Conducting ethnography* then refers to framing and conceptualising through an in-depth long-term study of a social group. Anthropologists, in particular, have 'owned' this approach. *Adopting an Ethnographic Perspective,* on the other hand, refers to applying an ethnographic approach to a specific situation. This approach is less comprehensive than a full ethnography and more appropriately describes what the participants were attempting to engage in through the workshop process which we describe in Chapter 5. *Adopting Ethnographic Tools* finally refers to using the tools of observation and participant observation to comprehend a certain situation, but without the general theory of culture and society that is involved in either of the other two approaches. The first such approach is characterised by the pure anthropologist who travels to an area and stays there for a number of years and then writes a major study on a community. However, there is a middle ground between highly specialised skills and the ethnography that we all learn as members of society. This can be characterised by disciplined and reflective ethnographic inquiry in which an ethnographic perspective is systematically applied to specific situations and processes. It is this perspective that is to be found in New Literacy Studies as participants, whether anthropologists, educators, practitioners in international literacy programmes or policy makers, attempt to describe and understand the literacy events and practices of those around them.

Some further concepts have proved helpful, as the methodological debates about use of ethnographic perspectives have been extended. For instance, the accounts offered by New Literacy Studies have led some to question the apparent lack of broader generalisation and over focus on the 'local'. Reports based on NLS have often found themselves subject to criticism from other social scientists, or more positivist-oriented policy makers, for not making clear the nature of their 'sample' and the 'typicality' of their subjects. One way of describing this conflict of approaches, is to draw upon Mitchell's helpful distinction between 'enumerative induction', and 'analytic induction' (Mitchell, 1984), where the former depends upon generalisation from a sample to a larger population and the latter aims to elicit theoretical insights rather than empirical extrapolations:

> An anthropologist using a case study to support an argument shows how general principles deriving from some theoretical orientation manifest themselves in some given set of particular circumstances. A good case study, therefore, enables the analyst to establish theoretically valid connections between events and phenomena which previously were ineluctable.
>
> (Mitchell, 1984: 240)

As my own fieldwork in Iran evolved, I made connections between local uses of literacy there and other social practices, such as identity, power, and commerce (see Street, 1984, especially Chapters 5 and 6). This work emerged as a 'telling case', of literacy as social practice, rather than an attempt to generalise about the whole of Iran or about literacy in general. If we are able to identify the kind of variety in literacy events and practices I noted in some Iranian villages, then we might be able to carry those questions and insights to other places. As a result, we might ask: are there different literacies in place here? Might there be some literacy practices associated with commerce, some with religion and some with education, as in this case, or might we find other 'types' such as the 'local literacies' identified by Barton and Hamilton in their study of the Lancaster environment in England? From this point of view, ethnographers of literacy will look for the ordinary or routine in each site and thereby identify for analytical exposition 'telling' instances of behaviour that elucidate, contradict, or expand relationships presented in earlier theories or field studies.

A further critique of the ethnographic approach in general, and of its use in NLS in particular, has been that the researchers have tended to be 'westerners' and that, in effect, they were still imposing an outsider view on their subjects. This is an issue that anthropologists in particular have been very concerned with in recent years, and their attempts to take it into account and to develop further conceptual tools have also proved useful for NLS work. The basic principle here is again that of reflexivity: even while doing observing and describing 'others', the researcher must remain conscious of her/himself. Through reflexivity, we can be aware of the reason for undertaking the research in the first place, of the experience, beliefs and values which we bring to the task – in the case of NLS identifying and understanding the literacy and numeracy practices which the subjects do within their own community, practices of which the researched may be completely unconscious. The researcher must go back and forth – enter the situation and then retreat to consider before re-entering again. Ethnography should be considered as cyclical, with forward and backward movement. It is not a question of the researcher abandoning his/her own belief systems and values but, as Todorov suggests, (1988), a matter of 'proximity and distance', a continuous process of movement backwards and forwards that one probably never gets out of once acquired. Anthropologists sometimes privilege their ability to act as a 'fish out of water', taking a distant view of local practices (a theme and indeed a metaphor that we will see developed further in the programme described in Chapter 5). Yet, they also give highest credit to colleagues who have immersed themselves in local practices and can think like the 'natives'. Todorov suggests that the issue is not just seeing the either/or but in recognising the full axis. Fieldworkers distance themselves from their home culture as they come into proximity with an unfamiliar social group. They then become more immersed before distancing themselves from their field site as they return home, drawing near again to their own culture. Many return to their field site, thus repeating the cycle of proximity and distance which becomes a reflex for all such engagement with difference and similarity. The 'ethnographic imagination' (cf. Comaroff and

Comaroff, 1992) is founded on this cycle and can be applied in micro situations of engagement and comparison, as well as larger ones, including those where researchers enter and leave sites of learning over a period of time. The terms *emic* and *etic* taken from the field of linguistic studies are often used in the field of anthropology to describe this proximity/distance relationship. As noted in Chapter 2, *emic* is used to describe the insider's point of view, while *etic* is used for the outsider's point of view. The ethnographer does not simply try to capture the local but rather attempts to understand their way of understanding using an *emic/etic* approach, not as either/or but exploring how the local and the outsider views are related. The *emic* sheds light on the local perspective, and the *etic* account may see it from outside, but the *emic/etic* axis or relationship will relate the two together.

Those who have adopted an NLS perspective, then, have helped to develop a series of concepts that move us well beyond the traditional approach to literacy as skill or 'illiteracy' as deficit. Some of these terms have been adapted from anthropology, such as *emic* and *etic*, proximity and distance, telling case and reflexivity, whilst the notion of an 'ethnographic perspective' has built upon anthropological accounts but broadened out to others not trained in that discipline. How these concepts are used for understanding literacy in different contexts is a question that is still being explored and one that we will come back to later in this volume as we seek to link approaches from NLS with those of Bourdieu and of classroom ethnography. At the same time, some of the 'new' concepts in the NLS field are more particular to literacy itself – terms such as 'multiple literacies', literacy as social practice, ideological and autonomous models and 'literacy events' and 'literacy practices', have all been developed in the last twenty years, as those in the field have engaged with the deep and complex issues associated with understanding the uses and meanings of literacy in different times and places.

A wealth of 'ethnographies of literacy' has emerged deploying and developing these and other key concepts in a variety of international contexts, including the UK (Barton and Hamilton, 1998); the USA (Collins, 1995; Heath, 1983); South Africa (Prinsloo and Breier, 1996); Iran (Street, 1984); India (Mukherjee and Vasanta, 2003); Mexico (Kalman, 1999); South America (Aikman, 1999); and multiple 'development' contexts (Street, 2001). The strength and significance of the approach, and the considerable literature it has generated, is attested by a recent spate of critical accounts that have addressed some of the problems raised by such ethnographies in general theoretical terms and, more specifically, for practice in educational contexts. The next section summarises some of these theoretical concerns and critiques and then turns to their applications to policy and practice.

Theoretical Concerns, Critiques, and Applications

In terms of theory, Brandt and Clinton (2002) have commented on 'the limits of the local' apparent in many NLS studies. They argue that NLS ought to be more prepared to take account of the relatively 'autonomous' features of literacy without succumbing to the autonomous model with its well documented flaws: this would involve, for instance, recognising the extent to which literacy does often come to 'local' situations from outside and brings with it both skills and meanings that are larger than the *emic* perspective favoured by NLS can always detect. Whilst acknowledging the value of the social practice approach, they:

> wonder if the new paradigm sometimes veers too far in a reactive direction, exaggerating the power of local contexts to set or reveal the forms and meanings that literacy takes. Literacy practices are not typically invented by their practitioners. Nor are they independently chosen or sustained by them. Literacy in use more often than not serves multiple interests, incorporating individual agents and their locales into larger enterprises that play out away from the immediate scene.
>
> (Brandt and Clinton, 2002: 1)

They also point out the important and powerful role of consolidating technologies that can destabilise the functions, uses, values and meanings of literacy anywhere. These technologies generally come from outside the local context: there is more going on locally than just local practices. Whilst researchers have learnt much from the recent turn to 'local literacies', they fear that 'something [might] be lost when we ascribe to local contexts (those) responses to pressures that originate in distant decisions, especially when seemingly local appropriations of literacy may in fact be culminations of literate designs originating elsewhere?'

I would agree with most of Brandt and Clinton's analysis here of the relationship between the 'local' and the 'distant'. Indeed, it is the focus on this relationship, rather than on one or other of the sites, that characterises the best of NLS. Brandt and Clinton's account here provides a helpful way of describing the local/global debate in which literacy practices play a central role. I would, however, want to agree with their caveat about the possibility of over-emphasising 'the local' whilst disagreeing with their labelling of the 'distant' as more 'autonomous'. The 'distant' literacies to which Brandt refers are also always ideological, and to term them autonomous might be to concede too much to their neutralist claims (see Street, 2003).

Brandt and Clinton's concern with the overemphasis on the local in some NLS accounts; their recognition that for many people the literacies they engage with come from elsewhere and are not self invented; and that there is more going on in a local literacy than 'just local practice', are all important caveats to deter NLS from over-emphasising or romanticising the local, as it has been accused of doing (cf. response by Street to McCabe, 1995 in Prinsloo and Breier, 1996). This important debate can, however, be continued without resorting to a claim that 'distant' literacies are 'autonomous' – as Brandt and Clinton imply in their attempt, to address certain 'autonomous' aspects of literacy without appealing to the 'autonomous model' of literacy. Distant literacies are actually no more autonomous than those of local literacies, or indeed than any literacy practices: their distant-ness, their relative power over local literacies, and their 'non-invented' character as far as local users are concerned, do not make them 'autonomous', only 'distant', or 'new' or hegemonic.

To study such processes both a framework and conceptual tools are required in order to characterise the relation between 'local' and 'distant'. The question raised in the early NLS work concerning how we can characterise the shift from observing literacy events to conceptualising literacy practices does indeed provide both a methodological and an empirical way of dealing with this relation, and thereby taking account of Brandt and Clinton's concerns.

NLS practitioners might also take issue with the apparent suggestion that distant literacies come to local contexts with their force and meaning intact. As Kulick and Stroud indicated a decade ago in their study of new literacy practices brought by missionaries to New Guinea, local peoples more often 'take hold' of new practices and adapt them to local circumstances (1993). The result of local–global encounters around literacy is always a new hybrid rather than a single, essentialised version of either. It is these hybrid literacy practices that NLS focuses upon rather than either romanticising the local or conceding the dominant privileging of the supposed 'global'. As we shall see when we discuss practical applications of NLS across educational contexts, it is the recognition of this hybridity that lies at the heart of an NLS approach to literacy acquisition regarding the relationship between local literacy practices and those of the school.

Collins and Blot (2002) are similarly concerned that, whilst NLS has generated a powerful series of ethnographies of literacy, there is a danger of simply piling up more descriptions of local literacies without addressing the underlying general questions of both theory and practice. In exploring why the dominant stereotypes of literacy are so flawed – such as the notions of a great divide between oral and literate, and the now challenged assumptions of the autonomous model – they invoke NLS but then want to take account of its limitations and to extend beyond them:

> Such understanding also has a more general intellectual value for it forces us to explore why historical and ethnographic cases are necessary but insufficient for rethinking inherited viewpoints ... although ethnographic scholarship has demonstrated the pluralities of literacies, their context-boundness, it still has also to account for general tendencies that hold across diverse case studies.
>
> (pp. 7–8)

They argue for 'a way out of the universalist/particularist impasse', which had troubled Brandt (as we saw above), 'by attending closely to issues of text, power and identity'. These issues are at the heart of current developments in NLS, from Bartlett and Holland's concern with identities in practice (see below), to Street's attention to literacy and power in the ideological model, and Maybin's (2000) refinement of Bakhtin's 'intertextuality' with respect to literacy practices. Writing in *Situated Literacies*, Maybin (2000) also links NLS to wider strands of social-critical work, offering a way of linking Foucauldian notions of 'Discourse', Bakhtinian notions of 'intertextuality', and work in 'Critical Discourse Analysis' with the recognition from NLS of 'the articulation of different discourses [as] centrally and dynamically interwoven in people's everyday literacy activities'. Gee (2000), in the same *Situated Literacies* volume, also located the 'situated' approach to literacies in relation to broader movements towards a 'social turn' which he saw as a challenge to behaviourism and individualism – a challenge which NLS has also pursued. Janks (2000), located in South Africa, likewise links Literacy Studies to broader social theory, invoking concepts of 'Domination, Access, Diversity and Design' as a means of synthesising the various strands of critical literacy education. Freebody, writing from Australia but, like Janks, taking a broad theoretical and international view, likewise writes of the relationship between NLS and 'critical literacy', an approach to the acquisition and use of reading and writing in educational contexts that takes account of relations of power and domination (Freebody, 2006)

Bartlett and Holland also link NLS to broader social theory. They propose an expanded conception of the space of literacy practices, drawing upon innovations in the cultural school of psychology, socio-cultural history and social practice theory. In locating literacy theory within these broader debates in social theory, they build on the concern of Bourdieu to focus on the relationship between social structures (history brought to the present in institutions) and 'habitus' (history brought to the present in person), and suggest ways in which NLS can adapt this approach, an issue that is of course central to the present volume and with which we will deal in some detail in later chapters. Applying a concept of 'figured worlds' – 'a socially produced and culturally constructed realm of interpretation' – to literacy practices, they suggest that such might include 'functional illiterates', 'good readers' and 'illiterates', any of which might be 'invoked, animated, contested and enacted through artefacts, activities and identities in practice' (p. 6). In the world of school-based literacy in particular, scholars have noted the tendency to invoke and deploy such figurings and identities to characterise children and their attainment. Holland and Bartlett enable us to see such characterisations as themselves part of what we should be taking into account when we try to understand literacy practices in context: we should be wary of taking these literacy practices at face value, a scepticism that will prove useful as we move towards applying social literacy theory to education in general and schooling in particular.

In her research on London families, Pahl (2002a, 2002b) has built upon Holland and Bartlett's use of habitus in relation to figured worlds in order to help her describe the multimodal practices of young children at home. She develops this approach further in this volume. Drawing also upon Kress for multimodality and Street for literacy practices, she describes the ways in which young children take from and adapt family narratives as they do drawings, create three-dimensional objects and write graffiti on walls. The work of 'figuring' these family worlds is done through a combination of oral, visual and written artefacts through which, over time,` key themes – such as a family's connection with the railways in India or with a farm in Wales – become 'sedimented' and persistent. Through these narratives, embedded in material and linguistic form, the identity of family members is constructed and adapted over time. There is here again a pedagogic message about how schools might recognise and build upon such home practices, but there is also an important theoretical contribution to NLS: namely that Pahl shows how any account of literacy practices needs to be contextualised within other communicative modes. Like Bartlett and Holland, and Collins, she develops a sophisticated analysis of how such practices relate to concepts of textuality, figured worlds, identity and power.

Another update and extension of NLS is to be found in Hornberger's edited volume (2002) in which the authors attempt to apply her conception of the 'continua of *biliteracy*' to actual uses of reading and writing in different multilingual settings: 'biliteracy' is defined as 'any and all instances in which communication occurs in two (or more) languages in or around writing', and is described in terms of four nested sets of intersecting continua characterising the contexts, media, content, and development of biliteracy. A number of the authors, as in the Martin-Jones and Jones (2000) book, draw out the links of NLS to such multilingual settings.

Applications to Education

The next stage of work in this area is to move beyond these theoretical critiques and to develop positive proposals for interventions in teaching, curriculum, measurement criteria, and teacher education in both the formal and informal sectors, based upon these principles. It will be at this stage that the theoretical perspectives brought together in NLS will face their sternest test: that of their practical applications to mainstream education.

Hull and Schultz (2002) have been amongst the first researchers directly to apply insights from NLS to educational practice and policy. They build upon the foundational descriptions of out-of-school literacy events and practices developed within NLS, to return the gaze back to the relations between in and out of school, so that NLS is not seen simply as 'anti school' or as interested only in small scale or 'local' literacies of resistance. They want to use the understandings of especially children's emerging experiences with literacy in their own cultural milieus to address broader educational questions about learning of literacy and of switching between the literacy practices required in different contexts. They:

> are troubled by a tendency ... to build and reify a great divide between in school and out of school [and that] sometimes this dichotomy relegates all good things to out-of-school contexts and everything repressive to school. Sometimes it dismisses the engagement of children with non-school learning as merely frivolous or remedial or incidental.
>
> (Hull and Schultz, 2002: 3)

In contrast to this approach, and drawing strongly on work in NLS, they argue for overlap or complementarity or perhaps a respectful division of labour. They cite Dewey's argument 'that there is much we can learn about successful pedagogies and curricula by foregrounding the relationship between formal education and ordinary life', that,

> From the standpoint of the child, the great waste in the school comes from
> his inability to utilize the experiences he gets outside of the school in any
> complete and free way within the school itself; while on the other hand, he is
> unable to apply in daily life what he is learning in school.
>
> (Dewey, 1899/1998: 76–8)

However, how are we to know about the experiences of the child outside
school? Many teachers express anxiety that the children in their classes come from
a wide variety of backgrounds and it is impossible to know them all. Hull and
Schultz respond by invoking the work of researchers 'who have made important
contributions to understanding literacy learning through ethnographic or field-
based studies in homes, community organisations and after-school programs'. Their
edited volume offers accounts of such research in a variety of settings. They are
aware of the criticism of such approaches that it might over-emphasise the 'local'
or even 'romanticise out-of-school contexts', and aim instead to 'acknowledge the
complexities, tensions and opportunities' that are found there. Nor is their aim to
provide an exhaustive account of such contexts – teachers are right to argue that
this cannot all be covered. Instead, they aim to provide us all, but especially those
responsible for the education of children, with an understanding of the principles
underlying such variation and with help in listening to and appreciating what it
is that children bring from home and community experience. Indeed, the book
combines both articles about such experience with comments by teachers and
teacher educators on their significance for learning. Here, NLS meets educational
practice in ways that begin to fulfil the potential of the approach but through
dialogue rather than simply an imposition of researchers' agendas on educators.

In Australia, the work of Peter Freebody and of Allan Luke, provide powerful
examples of the application of new theoretical perspectives on literacy, including
NLS, to education, especially work on curriculum and assessment in Queensland (cf.
Luke, and Carrington 2002; Luke and Freebody 2002). In another edited volume
on NLS, a number of authors from a variety of international contexts similarly take
on this challenge and attempt to follow through such practical applications of the
NLS approach (see Street 2005). As with Hull and Schultz's work, the authors are
conscious of the links between theoretical debate and the work of teachers in school
addressing literacy issues. The collection of case studies ranges from formal education,
including elementary, secondary and higher education, and informal sectors such
as community associations, international development programmes and workplace
literacies. Across these educational contexts, the authors are concerned, not just to
apply the general principles of NLS but to offer practical critiques of its application
that force us to refine its original conceptualisation. The volume is intended to
be not a static 'application' of theory to practice but a dynamic dialogue between
the two. In attempting to work through the implications of these approaches for
different sectors of education, the authors find limitations and problems in some
NLS approaches – such as the 'limits of the local' in educational as well as theoretical
terms – that require them to go back to the underpinning conceptual apparatus.

Theory, as well as practice, is subject to the critical perspective adopted there, so that both researchers and practitioners have either to adapt or reject parts of NLS as it is applied to such new tasks.

Such a challenge is raised by current research by Baker, Street and Tomlin applying literacy theory to the understanding of numeracy practices in and out of school (Baker *et al.*, 2003; Baynham and Baker, 2002). Numeracy, even more than literacy, has been seen as a 'universal', 'context' free' set of skills that can be imparted across the board, irrespective of children's background experiences and prior cultural knowledge. Recent approaches to 'situated learning', when allied to those from situated literacy suggest that such a 'banking' model of education, as Paulo Freire termed it, is inappropriate, especially in the multilingual, multicultural situations that characterise contemporary hybrid cultural contexts. The question that Street and Baker address is how far such a culturally-sensitive approach can be applied to numeracy education: can we talk of multiple numeracies and of numeracy events and practices as we do of literacy? Can we build upon cultural knowledge of number, measurement, approximation, etc., in the way that Hull and Schultz and those in the *Literacies across the Curriculum* volume believe we can do for cultural knowledge of literacies, scripts, languages? The questions being raised by NLS, when applied to new fields such as this, will again lead to critiques, not only of current educational practice but also of the theoretical framework itself. As with the critiques by Brandt, Collins, etc., NLS will be forced to adapt and change – the validity and value of its original insights and their applications to practice will be tested according to whether they can meet this challenge.

In an international context, the application of NLS to both schooling and adult literacy has also raised new questions and faced new problems contingent on the nature of the particular context: the aim of such 'applications' has not been to impose a pre-given template on to local work in the field but to enter a dialogue (cf. Street's 2001 edited volume of essays on literacy and development in a dozen different countries for detailed examples). The LETTER Project described in Chapter 5 builds on this work and links theoretical debate with applications in development education contexts. A central theme here is that, as with other 'applications' of NLS (cf. Rogers, 1994; Street, 2001), the local context generates it own new and unique problems that force us to rethink and adapt the initial conceptualisation. In this case, as in many development contexts, the problem arises as to whether there a conflict between theory and policy, and between the local and the needs of scale faced by administrators? The more that ethnographers explain the 'complexity' of literacy practices, the more policy makers find it impossible to design programmes that can take account of all that complexity. The more ethnographers demonstrate that literacy does not necessarily have the practical effects that the rhetoric has suggested – improved health, cognition, empowerment – the harder it becomes for policy makers to persuade funders to support literacy programmes. The more ethnographers focus on specific local contexts, the harder it seems to be to 'upscale' their projects to take account of the large numbers of people seen to be in need. The LETTER Project described in Chapter 5 is an attempt to bridge this apparent divide between policy and research in general, and in particular between large-scale needs and micro ethnographic approaches.

Policy Issues

Despite the willingness of the UK Department for International Development to fund such imaginative approaches to literacy work overseas as the LETTER Project (e.g. through the DELPHE Scheme), in the UK itself, as in the USA, the qualitative and ethnographic-style work that characterises NLS and underpins such an approach is currently out of fashion in higher policy circles. A number of commissions and panels have reviewed research on literacy in the light of a more outcomes based, 'scientific' approach effectively adopting an autonomous model of literacy to determine policy and educational practice; e.g. The National Academy of Science report *Preventing Reading Difficulties in Young Children* (Snow *et al.*, 1998); the *National Reading Panel* set up by the National Institute of Child Health and Human Development (NRP, 2000); and the US Department of Education's newly formed Institute of Education Sciences plan to evaluate research as part of its web-based *What Works Clearinghouse* project. Academic researchers, including those active in the field of literacy, are playing a leading role in these developments. For instance, in the USA Robert Slavin, the founder of *Success for All*, argued in a recent paper in *Educational Research* that: 'the use of randomised experiments that transformed medicine, agriculture and technology in the twentieth century is now beginning to affect educational policy'. He concludes from a survey of such research that 'a focus on rigorous experiments evaluating replicable programs and practices is essential to build confidence in educational research among policymakers and educators' (Slavin, 2002). In particular, this approach suggests ways in which what is known from experimental studies of literacy acquisition can be built into programs and policies for early schooling.

In both the UK and the US qualitative researchers in the literacy field in general, and those working in NLS in particular, have addressed the wider epistemological assumptions underpinning the 'scientific' move and the specific issues regarding acquisition of reading that are often the focus of such approaches (cf. Harrison, 2002). Joanne Larson's wittily titled volume *Literacy as Snake Oil* (2001) has a number of sharp criticisms of the way the Reading Panels have been set up, run and then invoked for policy purposes in the USA. The popularity of such a volume has led to a new edition in which there are also articles on the UK, including one by some of the present authors (Street *et al.*, 2007). These and other authors demonstrate some of the problems with the 'scientific' approach – its inability to engage with the nuances of cultural meanings, the variation in uses of literacy across contexts and the problems already highlighted with the autonomous model of literacy – and attempt to construct more meaningful solutions (cf. Gee, 2001; Coles, 2001). The present volume extends this work by considering ways in which the nuanced approach to 'practice' evident in the work of Bourdieu can be applied in the literacy context, refining the notion of 'literacy practices' and locating literacy in its social context where relations of *habitus* and *field* create a different dynamic – one not captured by dominant policy perspectives.

Conclusion

The effects of critical engagements with social theory, educational applications and policy are that NLS is now going through a productive period of intense debate that first establishes and consolidates many of its earlier insights and empirical work and, second, builds a more robust and perhaps less insular area of study. A major contribution arising from the work cited here has been the attempt to appeal beyond the specific interests of ethnographers interested in the 'local' in order to engage both with educationalists interested in literacy acquisition and use across educational contexts, both formal and informal, and with policy makers more generally. That practical engagement, however, must still be rooted in a sound theoretical and conceptual understanding if the teaching and studying of literacy are to avoid simply being tokens for other interests. We need to analyse and contest what counts as 'literacy' (and numeracy): what literacy events and practices mean to users in different cultural and social contexts – the original inspiration for NLS – but also investigate the 'limits of the local'; and how literacy relates to more general issues of social theory regarding textuality, figured worlds, identity and power. It is in this context that the present volume further draws upon the work of Pierre Bourdieu in order to develop analyses and interpretations that will enable us to further refine our understandings of literacy; whilst, at the same time, focusing on literacy as a case study, for such analyses can perhaps also help us extend and refine the application of the conceptual apparatus offered by Bourdieu. The next chapter addresses these issues with an account of Bourdieu's theory of practice and consequent method.

4

BOURDIEU, LANGUAGE, AND EDUCATION

MICHAEL GRENFELL

Introduction

This chapter is the third 'background' discussion to the three main themes of the book: classrooms, language and ethnography. Here, we offer an account of Pierre Bourdieu's perspective on language and education, since much of the later work in this book is presented in the light of his philosophical position and method. We are leading towards an account of a Bourdieusian ethnography of the language classroom. Language and Education are two separate fields, which need to be seen as being both distinct and integrated. The chapter consequently aims to show the degree to which the particular dimensions of one field also has implications for the other in terms of Bourdieu's general theory of practice. Since our concern is ethnographic, issues of context will never be far away from the discussion. The chapter considers Bourdieu's main theoretical positions, his 'key concepts' (see Grenfell, 2008 for further detail) and how these arose from and have implications for the study of language and education. It will contrast his approach to that of other writers in the broad area of 'language and education' and compare a Bourdieusian methodology with other approaches. The major aspects of adopting such a method will be discussed, together with the advantages they may have – in intent at least – over other methodological approaches. Education is itself a multidisciplinary subject. It will consequently be necessary to refer to issues from other cognate fields, such as history, psychology and sociology. Similarly, language needs to be understood as being central to such academic fields as philosophy and the study of language itself – linguistics (including sociolinguistics and social psycholinguistics). These disciplines will also be referred in the course of the discussion in this and later chapters of the book. Due to limitations of space, this chapter represents a summative rather than a chronological account of Bourdieu, language and education (see Grenfell, 1999 and Grenfell, 2010 for a fuller account). However, it is important, at the outset, to note that Bourdieu himself always insisted on a 'socio-genetic' interpretation of his work; in other words, that it should be read in terms of the socio-cultural, as well as academic context, from which it emerged. The first section of the chapter therefore places Bourdieu's work within his own personal and academic trajectory.

Bourdieu, Language, and Education: Background

Bourdieu's academic trajectory began at a time when matters of language were already dominating the intellectual world. Ferdinand de Saussure (1857–1913) had laid the foundations of contemporary linguistics. An essential feature of language, from a Saussurian point of view, was the distinctions between *langue* and *parole* and *signifier* and the *signified*. The significance of the latter was that any sign could in fact act to signify meaning, as long as there was common assent; the implication being that signs (language) were therefore arbitrary in nature. *Langue* is the totality of the arbitrary consensus on signs (words), whilst *parole* is the set of individual linguistic acts. It followed, for Saussure, that *langue* was the legitimate object for the study of language. The implications of this position were that linguistics should proceed according to an analysis of its formal structural properties. This view of language subsequently gave rise to a major new paradigm known as 'linguistic structuralism' which, through its advocates such as Leonard Bloomfield (1887–1949), was similarly concerned to study the formal structure of language – that is, grammar and its underlying structures – rather than speech itself.

Such developments in thinking about language had repercussions beyond the field of linguistics. For example, 'structuralism', as a system of thought, soon extended its applications to the study of the world itself. For example, Claude Lévi-Strauss (1908–2009) developed a structuralist form of anthropology, which attempts to read exotic cultures as if they were a language made up of underlying generating structures, a syntax of behaviour, and signs. Structuralism has significance for us here in terms of Bourdieu's response to it, and its influence on ethnography. For the moment, it is important to note that a radical form of structuralism was also later developed by such writers as the French Marxist Louis Althusser (1918–1990), who saw in such structures of society the class structures of capitalism. Structuralism is also to be seen as the precursor of post-modernism (post-structuralism) which took many of its grounding principles from extensions of Saussurian thinking about language and their extension to the realm of society as a whole. The French 'post-structuralist' Michel Foucault (1926–1984) often used a linguistic metaphor to talk about social systems as 'discourses'. Indeed, in some ways, we might conclude that the 'philosophy of man' in the twentieth century became the 'philosophy of language'.

These antecedents are extremely important in understanding Bourdieu's theory of practice and the way it developed through his early ethnographic studies (2008a/2000). Bourdieu's own training was as a philosopher, and he would have known the work of Saussure in depth. Lévi-Strauss and structural anthropology, along with existentialism, would have been amongst the major philosophical currents of his intellectually formative years. Wittgenstein's *Philosophical Investigations* had also been published in 1951, thus initiating the 'linguistic turn' which was about to overtake philosophy, with its insistence of seeing language as a 'form of life', the function of which could only be understood by its use. According to Wittgenstein, even cognition (mental processing) needed to be understood in terms of its social aspects. Such ideas became central to Bourdieu's own philosophical outlook. Other more decisive influences came from two direct and immediate personal experiences. The first arose in his own home environment of the Béarn. Here, a village ball led him to investigate the marriage strategies of bachelor farmers, questioning how it was that a section of the male populace seemed to be literally un-marriable. To answer this question, Bourdieu had recourse to detailed statistical analyses and thick ethnographic descriptions to explain how the patterns of culture and inheritance laws excluded certain male individuals from the marriage *field* (see Bourdieu, 2008/2002[1] for a summary of three seminal papers published in 1962, 1972, and 1989). The second experience came from experience in Algeria. Bourdieu was first sent there in 1955 in order to undertake his military service. The effects of being plunged into a cruel war of independence represented no less than a personal epiphany for him. As well as the obvious effects of the fighting, Bourdieu encountered a society divided against itself: large sections of the indigenous population had been uprooted from their lands and placed in 'resettlement' compounds; whilst town life revolved around clashes of tradition and modernity. The streets were filled with beggars and the dispossessed. However, a new, forward looking class had also emerged, the representatives of which could be seen as merchants selling their wares in the streets. In order to understand 'what was Algeria?' and 'what it was to be Algerian?', Bourdieu again undertook extensive statistical analyses as well as detailed ethnographic accounts of Algerian culture. He also took literally thousands of photos (see Bourdieu 2003) and, as well as publications of the time (1958, 1963, 1964), returned again and again to his Algerian ethnographies to develop further aspects of his theory of practice (for example, 1972/1977, 1980/1990).

These two experiences were formative for Bourdieu. He abandoned philosophy and embraced sociology as a professional discipline. Yet, his sociology was of a particular kind. First, it was heavily infused with the philosophical issues of the day and, as well as those listed above, we might add phenomenology and writers within the field of the history of the philosophy of science such as Bachelard and Canguilhem. Second, it was rooted in practical *field*[2] contexts; in particular ethnographies of everyday situations (indeed, it is arguable that Bourdieu might best be described as an 'ethnographer of France'). Third, it is one that begins with questions of the personal experience of the researcher – about which more later in the book.[3]

It is therefore perhaps unsurprising to see Bourdieu undertaking a similar approach and perspective to his early ethnographies of education and culture. In education, he showed a concern to understand 'What is this phenomenon that is a student?', 'How are they formed?', and 'What are the social forces acting upon them?' At the end of Le *déracinement* (1963), Bourdieu argued that the only way of overcoming both the colonial and revolutionary legacy in Algeria was by developing a policy of reconciliation between the demands of culture and politics. Education was central to such an aspiration. There were two clear issues: first, education as a means of providing a workforce which could respond to the economic needs of the modern world; second, education as a source of personal development and transformation. Such aspects applied as much in France as they did in Algeria. The early studies – *Les héritiers. Les étudiants et la culture* (1979/1964) and *La reproduction* (1977a/1970) – seem to explore the extent to which these two aspects were possible.

Culture was a second critical element to his investigation of education: how it is constituted, what it contains, and its presence and effects in pupils, teachers and students. We see similar methodological concerns in studies of art and culture (Bourdieu, 1990b/1965, 1990c/1966) as in the early ethnographies; to begin with a practical context and understand a phenomenon first in *its own terms* before any intellectual narrative is developed around it. The place of the researcher is also critical in his approach and, in a later study of French universities – *Homo academicus* (1988/1984) – Bourdieu offers an account of objectifying his own academic space. Of course, language, as the medium of education, also is a special focus on these ethnographies of education; both in terms of academic discourse itself and the way that language features at all levels of teaching and learning. For example, the 'categories of thought' that are expressed in language used to assess students' written work (see *The State Nobility* (1996/1989): 40–41).

Before looking at language and education from a Bourdieusian perspective in detail, it is worth noting that the concerns mentioned above preoccupied Bourdieu for the whole of his career. Much of his activism in the 1980s and 1990s can be read as a counter to the language of neo-liberal economics (see, 1998 and 1999/1993 for example), and he was always aware of the pernicious effects of language in misrepresenting the truth. He even warned the would-be researcher to 'beware of words' (1989: 54) because of the way they can become the repository of all sorts of 'historical assumptions', silent confusions, impositions, and particular academic interests. Even in response to a letter from a group of sixth-form (college) students seeking support for their cause, he warns them to reject any attempt by others to group them together in a general category such as 'youth', 'sixth-formers', etc., which, he argued, overlooks their true nature (2008b/2002: 181). But, it is time to look at Bourdieu's thesis on the nature and consequences of language in education in 'academic discourse' itself.

Language, Education, and the Reproduction of Society

As noted above, following the Second World War, there were high hopes for a new society in Europe and the role that education would play in its formation. Education was seen as a way to developing the economies and, to a large extent it was successful in this endeavour. Education was in the spotlight, as it still is, with the vocational element of schooling continuing to dominate policies around the world. However, in post-war France at least, the place of education in the development of individuals' culture and well-being was of almost equal importance. In this respect, education took on a much broader role in the passing on of skills and knowledge that would lead to a fuller and richer quality of life for modern man. In France, such an ambition can be traced back to the Catholic intellectuals of the 1930s and beyond, with their aim to develop the soul of modern man. Such a philosophy animated the Resistance groups in the Second World War and became enshrined in the policies of the Fourth Republic through a programme of popular education and Malraux's (the first Minister of Culture) *Maisons de la Culture*. Since, 'culture' and education were inextricably linked in post-war France, it was not surprising to see them featuring both in the pragmatic world of politics as well as attracting the attention of researchers in the fast-developing social sciences. Frequent international seminars on education were held. Bourdieu took part in several of these (see for example, Castel and Passeron, 1967 and Darras, 1966) where the issue of the unequal distribution of scholastic achievement, and thus profit, was addressed. Clearly, not all benefited from education to the same extent. In the Anglo-Saxon world, sociologists such as Musgrave (1966) and Banks (1968) had shown how scholastic success followed patterns of social stratification in terms of socio-economic groupings. This problem was seen initially as one of access and, certainly, in the past, education lasting into young adulthood was the prerogative of the rich. The post-war answer therefore seemed obvious: make schooling available to pupils in greater numbers and from a wider distribution of social classes. In a word, 'democratise schools'.

These issues of education and culture, the role of education, links with society and the economy, social differentiation, access and democratisation are those which faced Bourdieu, and which shaped his early studies: *Les étudiants et leurs etudes* (1964), *Les héritiers. Les étudiants et la culture* (1979/1964) and *La reproduction* (1977a/1970). In considering these works, it is important to keep in mind a series of key questions. Is the analysis a fair representation of reality? To what extent does it apply uniquely to France, and does it have common features with other cultural contexts? What evidence is there for the conclusions drawn? To what extent are the issues raised (over forty years ago) still relevant today? What are the implications for classroom ethnographies? What role does language play in the processes described?

The ethnographic dimension of Bourdieu's work is emphasised at the beginning of *Les héritiers*, which begins with an epigraph from the famous cultural anthropologist Margaret Mead in which she describes the practices of the North American Indians. At a certain age, apparently, the young men of the village were sent out into the wilderness where they fasted and experienced visions involving ancestral spirits. After a time they returned to recount what they had seen in their dreams, which were then interpreted by the elders of the tribes. However, it was explained to some young men that their dreams were not real at all, whilst others were recognised as genuine visions.

The analogy with modern education is obvious. As with education, there is a kind of 'rite de passage' through which all children and adolescents must pass. The required knowledge is available to all. However, according to the interpretations of society's elders, only some groups apparently successfully acquire it. It only needs to be added that the successful privileged few typically belong to the existing 'dominant' groups of the tribe and, unsurprisingly, those with 'inauthentic' visions come from less prestigious groups. In the same way, Bourdieu is noting in *Les héritiers* that whatever the issues of access – and the democratic school defined itself in terms of making educational opportunity more equitable – the pattern is that only 'the few' succeed, and that they seemingly always come from the same dominant sections of society. In fact, in a near polemic, Bourdieu denounces the whole notion of 'the democratic school', which he claims dated back to the Jacobin tradition born of the Great Revolution of 1789, and which paradoxically perpetuates inequality in the name of equality (2008b/2002/1966: 34ff.). Briefly, his argument is as follows: it is only necessary for educationalists to insist that everyone has equal access to all levels of education for social inequalities to play their part in operating a kind of social selection which excludes a large part of the school populace. So, anyone can enter the *concours* (a competitive exam for entry to the best schools, colleges and universities in France), while implicitly it is clear that only those with a certain education, prior experience and training stand any chance of passing it. Such a system of selection is in fact more effective when it operates in a covert manner than if privilege of birth were asserted at the outset. Indeed, within the systems operating in the democratic school, inequalities of social origin are retranslated and re-expressed as inequalities of talent, which allows for their *legitimation* in the face of the possessed and dispossessed. All the school has to do is ignore the content and teaching it transmits, the methods and techniques of that transmission, and the criteria of judgement it applies, for social inequalities to express themselves in the outcome of schooling. However, this imposed form of social differentiation requires more than that educationalists pass over in silence the selection which is operating before their very eyes. Such misrecognition also needs a medium for its operation, and this is where culture plays such an important role. Bourdieu makes the point that the content of the culture found, for example, in the teaching of literature – in French schools at least – was, at the same time, largely based around what he termed as 'aristocratic values'; in other words, those of the French literary tradition, with which the sons and daughters of the 'cultivated classes' had greater familiarity. The point is, of course, that the content and the values of the culture in place were in fact quite arbitrary. What is most important is that such cultural forms are unevenly distributed across the social hierarchy, and then established as core values for scholastic success. In this way, privileged like attracts privileged like, as a 'fish in water': a so-called 'elective affinity' of mutual recognition, valuation and *legitimation*. So, whilst the son of a top executive manager may have few obvious ways of inheriting his father's job, the attitudes, aptitudes and literacy required in the home will improve his chances of gaining access to highly prestigious universities; which in turn will create better professional chances. Success in one of the highly prestigious universities is then due to the aptitudes acquired in the home. This kind of sleight of hand is also a form of mystification since, in accepting social inheritance as social gifts, even the families of the dispossessed accept that their exclusion is socially right and justified. In this way, culture acts as a kind of 'capital' which buys position, access, and ultimately privilege. The term *cultural capital* is used to designate the way the operations of culture can have economic consequences. Bourdieu argues that social inequalities in relation to schooling can actually be more pronounced than economic inequalities in society; indeed, that awareness of cultural inequalities decreases as such inequalities increase. In this way, people are persuaded that, 'the distribution of degrees of merit corresponds to the distribution of degrees of culture' (1979/64: 39). The actual function of schooling is consequently occulted and misrecognised. And, contrary to schools' stated aims to train, educate, and develop, their principal function is rather to socially differentiate. In this sense, the 'democratic school' is in fact a socially 'conservative school' as it works to reproduce the established structures of society, but through a cultural mechanism rather than economic one (although the two are clearly always closely interrelated). But, how does this mechanism operates in the classroom and what is the part that language plays in it?

Academic Discourse

It is important to keep in mind that, for Bourdieu, the social world is a place of continual symbolic exchange. It is as if societies, communities and groups are in a perpetual state of valuation and re-evaluation with respect to each other. In a sense, this position is common to the Marxist view of modern capitalism, where everything is reduced to capital value, including labour. For Marx, what was social *was* economic. The same might be said of Bourdieu. However, for him, this view of economism – and this applied as much to neo-liberal economics as it did to the Marxist alternative – of everything being reduced to financial calculation of profit and loss, vastly underrated the actuality of 'economic' exchange. For Bourdieu, the 'economic' could be expressed just as clearly in symbolic exchanges, which might have just as significant consequences in terms of social positioning as any exchange of economic *capital*. Indeed, Bourdieu saw the whole social world as being articulated through the medium of forms and configurations of *capital*: social, economic and cultural (see 1986). All three are symbolic in that their possession is recognised within *social space* in terms of the power they each confer. *Economic capital* is the only one which is explicitly financial as it represents actual money wealth. *Social capital* is the term used to describe social networking, and how useful contacts can be called upon to gain entrance to prestigious positions in terms of society and professions. Bourdieu sees an evolution within communities and societies, where different forms of *capital* become more prevalent at different stages in their evolution. For example, he argued that *economic capital* had been displaced as the main medium of social reproduction within the *field* of power in contemporary France: and that displacement happened when cultural forms (initially most noticeable in educational achievement) took on an increasing significance as a way of establishing oneself within the social hierarchy. This phenomenon is understandable enough when seen against the background of the economic significance given to education because of the changes in society mentioned above. Bourdieu explains that such *cultural capital* was 'intended to account for otherwise inexplicable differences in academic performance with children of unequal cultural patrimonies and, more generally, in all kinds of cultural or economic practices' (2005/2000: 2). Basically, *cultural capital* is the expressed form of valued products arising from education and social standing. Such products may be acquired in the home, for example, the 'right' accent, or familiarity with 'high culture' as a result of access to the 'right' books, music, and cultural pastimes. However, it was in school (the democratic school!) that *cultural capital* was most explicitly bestowed on individuals. Certain qualifications can be seen to be *cultural capital* in that they offer an institutionally legitimised recognition of skills, knowledge and training which 'buy' professional position in the form of jobs. The higher the qualification, the more it buys. Similarly, attendance at certain institutions themselves hold prestige which rubs off on those who pass through them. Indeed, Bourdieu's own schools and colleges all come into the prestigious and privileged category of the most highly respected in France. However, these physical and personal attributes need also to be seen as forming part of the characteristics and behaviours of pupils and students, the language of education, and the very style and forms of thought itself.

As part of his early ethnographies of education, Bourdieu offers a characterisation – ideal type – of the then French *homo academicus* (1979/1964: 43). They are *cultural capital* personified. Such an individual is already the son or daughter (probably grandson or granddaughter) of teachers. They are studying philosophy and are aiming for the *École Normale Supérieure* with a view to becoming a teacher themselves. They are highly literate: they have read 'the whole of French literature by the age of 15' and have already distinguished themselves in academic competitions, such as Latin translation. They have also read all the latest writers, as well as recognising and acknowledging their literary tradition. Such individuals are clearly highly competitive, individualistic and precocious – a way of being that is fed both at home and school through particular forms of culture and language which act in symbiotic relationship to each other in a kind of game, but one which Bourdieu claims has deadly consequences in terms of the outcomes and life chances of individuals. It is a game in a truly Wittgensteinian sense as language is deployed according to function and situation. However, it is also a game in the very real sense of the word in that it has its own rules, playing fields, prizes, and players – albeit implicit and misrecognised as such – but where the odds are heavily stacked for and against certain groups of individuals who 'play' the game as a result of their own social provenance, and the extent to which this equips them with the necessary cultural prerequisites to survive and even come out on top in the competition. Indeed, as noted above, those without the necessary ways of speaking, thinking and doing accept and even collude in their own exclusion. Faced with what might be termed a 'charismatic ideology' of talent (p.71), those without it accept their lack of scholastic gifts in similar terms, thus conflating 'what' they are with 'who' they are. Mothers even reaffirm failure when they say of their sons, 'he is no good at French' (ibid.). For Bourdieu, this is a kind of negative illusion exhibiting three kinds of damage:

> Firstly, unaware that her son's results are a direct function of the cultural atmosphere of his family background, she makes an individual destiny out

of what is only the product of an education and can be corrected, at least in part by educative action. Secondly, for lack of information about schooling, sometime for lack of anything to counterpose to the teacher's authority, she uses simple test scores as the basis for premature definitive conclusions. Finally, by sanctioning this type of judgement, she intensifies the child's sense that he is this or that by nature.

(ibid.)

A family's misrecognition of the nature of educational success therefore works to preclude particular social groups from academic success. Of course, the point here is that the successful figure described is not *the* homo academicus, set out of time and across cultures. In fact, it is an actualisation that is in constant flux and which manifests differences of representation in times and places. However, the underlying cultural process is the same; one which legitimises one form of thought and practice (of a dominant group) and uses it as an implicit form of social selection through the mechanism of schooling and higher education.

Culture in terms of a particular form of education and language is therefore all for Bourdieu. At one points, he asserts that 'many of the distinguishing features of English "positivism", or French "rationalism" are surely nothing other than tricks and mannerisms of school' (1971a/1967: 204). Also, that the cult of team sports in English public schools both nourished and fed the 'anti-intellectualism of the British Imperial elite (1989: 74), as it encouraged loyalty to group and teamwork over individuality and independence – the latter values being more common amongst graduates of the French *École Polytechnique*. Even within the elite groups, there are noticeable oppositions which can be understood as characterising distinctions. So, between the ENS (*École Normale Supérieure*) and the ENA (*École Normale d'Administration* – a high level training college founded after the Second World War to train the new technicist elite required to drive the French economy) – there are differences in the way scholastic competence is defined. For example, in the oral exam of the ENA, mastery over complex situations is required – such as the 'official interview', or 'cocktail/dinner party'. At the ENS, on the other hand, academic excellence is defined more in terms of the presentation of written exams, which need to exhibit 'clarity', 'conviction' and a certain 'presence of mind'. But, it went deeper than even that. Bourdieu drew on the work of the art historian Erwin Panowsky (1957), who had showed that there existed a homological relationship between a certain style of Gothic church architecture and the style of scholarship found in the training schools of the architects involved. In both the buildings and the education that gave rise to them, there were symmetrical principles of 'clarity', 'literary presentation', 'order', and 'logic'. Mental habits were not so much replicated in practice as giving rise to genuine causes and effects in terms of dispositional structures, attitudes, and ways of organising thinking. In the same way, for Bourdieu, 'the school provides those who have undergone its direct or indirect influence not so much with particular and particularised schemes of thought [although they may do this as well] as with that general disposition which engenders particular schemes, which may then be applied in different domains of thought and action' (1971a/67: 184, my comment in brackets). In brief, men who are formed by a certain school have in common a certain cast of mind.

Contra the ethnologist Lévi-Strauss, however, Bourdieu does not see culture as providing a common set of codes or rules to answer recurrent problems in the world, but rather 'master patterns' through which problems are dealt with as an active part of invention. In other words, culture is less *rule-driven* than offering framing *principles* for developing *strategies* to think and act in a certain way. For the French, scholasticism had been characterised by the ability to abstract and generalise, to go for style over content, and to see human nature as eternal, immutable and timeless (ibid.: 201ff.). Such a position was not simply a scholastic mannerism. It had a moral dimension which characterised an entire *raison d'être* in the world: 'The phrase "I am master over myself and over the universe" is an ethical profession of faith in which a dominant individual justifies his domination in his own mind by referring to his *natural* capacity to nominate nature' (1989: 110 my italics). As such, a particular education acts as both a *consecration* and a *legitimation*.

Bourdieu saw these processes as being everywhere apparent in the actual language of education. In a reflexive study of students and their language, he makes a number of points about the nature and form of academic discourse (1994/65: originally entitled, *Rapport Pédagogique et Communication*, this book raises the pertinent question of the extent to which its findings are still valid – some forty years later – and how they contrast with different national contexts). Two key points are made by Bourdieu: first, that academic communication is predicated on the systematic misunderstanding of meaning between teachers and students; second, any one individual's particular use of language within a single context – whether teacher or student – is of less importance (significance) than their whole relationship to language (to which their own socio-cultural background and trajectory is intimately associated). Bourdieu's empirical investigations seem to show that students had a very 'poor' understanding of academic language in general (and even everyday language), and that competence varied according to such social categories as socio-economic background, gender, and professional specialism. 'Professorial language' and 'student language' are counter-posed. At the time, the ideal type 'professor' in France held a position of sartorial authority. If the 'toga' and 'ermine' had been abandoned, the style of language they employed (expressing underlying principles of thought) remained set within a certain way of expressing ideas, which itself was defined in terms of their specific position in the academic hierarchy (p.19). Indeed, the lectern from which the lectures were delivered itself seems to dictate a certain manner and tone to which there seems little resistance on the part of the lecturer (p. 11). Faced with this situation, students are often confronted by what is little more than a 'semantic fog' as they strive to adopt the language and thinking of the teacher. They mimic a style they have not really mastered:

> Student comprehension thus comes down to a general feeling of familiarity... technical terms and references, like 'epistemology'. 'methodology'. 'Descartes',

and 'sciences', shoulder each other up. He can quite naturally refrain from seeking clarification of each one of these…for his system of needs is not, cannot be, and up to a point must not be, analytical…the student is able to put together an essay which is apparently written in the same language of ideas, but in which the sentence 'Descartes renewed epistemology and methodology' can only be an impressionistic restoration. For outside this sentence, many students associate nothing with the word 'epistemology'.

(p.15)

Learning at best then becomes a loose familiarity with the content of education rather than a practical understanding. For Bourdieu, this is a kind of collective act of intellectual *mauvaise foi*. On the one side, the teacher is addressing their remarks to an ideal student that simply does not exist; on the other, the student is attempting to be someone they are not – except, of course, there is a closer cultural match between some students and the teacher than others. Academic discourse for Bourdieu is set up to exploit these differences in the very act of pedagogic exchange so that some students are able to cope and converge with the knowledge and style of language whilst others do not; the extent of this convergence being the 'social difference' between teacher and student: 'the world of the classroom where 'polished' language is used, contrasts with the world of the family' (p. 9). Yet, based on their authority, the teacher demands that all students learn whilst 'knowing' that the means of doing so has been withheld from a significant proportion of them. Bourdieu further argues that there are two contradictory principles in academic discourse: first, the need to maximise the quantity of information conveyed; and second, and as a consequence of this, the need to minimise lost of information (p. 6). The first leads to attempts by the teacher to reduce redundancy and repetition; whilst the second might actually require that these are increased. Both cannot be satisfied simultaneously and, according to Bourdieu, any attempt to do so is utopian because it runs counter to this fundamental relationship to the language of teaching that:

There is a visible abyss to be crossed between redundancy of a traditional nature, like musical variations on a theme, and redundancy of a rational kind, like conscious and calculated repetition (for example, in the form of the definition), or again between ellipsis by omission and understatement and conciseness guided by the need for economy.

(p. 6)

In other words, Bourdieu is arguing that a linguistic contradiction is at the root of academic pedagogy, one which only the 'literate' students can successfully surmount.

At this point, it is worth setting Bourdieu's original thesis on academic discourse in context, not as a historical aside but in order to emphasise the way that many of the issues that it raises are still pertinent today. Until the 1950s, educational research was essentially psychological and psychometric and often based, often based on experimental methods. However, this changed during the 1960s when there arose a new approach to research into education based around the so-called foundational disciplines: history, philosophy, sociology and psychology. In this way, educational research took a 'qualitative turn'. Before this time, even disciplines like the 'sociology of education' were dominated by academics who were sociologists first and interested in education second. Their approach consequently was often statistical, and sought to catalogue differences in academic achievement according to various pre-existing social categories. What Bourdieu's perspective did was in effect to focus on the actual process of knowledge formation in teaching and learning, and the causes and consequences of that process. In 1971, two of Bourdieu's papers – *Systems of Education and Systems of Thought* and *Intellectual Field and Creative Project* – were published in Michael Young's *Knowledge and Control* (1971), which acted as a seminal volume in the founding of this 'new' sociology of education. This collection set out with two primary aims: first, to develop new methodologies for the sociological study of education; second, to focus on the organisation of knowledge in educational institutions. Of course, Bourdieu's perspective addressed both issues, and it is therefore unsurprising that they should feature in the book. Across all papers, we see the emergence of a new preoccupation on the actual language of academic discourse and classroom ethnographies; although the two are still seldom integrated. Bourdieu was not a lone voice; for example, Basil Bernstein, in his work on theories of codes and classification of educational knowledge (1971: 47–69). Somewhat congruent with Bourdieu, Bernstein saw a distinction between what he termed the 'restricted' and 'elaborated' codes present in the language of pupils from various socio-economic categories: the former being characteristic of working class children, whilst the latter typified the language of the middle classes upwards. The significance of this thesis was, of course, that education demanded 'elaborated' codes, and thus implicitly favoured those who already possessed them (more or less). In another chapter, Nell Keddie was also looking at the way that subject and pupil orientation were dependent on the teachers' pre-formed categories of pupil abilities (pp. 133–160), which itself can be seen as complementing Bourdieu's view of the clashes between teacher and student world views.

Knowledge and Control can now be seen as part of a 'new wave' of educational research. Along with a direct interest in classroom discourse, researchers increasingly turned to naturalistic and so-called qualitative methods. Educational ethnographies were widespread, including both evaluative and non-evaluative case studies, action research, and reflective practitioner studies. Such trends also eventually embraced post-modernist and critical theoretical techniques. The number of classroom language studies also increased substantially. For example, researchers such as Douglas Barnes analysed the nature of group work and the way that teacher questioning affected pupil response (Barnes, 1976, and Barnes and Todd, 1977). Sinclair and Coulthard (1975) examined the structure of academic discourse and were able to see the patterns of pedagogic language: for example, the I-R-F (Initiation-Response-Feedback) sequences apparent in many teacher-pupil exchanges. They also quantified the amount and range of language use in the classroom. Furthermore, Flanders (1965) found that two-thirds of classroom activity was oral work, two-thirds of that oral work was teachers talking, and two-thirds of that talk was questioning. The tradition of studying classroom language eventually led to them embracing the work of the Soviet psychologist Lev Vygotsky (1962, 1978) with his focus of the social construction of knowledge as a form of individual cognitive control. Subsequently adopted by educational psychologists such as Jerome Bruner, Vygosky's concept of the Zone of Proximal Development – being the point where the *intra*-psychological interacts with the *inter*-psychological (and now reconceptualised as a pedagogical action, as *scaffolding*) became an important guiding metaphor for those interested in improving the effectiveness of classroom pedagogy though teachers' use of language. Edwards and Mercer (1987) and Mercer (1995) also saw classrooms in terms of the construction of 'common knowledge' between pupils and their teachers.

Many of these theoretical positions and practical observations would resonate with some aspects of Bourdieu's own view of language and education. However, there are two key points to be made – one epistemological, and one methodological.

The first of these concerns the radical or critical nature of Bourdieu's position. Bourdieu wrote at the end of *Les héritiers* about a 'rational pedagogy' – one having, 'the unconditional goal of enabling *the greatest possible number of individuals to appropriate, in the shortest possible time, as completely and as perfectly as possible, the greatest possible number of the abilities which constitute school culture at a given moment*' (p.75), a goal which would neutralise social and cultural factors apparent in educational inequalities. However, this would require teachers to step outside their 'linguistic and cultural ethnocentrism' (1994/65: 22), something they would seem unlikely to do as it went against the very nature of the generating principles of the academic discourse to which they belonged. It would need teachers to give students the means to satisfy the demands put on them, by making explicit the presuppositions underlying academic manipulation of language in teaching and learning contexts, which runs against the scholastic logic of practice outlined above. Of course, Bourdieu's critical position was in keeping with the intellectual trends of the day. Many writers of the time were used to using terms such as 'power', 'ideology', 'opposition' and 'resistance' in their discussions of education. As noted, *Reproduction* itself can be read as a quasi-Marxist account of the ways by which education contributes to the construction and perpetuation of class structures in societies. No wonder therefore that many educationalists were talking about *deschooling*, as a way of reducing the pernicious effects of education. Some contributors to *Knowledge and Control* also acknowledged the need for some *unstreaming* and *unorganisation* of the curriculum in schools. The prime cause of scholastic inequality, it was argued, resided in differences between the culture of schooling and that of various groups within society. The logical consequence was therefore to change the relationship between culture and schools. Such a change came under three headings: celebration, compensation, and confrontation. Either the 'counter culture' was celebrated as a rich alternative; or policies were introduced to compensate for the relative cultural deprivation it implicitly imposed; or it was used as a form of resistance, as a counter-attack against the dominate hegemony. It would be fair to say that Bourdieu flirted with each of these in the course of his career. In some ways, he struggled with the logical consequences of his own theoretical conclusions. In a sense, if he was correct, any move to change to a new situation would be doomed to failure as it would go against the whole *raison d'être* and logic of the practice of education as it was originally constructed. A different social group might well achieve dominance but inequalities based on culture and school would persist. At the same time, something had to be done.

The second concern – a methodological one – is connected with the use that could be made of Bourdieu's perspective. The 'new' sociology of education entered a *field* that was seeing the expansion of teacher education. Many of the school ethnographies and classroom discourse analyses carried out took a mainly positive approach in analysing what was occurring in the structures of teaching and learning with a view to suggesting the ways in which pedagogy could be improved. There was then an onus on increasing the effectiveness of pedagogy. For Bourdieu, classroom efficiency was not the main issue, but the whole tenor of educational philosophy and its consequences; a position that struck at the heart of modern capitalist society and the role that education played in the reproduction of social inequalities. Such a position can be read as a neo-Marxist critique. Yet, there is another reading – critical with a small 'c' perhaps – that offers the same insights without the socio-political implications and ramifications. The point here is to analyse the nature of academic discourse in order to disclose underlying operations and their provenance, and thus to facilitate pedagogic communication, rather than expressing it simply in terms of capitalistic class relations (Bourdieu eventually took a similar line with his work on reforming the curriculum. See 1992a/1989). In fact, the preoccupation with effectiveness and efficiency was at the core of the analyses of the educational discourse discussed above, even in their more radical guises. However, methodologically, this led many such researchers to see answers in the nature and form of the discourse itself – within the language of pedagogy and the way it was expressed differentially between teachers and students. Bourdieu's approach goes beyond this and focuses on the provenance of such language, the classroom, and the backgrounds of the pupils and teachers. Which historical factors, for example, led to the construction of the classroom in this way? What were the explicit links with curricula and syllabi, and how were these played out in the classroom? In what ways were cultural forms differentially expressed – ethnographically and linguistically – and how demonstrable were they in the classroom? What were the consequences? What influence do the biography and training of the teachers have? What about the pupils' social origins? In order to answer these questions from a Bourdieusian perspective, we need to be able to track learning from the individual cognitive act in a particular cultural environment through to the more generic learning context and to the educational *field* as it is placed within society as a whole.

Habitus, Field, and the Processes of Teaching and Learning

So far, this chapter has looked at a range of the elements in Bourdieu's approach to language and education: there are the early formative ethnographies in Algeria and the Béarn; the centrality of education as a phenomenon for analysis in Bourdieu's work; a particular view of culture and the way its conspires to affect social selection; and the nature of academic discourse itself. All of this is underpinned by Bourdieu's own background as a philosophy graduate and his embracing of sociology as a discipline. This background is crucial to understanding the potential of Bourdieu's work. The present section now takes forward these perspective by developing the links between individuals and the socio-cultural environments which surround them. In the course of this discussion, the connection between the psychological and sociological will be raised, as well as the way that language mediates these relationships on a number of levels. Each of these issues is central to a Bourdieusian approach to educational ethnography.

Bourdieu's approach requires that any individual can be understood as being inextricably connected with their own particular broader socio-cultural environment. But, this relationship is always a dialectic, where the two are seen as dynamic and mutually constitutive. At one point (1968), Bourdieu borrows a phrase used by Berger and Luckmann (1967) in their *Social Construction of Reality* – 'the externalisation of internality and the internalisation of externality' – to express this dynamic. It is worth noting that Berger and Luckmann's thesis was itself constructed from a synthesis of the founding fathers of sociology – Marx, Weber and Durkheim. Later still, Bourdieu referred to his methodological approach as being based on a principles of 'structural constructivism' or 'constructive structuralism' (1989). But what does he mean by *structure*, and in what way do structures inter-relate with each other?

Bourdieu was enough of a phenomenologist – he was a student of the French phenomenologist Merleau-Ponty – to see the primary act of consciousness in structural terms. When we direct thought at anything, intention is involved which creates a structural relation between the thinker (subject) and the object of their thought. This process begins at birth and builds throughout life. Gradually, individual acts of perception are made in the light of a pre-existent and constantly growing pool, or reservoir, of knowledge (both conscious and unconscious) – a distinction that the German philosopher Husserl would later refer to as the *noesis* and the *noema*. In a sense, it is also part of a process of 'control,' or acquiring social equilibrium and, of course, it is one in which language is actively involved. If we think something, we can name it. If we can name it, we can objectify it. If we can objectify something, we can control it – internally at least. Structure at this level then is bound up with individual subjective knowledge and thinking. However, such knowledge is also clearly formed in relation to the external socio-cultural environment – including what is already 'known' within a particular culture. In this sense, knowledge can be seen as an 'objective' phenomenon, and as one to be understood in structural terms.

For Bourdieu, there are two salient traditions in the understanding of culture: one which sees it as a *structured* structure, and the other as a *structuring* structure. The first consequently studies cultures in terms of observable structural relations. The ethnologies of Lévi-Strauss are good examples of this tradition: based around Saussurian structural linguistics and 'reading' cultures in terms of their observable signs, rules, and systems. The second tradition sees culture in terms of its ideational infrastructure, and the way this functions to direct human action. The sociology of Durkheim and Parsons would come within this tradition, as both are preoccupied with the moral health and integration of society and, consequently, how it is that social agents behave in the way that they do. Paradoxically, the radical sociology of Marx also sees culture in this way; except that in this case, the moral state of society is capitalist, and therefore alienating, and individuals behave largely as a result of *false consciousness*. These two traditions express culture in terms of objective structures. Bourdieu is critical of both: the first for being simply too rigid and static, and underestimating the creative aspect of human facticity; the second for being idealist, for example, seeing ideology as an imposition of the ruling class in the critical tradition, or moral authority and social control in the positivist one. Bourdieu is seeking to go beyond both traditions in order to 'arrive at the basic principle behind the efficacy of symbols, which is the structured structure which confers on symbolic systems their structuring power' (1977b/1972: 3).

Bourdieu developed such theoretical views as a direct result of immediate ethnographic experience and, at one point, argues that his perspective should be seen as constituting a series of 'breaks' (ibid.). He wants to break from naïve, everyday, practical knowledge in order to understand what is actually going on in empirical contexts. However, he also wants to break from subjective forms of theoretical knowledge (phenomenology, etc.) and objective forms such as structuralism, positivism, etc. Indeed, at one point he refers to the opposition between the subjective and objective in the social sciences as 'the most fundamental, and the most ruinous' (1990a/1980: 25).

Bourdieu was not alone in this endeavour. As mentioned above, the Soviet psychologist Lev Vygotsky was also interested in a form of constructivism that saw knowledge as a product of the relationship between any one individual and the socio-cultural environment in which they found themselves. Bourdieu's version, however, has a radical twist in that if individual knowledge is formed through the interaction with their socio-cultural surroundings, then it must also necessarily be partly formed by structures saturated with pre-existent values, principles, and ways of thinking. Moreover, the latter can be seen in terms of their proximity to, or distance from, orthodox forms. In other words, knowledge is never value-neutral but comes as representing the particular social environment from which it emerged. There is then an *interest* expressed in knowledge, of one group or another, which can subsequently be recognised (or not) by others sharing (or not) the same social provenance (see Grenfell, 2008). This argument is at the core of Bourdieu's thesis on education: that scholastic culture has an *interest* that is shared by some – but not all – socio-economic groupings within the *social space*. A key feature of Bourdieu's approach is then to see such *interest* (values, principles, etc.) in terms of the structural homologies shared between individuals' knowing and the knowledge bases with which they engage.

Bourdieu's methodological approach is therefore based, not on theoretical suppositions, or simply practical ethnographies but a 'theory of practice' which aims to synthesis both of these into one integrated worldview. Such an approach constitutes a 'science of the dialectical relations between objective structures... and the subjective dispositions within which these structures are actualised and which tend to reproduce them' 1977b/1972: 3) – and, we might add, to do this in the context of real-life ethnographies. It is worth emphasising that the whole of Bourdieu's conceptual terms were developed as a result of the necessity to make sense of and understand practical situations in terms of the scientific ambitions expressed above. In order to bridge the subjective–objective divide two terms in particular were used by Bourdieu to elucidate empirical data: *habitus* and *field* (space does not allow for a full explanation of the way these evolved in the course of Bourdieu's *field* work, but see Grenfell (2006)).

Habitus expresses the subjective side of the equation and is defined by Bourdieu as:

> Systems of durable, transposable dispositions, structured structures predisposed to function as structuring structures, that is, as principles which generate and organize practices and representations that can only be objectively adapted to their outcomes without presupposing a conscious aiming at ends or an express mastery of the operations necessary in order to attain them.
>
> (1990a/1980: 53)

Whilst *field* is defined as: '... a network, or a configuration, of objective relations between positions' (1992b: 97). As such, education can be seen as a *field* in that it is bounded, structured and conforms to its own organisational logic. Any methodological approach conducted from a Bourdieusian perspective therefore would proceed in terms of an analysis of *habitus* and *field*. Indeed, a four-stage methodology is therefore implied in that any ethnography must look a *social space* in terms of: first, the *fields* represented there; second, the structure of the *fields* themselves; thirdly, the structural relation between *fields*; and, fourthly, the *habitus* of the individuals involved in each of them. Bourdieu's account of education, as outlined above, can be seen as an expression of this approach (see Grenfell, 2007 for further discussion).

It would be possible to give further exemplification of ethnographies using Bourdieu's concepts and theory of practice, and the chapters in part II do just that. The later sections then assess these applications in terms of the overall themes of the book – New Literacy Studies, Ethnography and Education. The last section of this chapter, however, considers what language looks like from the perspective of *habitus* and *field*.

The Linguistic Market and Education

In a sense, it would be very easy to superimpose Bourdieu's theory of practice, with all that entailed in terms of the issues surrounding 'structure', onto language. Indeed, Bourdieu employed the term *linguistic habitus* to designate individual speech characteristics. Just as in the case of *habitus* per se, *linguistic habitus* is formed from any one individual's (linguistic) background and environment and shares features in common with others within the same socio-cultural milieu. Indeed, in theory, the linguistic features of *habitus* can be expressed at any linguistic level – phonetic, phonological, morphological, syntactic and semantic – and may even extend to the meta- and para-linguistic: language is also a bodily feature for Bourdieu, and therefore forms part of any individual's *hexis*. *Linguistic habitus* is similarly 'structured' in both the phenomenological and cultural sense of the word, and exists in a homologous relationship with the surrounding *field*. For Bourdieu, however, the 'linguistic *field*' is expressed in terms of a *linguistic market*. This is an extended econometric, rather than economic, metaphorical tool to draw attention to the way that language has value within a *field* context, is the product of investment (at home and in school) which draws profits, and 'buys' position as a result of the prestige it attracts to itself from the *field* by being recognised as such. In short, just as the relation between *habitus* and *field* is never value-neutral, neither is language – and the relation between culture and learning expressed through language. It always comes with an autological self-definition in terms of its proximity to what is regarded as the *consecrated* (most highly valued) linguistic norms of the *field* context. Basically, any social space – even deviant sites – has an acknowledged way of expressing language at its various levels: therefore, linguistic norms or *legitimate language*. The most obvious example of the latter is the recognised norms of language and literacy acknowledged at a national level; for instance, Received Pronunciation in English or *Academie* French. For Bourdieu, such linguistic features should furthermore be regarded as *capital* – *linguistic capital* – and forming a part of *cultural capital* as the dispositional prerequisites individuals hold to mediate position within the social hierarchy. However, behind this perspective on language lies a more fundamental critique of the sciences of the study of language itself.

As mentioned earlier, the founding father of contemporary linguistics was Ferdinand de Saussure who, with linguists such as Bloomfield, defined the study of language in terms of its formal, structural properties. Even the Chomskyan revolution of the 1950s is predicated on the notion of an 'ideal' speaker and, thus perfect competence. For Bourdieu, this model is simply something that does exist. Moreover, the consequent methodology that seeks to see sense and significance in terms of an 'internalist' reading of language itself basically overlooks all the contextual (social, cultural) components that give linguistic events their meaning:

> (it) … reduces individual practice, skill, everything that is determined practically by reference to practical ends, that is style, manner, and ultimately the agents themselves, to the actualization of a kind of historical essence, in short, nothing.
>
> (Bourdieu 1990a/1980: 33)

The normal constructions of linguists – which sees the study of linguistic form as an end in itself – therefore needs to be reconceptualised. Bourdieu's alternative is as follows:

> In place of *grammaticalness* it puts the notion of *acceptability*, or, to put it another way, in place of 'the' language (*langue*), the notion of *legitimate* language. In place of *relations of communication* (or symbolic interaction) it puts *relations of symbolic power,* and replaces the *meaning* of speech with the question of the *value* and *power* of speech. Lastly, in place of specifically linguistic competence, it puts *symbolic capital*, which is inseparable from the speaker's position in the social structure.
>
> (Bourdieu, 1977c: 46 italics in the original)

This reconceptualisation of language needs to be considered in the light of what was said above about language, culture and education. So, the grammaticalness demanded in academic texts becomes an imposed notion of *acceptability* which is quite arbitrary and expressive of a particular group within society – and one which some students are more prepared for than others according to varying degrees of literacy. Literacy then means possessing sufficient and appropriate linguistic *capital* to occupy a desirable *field* position. Scholastic language will always presuppose a certain form of *legitimation*, *consecrated* as such by being enshrined in texts, school books, curricula, etc. Classroom relations becomes systems of power as hierarchies are set up between in- and out-groups defined in terms of their proximity to the legitimate cultural prerequisites as expressed in discourse between teachers and students. Meaning is always defined according to what is and is not valued by this culture. This actual linguistic competence is always only ever a particularly valued form of language, as defined within the educational *field*. A Bourdieusian view of literacy therefore takes account of the individual in terms of their history, dispositions, qualifications and the *field* position they currently occupy, and their structural (principled) relationship with linguistic *field/* market and the *field* of power. Clearly, this is a radical and critical line to take on language and education, and does raise a number of methodological and theoretical issues concerning ethnographies that can be constructed around such an approach. Certainly, bearing all this in mind, it is perhaps unsurprising to see Bourdieu adopting strong language in his descriptions of the education process: 'Pedagogic Authority', 'Symbolic Violence', 'Power Relations', 'Work', etc. (see Book I of 1977a/1970).

Conclusion

This chapter has given a brief account of Bourdieu's approach to language and education. In order to understand these two, and the links between them, it is also necessary to understand the ethnographic field work that Bourdieu undertook, the problems and issues with which he was faced, and the way that his conceptual tools were developed to account for what he observed from real-life empirical data. However, it is also necessary to understand the philosophical and sociological ideas he had at his disposal, and which he synthesised in seeing the world through this point of view. We have seen that Bourdieu developed his own language to express this particular perspective, and how terms such as *habitus*, *field* and *capital* are used to elucidate social contexts. However, a note of caution is needed here. These terms, these tools should not be taken to be simply analytic metaphors – basic heuristic devices to gloss empirical data. Rather, they are highly charged epistemological matrices used to convey structural relations at various levels within social phenomena, and we have seen that 'structure' for Bourdieu needs to be understood in terms of the cognitive, the phenomenological *and* culture. For Bourdieu, 'the real' is relational because reality is nothing other than *structure*, a set of relationships, 'obscured by the realities of ordinary sense-experience' (Bourdieu, 1987: 3). The alternative is to treat things as 'pre-existing entities' – with essential properties. In short, there is an important distinction to be made here between *relational* and *substantialist* thinking. What Bourdieu is trying to do is to found a relational approach to the social sciences against all substantialist methods.

Relational thinking requires a kind of dialectical way of thinking which is opposed to uni-linear thought – to hold more than one theoretical and practical pattern in the mind at one and the same time. However, clearly, it is only ever one thing at a time. In a way, the three main components of this chapter – language, education, and ethnography – are all co-terminous and exist simultaneously in the multidimensionality of social time and space. As we have seen, Bourdieu's basic theory of practice, together with his conceptual 'thinking tools', can be applied equally to language or education as we are encouraged to think of both of these in terms of the same basic epistemology – a relational one. But, all of these, at least from a Bourdieusian perspective, can never be studied simply as stand-alone phenomena, and 'internalist' readings should also be fought against. Rather, they form part of natural contexts which are equally active in shaping what is occurring on the ground. To this extent, ethnography – in some shape or form – is a natural prerequisite for a Bourdieusian methodology.

Of course, there are many questions. Substantively, we need to ask whether or not Bourdieu's approach to language and education is justified? As raised before, is it a perspective that transfers across time and national boundaries? And, if is true, what can be done about it? – what could be done by the teacher or researcher to make use of these insights? Bourdieu's work on education and language – from both a 'critical' and 'non-critical' perspective- also mostly involved students in higher education. How might the approach transfer to other types of students – primary, secondary and adult learners, for example? These are the sort of question that will be taken up in the latter part of the book. On a purely research methodological level, however, we should also note that the sort of 'in the field' experience which Bourdieu personally had in the Béarn was very different from his Algerian encounters: and, the type of data he collected on education and culture were very different again. What these contexts – and others – shared, however, is a commitment to 'think relationally', to look beyond surface relations, and to consider deeper structures in *field* contexts. Such an approach sought to see *social space* as bounded in terms of a series of *fields*, each with their own *logic of practice* and represented through what was valued within them. The structure of *social space* is therefore extremely important in any Bourdieusian ethnography, as are the relations between *fields*, and the *habitus* of agents active within it. This is true of education, as it is of the language used to mediate its operations. In a sense, Bourdieu's thesis on language was four-fold: first, there is his conceptualisation of language itself; second, is the way language is employed in separate *fields* – for example, education; third, is his critique of the conventional approaches of the sciences of language – linguistics, etc.; and fourth, is his own conceptual vocabulary, developed to break with everyday language, the language of other academic disciplines, and to represent the theory of practice he developed at the juncture of his philosophical training and practical ethnographic experience. The rest of this book aims to explore the ways this perspective fares when compared to other theoretical and practical traditions, including New Literacy Studies, and to do so in the light of actual empirical exemplification.

Notes

1 It is my habit to give both the English translation and the original French publication dates when referencing Bourdieu in order to preserve the 'socio-genetic' aspect of his various works.
2 Key concepts used by Bourdieu – field, habitus, capital, etc. – are given in italics in order to remind the reader that they have a particular Bourdieusian sense distinct from their everyday use.
3 A more detailed account of Bourdieu's intellectual background and training can be found in Grenfell (2004).

PART II

Language, Ethnography, and Education – Practical Studies

Part II of the book offers a series of case examples drawn from particular practical situations. Each case is framed by a unique socio-cultural context. As such they are liable to study and interpretation in terms of the approaches outlined in Part I. Each author writes from an 'ethnographic' perspective, drawing on ideas and principles derived from New Literacy Studies (NLS) and Bourdieu. The projects presented here focus on different forms of literacy in a range of classroom settings. The intention in this part is to provide practical exemplification of the type of methodological principles addressed in part I.

Chapter 5 presents development work undertaken in Delhi, India and later Ethiopia with local trainers interested in ways of working with and recognising local literacies prevalent amongst dominated social groups, such as Dalit women. The account explores some of the issues which arise when teachers and local women from a locally defined socio-linguistic field activity engage with trainers and researchers from a broader international field of language. The case study in Chapter 6 is based on a long-term investigation of a UK classroom. Here, an ethnographic approach to the classroom is adopted by the researcher. Whilst her perspective has been formed from a NLS tradition, she extends this with reference to key concepts derived from of Bourdieu to investigate the material relationships between children and their art work and the linguistic relations demonstrated through extracts of learners' talk. Textual practices are juxtaposed with situated accounts of creativity in relation to the particular events and practices in one classroom with one teacher. The difference between the teacher's and the researcher's concerns are also highlighted in this chapter as part of its reflexive account.

Chapter 7 is located in the USA. The chapter explores the effect of changing the medium of language/literature learning for five students who have previously failed to achieve well in lessons. The author notices that, by using a range of audio and visual modes of recording, the students are able to locate themselves in relation to the story of a particular journey – that of Odysseus. In their efforts to engage personally with the story, the students begin to reveal fragments of their own stories and histories. The author explores the way these fragmented attitudes and experiences can be seen as elements of their 'habitus' or, as Pahl names them, their 'fractal habitus'. Chapter 8 is also a USA-based case study. This chapter is also based on ethnographic data, including lesson transcripts from a year-long collaborative project which focused on literacy in the context of African American teenagers learning to read literature. By analysing excerpts of classroom discourse, the authors examine the dilemmas which arise for a particular teacher, and for educators in general, when a prescribed literacy curriculum, typically based on the dominant culture, does not address the more local literacies of an African American community. In other words, the chapter considers some of the issues which arise when 'pedagogic action', intended to support students in acquiring attitudes and behaviours (habitus) which will sustain their future success, takes place in several distinct field contexts at the same time – here the school, the local community and culture, and the broader social space of USA. In a strong parallel to Bourdieu's work on language, the pedagogic role of the teacher is described as a (jazz) 'improvisation', as she moves between two literacies: that of the dominant (*la langue*), and that of the African American community (*le parole*).

No one author would claim to provide a definitive or comprehensive account of classroom language ethnography from a NLS and Bourdieusian approach. Rather, the project reports need to be seen as explorations of practical situations in terms of these perspectives. They demonstrate the way that key principles derived from these sources may highlight issues not readily seen from more conventional methods. Part II needs to be read as a kind of bridge between the introductory accounts of Part I, and the extended methodological discussions in Part III.

5

LETTER

LEARNING FOR EMPOWERMENT THROUGH TRAINING IN ETHNOGRAPHIC-STYLE RESEARCH

BRIAN STREET

Introduction

This chapter describes an experimental project designed to assist adult literacy practitioners to engage in ethnographic-style research about the literacy and numeracy practices of the communities from which their literacy learners come. It is presented in two sections: first, an outline of the project, its rationale and progress made so far; second, a preliminary analysis of the relation of this practical and applied work to the theoretical constructs in this volume.

The Project

The Learning for Empowerment Through Training in Ethnographic-style Research project (LETTER) started in 2001 in response to an approach from Nirantar, a women's organisation in Delhi, India dedicated to the empowerment of rural Dalit women through education.[1] The request was for some training in ethnographic approaches to investigate the existing literacy and numeracy practices of the women involved in their programmes and the epistemologies on which those practices were based. Initial discussions with Nirantar on this project were held during a seminar in Delhi on Urban Literacies organised by Uppingham Seminars in association with J.N. University, Delhi.

Nirantar is an organisation engaged in developing alternative adult learning programmes with a group of Dalit women in southern Uttar Pradesh, India. They had discovered that the women held alternative ways of looking at the world of which Nirantar knew little and of which the teachers were sometimes disparaging whilst the women themselves were to a large extent unconscious of their distinctiveness. For example, the women said they believed that rivers were animate objects rather than inanimate, as Western scientific categories held. Not knowing what views were held, but aware that there were often sensitivities in how such views were perceived across different groups of people whom the learners encountered, the Nirantar staff felt that careful study needed to be made of the practices and language of the communities with which they were working. They also felt that ethnographic approaches would form a foundation for such research and a basis for more respectful relations across the participants.

Background

The approach that I used in the project was that taken from New Literacy Studies and ethnographic research as shown in a number of publications (see Chapter 3 for a fuller account of these approaches). Alan Rogers, as an adult educator, brought an approach to adult learning that stressed the importance to those who help adults to learn of understanding the need to 'start where they [the adult learners] are', the necessity of building on the prior learning (formal and informal) that adults bring to their new learning programmes; likewise he brought to the project extensive international experience of working with learners and facilitators in this way (Rogers, 2002; Rogers, 2004). But, while those who train adult education practitioners exhort to the tutors/facilitators the necessity of finding out about the existing practices and knowledges of their participant learners, they have more difficulty helping them with understanding *how in practice* such information is to be collected. As Alan Rogers argues: 'That one cannot just ask the learners about it is clear'. He suggests three reasons for this:

> For one thing, many (but not all) adult learners come to adult learning programmes believing that they know nothing about the subject matter of the programme, that they have nothing to offer in the way of knowledge or experience to the programme, often accepting the outside stereotype that they are mere 'illiterates' (cf. Nabi, *et al.*, 2009) Or, secondly, even if the participants do feel that they know something about the subject matter, direct questioning of adults will often result in what is known as the 'echo effect', that is, the respondents will tell the researcher what it is felt the questioner wishes to know. Making judgments about each other is part of the relationship between researched and researchers built up during the research encounter. The researcher controls the situation, provoking resistance (often unconscious) among the respondents; and this resistance sometimes expresses itself in the form of echoing back to the researcher the language and concepts for which the researcher is seen to be searching.

Recent advances in 'reflexivity' in ethnographic research have addressed this issue head on, and it requires researchers to be more conscious of the 'effects' their very presence has on their informants, a principle that we outline further below (cf. Foley, 2002). The third reason Rogers puts forward and, as he suggests it is the most important, builds upon recently developed understandings of informal learning which all adults pursue throughout their lives (Eraut, 2000; Coffield, 2000; Hager, 2001). These have led to a realisation that adults have built up through experience very extensive amounts of 'tacit knowledge' and 'hidden skills' – knowledge and skills which form the basis of the practices they engage in and the discourses they use. But, this is largely unconscious – the participant-respondents will often not know what epistemologies they hold, what 'funds of knowledge' (Moll *et al.*, 1992) and banks of skills they have built up through this informal experiential learning (Rogers, 2008). There are in this links to Bourdieu's notion of 'habitus'. These will be elaborated on after further background detail on the LETTER Project itself.

So, practitioners in adult educational programmes cannot simply ask the participants about their existing literacy practices. Informal discussions with learners will, however, form part of the battery of research methods practitioners will bring to the task of trying to find out about the existing ways of knowing of their participant learners. They need to do more. The LETTER Project argued that, through developing 'ethnographic-style' approaches to this research, a surer foundation could be laid for building any new learning programmes for adults that take into account the existing practices and knowledge systems of the learners (see Papen, 2005). Many educators are apprehensive about the term 'ethnography' and sense that it belongs already to the discipline of anthropology. They do not want to become anthropologists, who spend a number of years 'in the field', living with their subjects, learning the language and using a variety of methods to penetrate more deeply into the meanings and concepts of the culture. The LETTER participants, like many in education, do not want to be accused by anthropologists of doing a poor job by adopting 'ethnography' in this sense and so may be wary of the term. However, we introduced the notion of 'adopting an ethnographic perspective', borrowed from Green and Bloome (1997) which allows for non-anthropologists to make good use of many of the features of ethnographic approaches without having to become fully fledged anthropologists. An ethnographic perspective involves a set of principles and methods that may be applied to the contexts that adult literacy educators are working in. These may include taking account of the following principles:

> *Local meanings* – what do local people mean when, for instance, they say 'the river has feelings', rather than how do outsiders view such statements.
>
> *Reflexivity* – recognising that the observer is bringing assumptions to bear on the local accounts and questioning how far these are appropriate and how they might need to be changed – for instance, adult literacy practitioners might see locals as 'illiterate', but a more reflexive approach would have them question these assumptions and instead ask, in keeping with the LETTER spirit, 'what literacy practices are the locals engaged with?'
>
> *Practices* – how might the particular events being observed locally, such as fishermen keeping notes of their catches in Lake Victoria in Uganda, be seen as part of a wider pattern of 'practices' – in this case commercial or 'workplace' literacy practices, some of which may not be recognised or acknowledged by

the economic enterprises or educational institutions that are beginning to oversee such local practices.

In addition to such principles, as part of an 'ethnographic perspective' on 'what is going on', participants learn to develop a variety of methods for addressing the questions that this raises. Not all of these need necessarily be adopted – the important point is to ask which ones will help the observer to understand the issues they are addressing with local people. The methods include:

> *Observation* – which means in this context a more systematic way of watching what is going on. As the Ethiopia LETTER Report (Gebre *et al.*, 2009) indicates: 'Observation of the practices used within the communities from which they come and which they share, analysis of the language used by the participants, collections of artefacts used in expressing their culture as well as informal discussions with participants – these form the basis on which judgments and interpretations by learners can be built'.
>
> *Photographs* – for instance, if the observer wants to explain to colleagues in the LETTER class how local people make use of writing on different surfaces, such as on the walls of their house, then photographs might prove a helpful way of showing 'what is going on' (see photos).
>
> *Questions* – this may involve not just asking direct questions, which local people may be resistant to, but rather engaging in informal discussion and questioning and also LETTER practitioners questioning, in the spirit of 'reflexivity', their own prior assumptions.
>
> *Field notes* – in most cases, it will be useful for the observer to keep notes, maybe in an exercise book available as part of the local educational setting; from these notes they will be able to make reports to colleagues and to their educational institutions and also maybe to write up reports for publication. Two of the recent LETTER programmes have been published by local practitioners, with abundant photographs and details of observations drawn from field notes.
>
> (see Nirantar, 2007; Gebre *et al.*, 2009; Nabi, *et al.*, 2009)

A key way of thinking about ethnography that was called upon during the LETTER training programmes is *turning my world upside down*, to try to take the point of view of another person (cf. Gebre *et al.*, 2009). Ethnography is presented as being about understanding an activity through someone else's eyes. It can be seen as changing position, trying to see the world as someone else sees it; it is learning about someone else or about something, not from the outside but as far as possible from the inside.

During the first workshop in Ethiopia[2] this need to abandon one's own position and adopt that of another was illustrated with the story of the turtle and the fish:

> To illustrate the error of ethnocentrism, Buddhists use several versions of the story of the turtle and fish. One story goes like this:

One day the turtle decides to go for a walk on dry land. He is away from the lake for a few weeks. When he returns, he meets some fish who ask him: 'Mister Turtle, hello! We have not seen you for a few weeks. Where have you been?' The turtle says, 'I was up on the dry land'. The fish are puzzled: 'Up on dry land? What is this dry land? Is it wet?' The turtle answers, 'No, it is not'. 'Is it cool and refreshing?' the fish asks. 'No, it is not'. 'Does it have waves and ripples?' 'No, it does not have waves and ripples'. 'Can you swim in it?' 'No, you cannot'. So the fish say: 'It is not wet, it is not cool, there are no waves, you can't swim in it. So this dry land of yours must be completely non-existent, just an imaginary thing, nothing real at all'. The turtle says: 'Well, that may be so', and he leaves the fish and goes for another walk on dry land. (www.beyondthenet/dhamma/nibbanaTurtle.htm, accessed April 2007).

A further take on this interaction is signalled by the attempt to avoid simply describing local cultures as 'lacking' 'in deficit' – 'they do not have …'. When the turtle returns from dry land to water, and the fish question him, the turtle answers only by saying that the land has no waves, no seaweed, etc. The fish admonish: 'Don't tell us what it's *not*, tell us what it *is!*' The longer version of the story is more hopeful than our brief account, for the return 'walk on dry land' takes with it refined questions and the intention this time 'to see what is there' (see Heath and Street 2008). The accounts of 'literacy' and 'illiteracy' in development contexts represent a classic case of outsiders stating what the locals 'do not' have – they do not have 'literacy' and that after all is the basis for the development of literacy programmes in many parts of the world (cf. Unesco GMR, 2006).

In ethnography, therefore, we will try to see the dry land still through the eyes of a turtle but one who has come to see that water is not the only context for living, and who is trying to find new words to describe it to himself and to others. One danger of the story of the turtle and the fish is that it may suggest that an ethnographer is only interested in the strange, the 'other' – in 'making the strange familiar'. But ethnography will also look at what is to us 'normal'. The turtle could use ethnography to look at the fish as well as the strange dry land; it can be used *to make 'the familiar strange'*.

Putting people into two categories of literate and illiterate means that there is a danger that only illiterates tend to be studied. But, as George Openjuru stated in relation to the study of local literacy and numeracy practices: 'Ethnography is not only about indigenous knowledge systems, but also about what all people are doing. We are not questioning aspects of how primitive people are negotiating modern systems of knowledge. We live in a literate environment and we all have to interact with the written world. There are certain aspects of their life that interact with the written world and we need to investigate these things, what practices are they using to deal with this?' Ethnography is not just about those who are not literate; it will need to cover the whole spectrum of literacy.

The LETTER report goes on to say:

Within this field, however, we cannot decide in advance exactly what we are looking for (although we have the general field of study), because we do not know what is important to the other. An ethnographer avoids determining in advance what to look for, imposing his/her value system on the informants. For example, one of our case studies explored attitudes towards the benefits of microfinance through the eyes of women borrowers, and found one person who said she 'hated it'. In one or two of the case studies, the respondents were said to be 'illiterate'; but in most cases, this is the researcher speaking. Instead of making such judgments, looking down on other people and saying, 'We can help you', we are trying to understand them, to see their value and belief systems. By getting as close to the respondent(s) as possible, we are trying to make the things that are important to them become important to us. We must not under-estimate how difficult this is – it takes time and we will never do it completely, but this is what we attempt to do.

(Gebre *et al.*, 2009)

In the training programmes, with Nirantar, and then in Ethiopia and in Uganda, much of the discussion centred on two matters: first, the training of literacy and numeracy practitioners in ethnographic-style approaches to literacy and numeracy; second, the relationships between ethnographic-style research on local literacy and numeracy practices and the teaching of literacy and numeracy to adults. In the Ethiopian programme, the following principles were set out:

- What are the politics, the theory, the methodology, ethics and procedures, and the pedagogical perspectives that closely relate to the challenges of the LETTER approach?
- How do we critique, identify and deal with the challenges of the LETTER approach?
- How can the LETTER approach be taken forward?

The aim of the LETTER Project was, therefore, to train some adult education practitioners (programme planners and trainers) in ethnographic-style research as described above (Green and Bloome, 1997), taking as a focus the literacy and numeracy practices of the learners and the communities from which they came. The trainers then would train the facilitators (adult teachers) to conduct such research with their own learning groups. In this way, all those who teach literacy and numeracy to adults, by seeking to learn about and build on the existing experiences of their learners in these two fields, would engage in their own ways in practitioner research.

The Project: Part 1: Delhi 2002–3

The above set out the thinking that lay behind the programme originally worked out between Nirantar and Uppingham Seminars in Development, the organisation facilitating the project from the UK side. It became known as LETTER: Learning for Empowerment Through Training in Ethnographic-style Research. In association with ASPBAE (Asia South Pacific Bureau for Adult Education), Nirantar obtained enough funds to ensure that a small group of about twenty participants drawn from the various countries in part of the region covered by ASPBAE (Nepal, Bangladesh, Afghanistan, Pakistan and India) came together for two workshops held in Delhi in 2002 and 2003. Brian Street led the resource team, Alan Rogers contributed from a distance, and Dr Dave Baker of the Institute of Education, London, contributed insights into numeracy as social practice that complemented the literacy focus (see Baker *et al.*, 2003).

The first one-week workshop concentrated on what is meant by ethnographic-style research, as outlined above (Green and Bloome, 1997; Heath and Street, 2008). It was stressed that what was needed in this context was not a full ethnography, for that would take too long and require a much greater investment than would be available and in any case we were not training the participants to be anthropologists, rather to be more culturally sensitive educators. To this end, adopting an ethnographic-style approach, an ethnographic lens, would help the practitioner to gain insights into these practices which would challenge many of the sweeping assumptions on which

FIGURE 5.1 Measuring Mehroni crops (photo: Dave Baker). This photo shows a woman holding a container in which she might collect grain or liquids and then sell as a unit; the numeracy point here is that she does not use/need metric arithmetic schemes as she, like many people in the world (including my own local Greengrocer in Brighton) sell and 'measure' by container.

so many existing adult education programmes are built (for details see the Nirantar publication 2007). It would provide nuances to the generalisations often made about adult illiteracy and innumeracy. This workshop progressed through sessions devoted to discussion in plenary and small groups, through readings given out and discussed (including Uta Papen's 2005 book *Adult Literacy as Social Practice)*, and through a small-scale practice session of field work. The participants were sent out into Delhi for an afternoon to see what they could find out about the literacy and numeracy practices in the area. They then returned to present and debate their findings to each other. The latter part of the week was spent designing a somewhat bigger research project to be conducted individually or in very small groups between the first and second workshop, when the participants returned to their home sites.

These larger research projects (mostly into local numeracies) were then brought to the second workshop. A good deal of time during this workshop was devoted to finalising the reports on these topics, and a start was made on working out how to use the findings of these local projects in developing ways of helping adults to learn new literacies and numeracies.

The Nirantar project, which was the first of the workshops, was written up by Malini Ghose, one of the directors of Nirantar. At a workshop in Ethiopia she provided a report on the Nirantar events, which was in turn published as part of the Ethiopia report. She focused on the background of Nirantar as a non-government organisation aiming at empowering Dalit women around the issues of land, etc. She

FIGURE 5.2 Delhi LETTER banner in India (photo: Brian Street)

described how they came to thinking about ethnography and the LETTER workshop and how LETTER was expanded to the region in association with ASPBAE. The training started with the application of theory and reflection. The training provided for the reversal of roles and power, new lenses for listening, observation, stepping back and collective listening. The Nirantar training was implemented in two phases: a workshop on ethnographic approaches (with field work), followed by a small piece of research work done at the home of the participants; and a second workshop which finalised the case studies. Nirantar finalised the report (*Exploring the Everyday: Ethnographic Approaches to Literacy and Numeracy Practices*, published by Nirantar and ASPBAE, Delhi 2007). Malini then described how the work of the programme had developed in the Nirantar programme, as they first explored the local literacy and numeracy practices of the participants in their classes – for example, the uses of calendars – and then used these practices to create a new curriculum for their classes with the women learners.

Part 2: Ethiopia 2007–8

The project then moved to Ethiopia, where ANFEAE (Adult and Non-Formal Education Association of Ethiopia) and PACT, made a request for a LETTER programme in that country. ANFEAE, led by Alemayehu Hailu Gebre, raised the funds for the project, this time building into the schedule a third workshop to develop further the applications of the projects to specific educational programmes. Again, some twenty participants came together, this time all from within Ethiopia.

As in the initial Delhi LETTER programme, the aim was to encourage the trainers of adult literacy facilitators to develop an expertise and experience of ethnographic-style research as outlined above and then to train the facilitators so that they could engage in practitioner research. There was a small-scale field exercise in both the first and second workshops, and larger scale research projects were compiled by the participants between the first and second workshops and revised between the second and third workshops. In the end, some ten research reports into local literacy and numeracy practices were compiled (published as Gebre *et al.*, 2009). The first workshop concentrated on ethnography, what it is, why it is important and how it is conducted. The second was largely devoted to the research projects.

In the third workshop, with Malini Ghose[3] outlining the progress made by her Nirantar project as described above, the LETTER Project made further advances in educational terms, especially in considering how to adapt the research findings for adult teaching and learning programmes. Malini's group in India had identified certain literacy and numeracy activities in the area they were working in as suitable for building new learning programmes on. One such was 'calendars'. They found that many homes and offices in the area had calendars and they collected these up and debated them with the learners. The discussions included issues such as the difference between local ways of measuring time (a lunar system) against the formal printed measures (a solar system); how these calendars were used, for example, how

FIGURE 5.3 Ethiopian wall writing (photo: Brian Street)

far they were used for recording past events and how far for planning future activities; gender differences in the approach to calendars were considered; the languages and scripts in which these calendars were presented, and the balance between numbers and words; the cost of the calendars; the difference between religious and secular calendars (see Figure 5.4). During these discussions, new ways of looking at time, new numeracy and literacy activities were devised, and new learning took place. Formal 'schooled' practices were introduced alongside the local practices.

Drawing upon such experiences from other sites, the Ethiopia workshop participants worked out a general process of using the findings of the ethnographic research on local literacy and numeracy practices, building new adult learning programmes on them. In this context, the procedure was called the collect-reflect-build on approach (or discover, discuss and develop approach). The chosen local practices would be collected, observed and described; they would then be discussed fully in class in a critical way (including issues of equality and justice, gender and power); and on these practices and discussions, new ways of knowing and doing would be built, the more formal and standardised ways of the classroom alongside the local and more informal practices. This, then, was what was meant by 'starting where they are, taking into account what they already know and do' and then building further. Each group then looked at their own research projects and chose four areas which they found in their case studies and saw as being suitable for such an approach:

FIGURE 5.4 Panchang (religious calendar) (photo: Purnima Gupta, used by permission Nirantar, India. Compare Nirantar 2007: 48). Calendars were available in a number of homes. 'Panchang is a type of calendar used by Hindus and has lunar days marked as well. ... A few people said these calendars were used to mark or read dates of important "official" events ... School going children referred to calendars to find out when school holidays were on. Some women read calendars so as to remember dates of meetings or trainings'. So, these can be considered as both literacy and numeracy events, in the home – often in contexts where outside educators and officials assume everyone is 'illiterate'.

- different ways of counting (for example, the use of sticks or beans, and different ways of using finger counting, etc.);
- different informal ways of measuring, including uses of containers (see Figure 5.1) (cf. Saraswathi) (some purely individual, others common to all the traders in one local market but different from other markets) and the code switching of the traders between these and the more formal standardised ways of weighing and measuring;
- different ways of calculating income and expenditure (the difference between unwritten household accounts which start with income and determine the expenditure, and the accounting system of small businesses that begin with how much is spent, which in turn determines what income is needed);
- and proverbs, sayings and songs/poems which were found in the local communities, sometimes painted on the walls of buildings (see Figure 5.5),

acting as a community 'glue' and especially building inter-generational relationships (grandparents teaching children traditional sayings and children teaching grandparents new songs).

All of these could be collected, used by local trainers and debated fully and critically in the class, and more formal literacy and numeracy practices could further be built on them. This represented what the project team saw as 'relevant learning', 'starting where they are', using teaching-learning materials which come from the local communities in which the learners live. Such learning is seen not just as exportable from the classroom into the community, as in standard educational models, but also as coming into the classroom from the community: learning, is then mediated there by educational practices, and returns to inform and enhance everyday activities. Here, learning is envisaged as not only useful for educational and measurement purposes but as something that can be used in the everyday life of the learners.

More recently, the LETTER Project has been adapted for use by facilitators and learners in Uganda. Demands for training in such an approach have also come in from adult literacy agencies in Mexico (in Spanish) and Pakistan amongst other enquiries.

Bourdieu and LETTER

As we go over these accounts, the reader will no doubt recognise aspects of a Bourdieusian perspective. For instance, Malini Ghose's reference to 'reversal of roles and power, new lenses for listening, observation, stepping back and collective listening' are evocative of Bourdieu's concern to challenge dominant discourses and to penetrate more deeply local ways of making meaning. To some extent, the 'ethnographic perspective' can be seen as in the spirit of the kind of more anthropologically explicit approach found in Bourdieu's accounts of the Kabyle House and of his own home village context in the Pyrenees (1977b; 2008a). The designers of the LETTER programme were themselves influenced by Bourdieu's ideas, both explicitly and implicitly. His work with the French Academy was a telling case of the link between such theory on the one hand and the engagement in policy and practice on the other, which is exactly how the LETTER programme developed. And, at the same time, it is possible to reflect on the whole process with the help of Bourdieu's ideas, as we will do below, drawing for instance on the concepts of habitus and field and their relationship – at the wider level of international programme development and of local practices such as the LETTER approach.

What does Bourdieusian theory contribute to our understanding of the LETTER Project and how does this example of practical studies in ethnography and education help us to clarify and develop our understanding of this theory? In particular, how does the literacy dimension of such activities help us to extend the links being made in this volume between Bourdieu and New Literacy Studies?

Bourdieu's conception of the relationship between habitus and field can offer a way of relating the LETTER approach to others in the field of literacy. As Rowsell

FIGURE 5.5 Ethiopian wall writing: 'I became lonely in order to make my life easier [because] today's friend is tomorrow's enemy' – one of a number of sayings seen on the walls of houses, collected by Negussie Hailu, Ethiopia (photo: Negussie Hailu). Writing on the wall of a house in Debre Zeit, Ethiopia in April–May 2008. Again indication of 'local literacies', in this case calling upon well known stories and sayings. Some people, passing by, may read such accounts, others like the owner of this house will write on surfaces not usually seen as 'officially' appropriate for writing – literacy classes often restrict where people can write to official sites such as posters on the wall of classroom, removable pieces of paper, notebooks etc. One theme this raises for discussion is what 'genres' people write in – in this case a kind of notice/warning – and where it is considered appropriate to inscribe in different genres.

(2008) argues: 'The dialectic between habitus and field, or in other terms, between agent and structure is central to looking at how artistic practice operates in social context'. We might extend these ideas to educational practice. At the first level we might see dominant approaches as a 'field' context of literacy working with institutional sedimented notions of skill, etc. Such a context needs to be understood as moves from international, usually Western, contexts 'downward' to local contexts assumed to be in 'deficit', 'illiterate' etc. We call this Field 1 in the Figure 5.6. In contrast, an ethnographic perspective attempts to begin within the field of local institutional practices – Field 2 in the diagram – in different contexts, to describe and engage with local habitus of participants, to recognise their practices and then to work outwards towards what new literacy practices they may wish to adopt. The contrasting perspectives may be represented in terms of field/habitus relations.

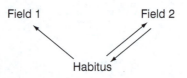

FIGURE 5.6 Field and habitus

In Field 1 relations, the arrow moves in a single direction; whilst in Field 2, the kind of perspective represented by LETTER, the arrows move in both directions – relations are dialogic.

Bartlett and Holland (2002), in response to Bourdieu's (1977b) account of education *Reproduction*, suggested a further use of Bourdieu and how it might apply to the study of literacy:'Bourdieu's theory suggests we analyse literacy events with an eye to the ways in which historical and social forces have shaped a person's linguistic habitus and thus impinge upon that person's actions in the moment'.This approach might capture something of what the LETTER project attempts to do, asking literacy trainers to observe and describe the literacy events in which learners engage during their out of class lives. Bartlett and Holland extend such a theoretical apparatus in ways that are particularly appropriate for the LETTER work:'Bourdieu's theory remains limited by his tendency to underplay the importance of culturally produced narratives, images and other artefacts in modifying habitus. We propose to strengthen a practice theoretical approach to literacy studies by specifying the space of literacy practices, examining in particular the locally operant figured world of literacy identities in practice, and artefacts'.What they mean by 'figured worlds' is;'a socially produced and culturally constructed realm of interpretation in which a particular set of characters and actors are recognised, significance is assigned to certain acts and particular outcomes are valued over others' (Holland *et al.*, 1998: 52). From this perspective,'a figured world of literacy in the LETTER project might include 'functional; illiterates','good readers' and 'illiterates' who struggle to become literate or demonstrate their literacy in a variety of settings, including the classroom, the market place and home. The ethnographic-style accounts of local people in the marketplaces of Ethiopia, India and Uganda could be taken as case studies of these 'figured worlds' – the world of the international agency might classify all of the people observed as 'illiterate' and in need of 'literacy classes' and training. The accounts by LETTER participants as they walked the streets around their workshop sites, might be seen as indications of different 'figured worlds' – those of the local people, putting up calendars in their homes, writing on walls, exchanging goods in market places with the help of written notations regarding price and quantity or keeping records of their fishing, agricultural and taxi driving activities. Bartlett's own ethnographic research in Brazil is illustrative of the application of these ideas to local contexts, of the kind that the LETTER Project, also addresses. Figured worlds, she suggests, are invoked, animated, contested and enacted through artefacts, activities and identities in practice' (Bartlett and Holland, 2002: 11, reprinted in Street and Lefstein, 2007: 153).

Rowsell's account of 'Artifactual English' (see Chapter 7) demonstrates a way of teaching and learning English that takes account especially of the emphasis here on artefacts. The LETTER project, likewise, builds on the notion of 'culturally produced narratives', as evidenced in the emphasis on how literacy trainers elicit from their learners accounts of the way literacy is figured in their worlds. In addition, the trainers enter those worlds using ethnographic perspectives as they attempt to describe literacy events there. In India, as the volume 'Exploring the Everyday' indicates, the members of the workshop went out into the streets of Delhi and observed and talked with taxi drivers, street vendors, etc., whilst in Ethiopia groups went to mosques, churches and shops both describing artefacts and electing narratives. In this way, the local disposition and practice are figured into the work of the training programme in ways that model how literacy programmes in other sites might work. Everyone then is more conscious, in Bourdieu's terms, of the cultural capital and its relation to different fields – whether those valued by outside agencies and educational institutions or those in which local people engage. Applying Bourdieu to educational programmes using ethnography in this way, draws attention especially to the relationship between the local literacy events and practices and the wider field of education and other institutions – often commercial as Bourdieu frequently recognised in his own accounts of such practices – that frequently press down upon learners. An understanding of that relationship can be used to consider educational practices and also help the learners to balance in more socially sensitive ways exactly what they are getting out of such engagement with educational practices. In this way Bourdieu's theory can be used both to extend and develop the NLS perspective and its applications and to extend our understanding of educational developments, at a time when standard approaches often seem lacking in such insights (cf. Unesco, 2006). What they lack is, perhaps, exactly what a combination of Bourdieu and NLS can offer.

Conclusion

Readers may wish to bring further conceptual tools to bear on these data, drawing upon other aspects of the theoretical perspectives being developed in this volume. We have noted here ways in which Bourdieu's concepts of habitus and field might help make sense of what is going on in the LETTER[4] programmes. A further elaboration of his ideas, via Bartlett and Holland's notion of 'figured world', has also been applied to some of the data signalled here. We have also drawn briefly on the accounts of 'artifactual English' in Chapter 7, to indicate how the learning of literacy in programmes such as LETTER also involves manipulation of material objects, such as the container seen in the photo. Lurking more implicitly are concepts of power and ideology – on the one hand, the relation between international claims and programmatic statements regarding 'illiteracy', entailing the need for formal and generalised 'literacy' programmes, and, on the other, the need to build on local development of literacy practices and often 'invisible' engagement with reading and writing, – what Nabi *et al.* (2009) term 'hidden literacies' – represents the most obvious site in which a Bourdieusian perspective on power and ideology could help inform our understanding. The account in Chapter 4 of the relation between language and education, and the accounts of classroom practice to be found in Chapter 2, might also be constructively brought to bear on these data. In the final section of this volume, we will bring together the various sets of data outlined in it, with the various conceptual issues raised in the discussion of Bourdieu's work. These accounts make evident the value of bringing together such accounts in relation to Bourdieu's seminal work with the approach to reading and writing practices evident in New Literacy Studies. We also indicate there some possible future directions in deploying Bourdieu's work, and our developments of it, in the field of language and education.

Notes

1 This approach was made to Brian Street and Professor Alan Rogers (Uppingham Seminars in Development UK: (www.uppinghamseminars.com)).
2 In the Ethiopia workshops, Dr George Openjuru from Uganda worked with Brian Street in the first workshop and with Alan Rogers and Dave Baker in the second workshop whilst Alan Rogers was present at the second and third workshops; and Dr Rafat Nabi from Pakistan (see Nabi et al., 2009), a post-doctoral fellow at the University of East Anglia (UK) working with Alan Rogers and Brian Street on literacy and numeracy practices in her country, attended the second and third workshop, at first as a participant and later as a resource person; and connections with LETTER Delhi were maintained by Malini Ghose from Nirantar coming to the third workshop. Reports of each of the Ethiopia workshops are on the ANFEAE and Uppingham Seminars websites; and a publication is available cf. Gebre et al., 2009.
3 Malini Ghose of Nirantar drew the first two LETTER workshops in Delhi together into a report which Nirantar and ASPBAE jointly published under the title *Exploring the Everyday: ethnographic approaches to literacy and numeracy* (Nirantar, Delhi, and ASPBAE, Mumbai 2007; www.nirantar.net; www.uppinghamseminars.com).
4 LETTER publications include: Gebre et al. (2009), Nirantar (2007), Street et al. (2006). Nabi et al. (2009).

6

SEEING WITH A DIFFERENT EYE[1]

KATE PAHL

Introduction

In this chapter I focus on a group of children in a classroom and the work of one teacher, Sally Bean, who taught in a class of 6–7-year-old children, in an infant school in the North of England. The school was situated on the outskirts of a town with a history of coal mining and farming. The study was ethnographic, and took place over a two year period (2005–7). I collected a wide range of data: interviews with Sally drawing on her own research notes as she reflected on her practice, my own fieldnotes, and photographs, building up a linguistic ethnography. Using this data, I developed a dense and many layered picture of the context of Sally's work, the way she enacted her beliefs and dispositions in the classroom and how the children responded to her work. I attempt to trace the enactment of her *pedagogic habitus* (see Grenfell 1996 and this volume) in the context of an initiative to promote creativity in the classroom. I focused on literacy events and practices, with a particular interest (mine) in the children's *multimodal* text-making, and seeing this process of text-making as being ideologically situated (Grenfell Chapter 4 this volume; Pahl 2007; Street, this volume).

I begin by situating the study in a context, which was of the Creative Partnership (CP) policy (a UK initiative). The policy initiative is a background to the study but also, is the 'field of play' in which Sally enacted her *pedagogic habitus*. To make sense of this field-setting, I pay attention to those research monographs and documents that were commissioned by CP. I bring my own reflexive understanding to the data-analysis process and the report-writing. I move between an ethnographic account of the classroom ethnography and the emerging findings from that study. By linking the enactment of CP in the classroom, to the CP policy documents and writing on creativity, to the wider field of creativity as a concept, I demonstrate how this kind of analysis is useful to unpack enactment of policy in the classroom (see also Lefstein

2008). I draw on discussions of creativity that were current at the time of doing the research (Heath and Wolf 2004; Jeffrey and Craft 2006).

The children were engaged in making panoramic boxes, dioramas, which were natural environments such as the ocean, jungle or desert, peopled by animals. Close analysis of the classroom interaction was possible, as I carried out an in-depth study, conducted sequentially over two years. I drew on data from a wider study, also lasting two years, in which teachers, artists, pupils and parents were interviewed and a number of ethnographic observations undertaken within the school. My involvement, as a researcher, was also subject to analysis and to a form of objectification in relation to my own perceptions of the field of creativity (see Grenfell later in this volume) situating myself within the field. The class teacher also researched her own practice so that her understandings drawn from her research diary, is woven into the analysis. Part of the task of this chapter is to construct an analysis both of the relational construction of the classroom, but also to trace back the thinking I did alongside the class teacher's construction of her site, the classroom. Grenfell (in this volume and elsewhere) has consistently argued that this kind of analysis and thinking can be realised in educational research through drawing on Bourdieu's logic of practice.

I discuss the 'field' setting of the classroom as the place where the teacher deployed her *pedagogic habitus*, which was in turn shaped by the artists who worked in the school and her understanding of the 'value' of creativity. I then discuss the relations Sally's work and what I conceive as the world of Creative Partnerships, its policy documents, research papers and pronouncements, particularly those published between 2002 and 2005. Finally I look at a much broader level, which I consider to be the concept of 'creativity' as expressed over a period of time, and which has been discussed in a recent monograph by Ken Jones (2009). Bringing these all together is the task for the chapter.

Using a relational framework in a classroom ethnography context can provide a helpful lens to unpeel the way in which habitus and field interact. This can be done by looking at the language the teacher uses in the classroom but also the language the children use. By focusing closely on multimodal events and practices in the classroom in the context of recorded interaction, the arena that Creative Partnerships set up can be unravelled and dissected. Different versions of creativity were also at play which could be seen in the analysis of the classroom data.

While I, Kate, focused on how narratives could be found *sedimented* within multimodal texts, the teacher, Sally, focused on creativity as being about problem solving in the material world. In my case, New Literacy Studies (Street this volume) helped my analytic frame by offering the lens of events and practices. By tracing our definitions of creativity back to the literature from Creative Partnerships, and drawing on Jones (2009) who offered a number of accounts of creativity as instantiated within different traditions, it is possible to see how Creative Partnerships itself was driven by a number of discursive domains of practice.

New Literacy Studies

New Literacy Studies takes as its starting point the notion of literacy as a set of events and practices (Street 1995 and this volume). Here, in this chapter I focus both on literacy as being about narrative texts within the classroom, as where children told stories that were then represented multimodally within the boxes, and as a set of practices, that is the recurrent experience of the children as they realised their visions of the boxes in a textual form. This can then be linked to box making as a situated textual practice. My account of literacy is shaped by Kress (1997, 2010) and his view of semiosis as inherently multimodal. I understand the children's meaning making to reside just in one mode, that is reading, writing and oral narration, but look across the modes to understand the meaning making of the children. In that, I share with Street (2008) a focus on multimodal events and practices. As Flewitt (2008), I take as my focus the concept of 'multimodal literacies' that is literacies that range across modes and are focused on meaning making in all its diversity, and then home in on the unfolding of that meaning making in the classroom.

Context for the Study

Creative Partnerships is the UK Government's flagship creativity programme for schools and young people, which was set up in May 2002, managed by Arts Council England and funded by the Department for Culture, Media and Sport (DCMS) with an additional support from the then Department for Education and Skills (DfES). It was developed as a result of the ground-breaking report, from the National Advisory Committee on Creative and Cultural Education called 'All Our Futures: Creativity, Culture and Education' which urged the importance of a national strategy for creative and cultural education to unlock young people's potential. Following this report, in 2000 the Qualification and Curriculum Authority commissioned a review of creativity in other countries and developed a 'creativity' framework. There was a hypothesis that 'creativity' could both enhance economic productivity and create a framework for learning that would increase pupil motivation and lead to increased literacy achievement. It was a response to the concerns from many educationalists that the National Literacy Strategy was over-prescriptive and relied on a skills-based, 'autonomous' model of literacy (Street, this volume). Creative Partnerships was initially focused on particular areas of the UK, where there were considered to be higher pockets of deprivation.

The area where this study took place, Rotherham, Doncaster and Barnsley, was characterised by considerable economic disadvantage after the closure of the mining industry in South Yorkshire and the consequent loss of confidence in older industries such as steel and manufacturing. At the time of the study, 2005–7, there was some economic activity in the field of building and light industry, but at the same time, there was a concern that children's speaking and listening skills, particularly in the school where the study took place, were not being fully developed. The study itself was funded by Creative Partnerships in order to find out what was the impact of a group of artists, Heads Together, on teachers' practices in a small infants' school on the outskirts of a northern town in the UK.

Creative Partnerships as a scheme had wide and far reaching aims. It aimed to develop:

- the creativity of young people, raising their aspirations and achievements;
- the skills of teachers and their ability to work with creative practitioners;
- schools' approaches to culture, creativity and partnership working; and the skills, capacity and sustainability of the creative industries.

(Creative Partnerships: Approach and Impact 2007)

At the core of the programme was the notion of artists and teachers working alongside each other to inform each other's practice. The ideologies behind the scheme were progressive and hopeful, with a focus on the unexpected and celebrating children's ability to learn and move forward using new and unusual paths. There was, however, within this, an equal interest in the role of the arts in education and ways of engaging all children in the highest forms of the arts. The Creative Partnerships initiative has been analysed by Jones (2009) as having its roots in three traditions:

- a cultural conservatism for which tradition and authority are important reference points;
- a progressivism concerned with child-centred learning;
- and a tendency whose belief that 'culture is ordinary' [which] led to an insistence that working-class and popular culture should be represented in the classroom.

(Jones 2009: 7)

Jones recognised that Creative Partnerships coincided with a new 'enthusiasm for creativity' that was accompanied by an equally enthusiastic response from the academic sector (Thompson and Hall 2008) in which the New Labour progressivism simultaneously tried to set up the National Literacy Strategy alongside a more radical, creative approach to learning.

Creative Partnerships made an effort to question its own dogmas. David Parker and Julian Sefton-Green commissioned a series of studies that critically reflected on the more enthusiastic tenets associated with creativity, and their stance has resulted in some publications that tend to scepticism, informed by such thinkers as Willis (1998) and Sutton-Smith (1997). Following the *Rhetorics of Play* (Sutton-Smith 1997) Sefton-Green commissioned a study on the *Rhetorics of Creativity*, which argued that creativity itself was really a kind of 'rhetoric' that could be identified with a number of different traditions (Banajai *et al.* 2006). Much of the Creative Partnerships funded or inspired research focused on the spaces such initiatives opened up for innovative teaching and learning. Anna Craft and Bob Jeffrey (2006) were particularly at the forefront of this academic field of 'creative teaching and learning'. From these discussions, a view of creative learning emerged, and argued that creative learning involves:

- Relevance. Teaching that contains this is operating within a broad range of accepted social values while being attuned to pupils' identities and cultures.
- Control of Learning Processes. The pupil is self-motivated, not governed by extrinsic factors, or purely task-oriented exercises.
- Ownership of Knowledge. The pupil is self-motivated, not governed by extrinsic factors, or purely task-oriented exercises.
- Innovation. Something new is created. A major change has taken place – a new skill mastered, new insight gained, new understanding realised, as opposed to more gradual, cumulative learning, with which it is complementary.

(Jeffrey and Craft 2006: 47)

This perspective about creative learning is echoed by Burnard *et al.* (2006) who also have an understanding of creative learning and teaching focusing on ways in which teachers could create the optimum conditions for creativity to happen in the classroom. In particular, they focused on *learner agency* as critical to creative teaching in the classroom.

Thompson and Hall (2008) identified the bringing in of 'funds of knowledge' (Gonzalez *et al.*, 2005) as part of the possibilities of Creative Partnerships type teaching spaces, as opposed to the more restricted national curriculum. The possibilities offered by listening to children's funds of knowledge also opened up more difficult questions of censorship and directly, at times, clashed with priorities that the schools had set in other domains of practice.

The world of creativity has its own 'rules' (see Grenfell in this volume and Grenfell and Hardy 2007) and taken for granted textual practices. When consulting the literature on creativity, using the Creative Partnerships publications, many quotes were in bright, primary school type colours, in slightly larger print, as if I might be an excited creative child, rather than an academic used to the demands of article searching and reading dense black and white text. Many publications, even those that purported to be of strong academic relevance such as Heath and Wolf's (2004), were printed on bright yellow, thick paper, with lots of white space. 'First Findings', the review of creative learning from 2002–2004, had many large images, mostly photographs, of creative practitioners, alongside facts and figures represented in handwritten notes. Children's drawings and blurry impressionist images of children's faces, lit up by light and learning in new and unusual ways, were prevalent in these publications, even the more academic ones. Ken Jones' review, while highly academic, was printed in turquoise. In terms of a multimodal analysis of these texts, they *instantiated* these discourses of creativity as a bright, progressive, primary school type quality, in which children's own perceptions and colour ways were at the core of the offer.

Literacy and language were a key part of the intended outcomes of the Creative Partnerships initiative. There was an effort within the sector to argue for the benefits of creativity for increasing interaction and linguistic competence, as its director, here attests,

> [Creative Partnerships] is about creative education, by which I mean helping teachers teach more creatively, using creative journeys as education drivers and developing creative skills in young people. Creative education will for me achieve a range of benefits like linguistic development, more confident students, more motivated students who are more committed to education, more emotionally literate students, more curious students, imaginative kids with lots of ideas, students with an improved capacity to take intelligent risks, etc.
>
> (Paul Collard, interview Jan 2006 quoted in Sefton-Green 2007: 3)

A focus on meaning making as well as a progressive interest in the everyday as a site for change enabled many progressive academics and educationalists to become more visible within the sector. Language and literacy were in many projects the site for this research impetus. New Literacy Studies were a helpful lens with which to look at textual practices, and to situate accounts of 'creativity' in relation to events and practices (see Pahl 2007).

Methodology of the Study

The study was conducted drawing on 'linguistic ethnography' as a methodology; that is, following from Maybin (2007) and Lefstein (2008), I conducted a situated analysis of linguistic interaction in the classroom. I used tape recorders on desks to record children's meaning making and recorded, using cameras, often with the children as photographers, the multimodal texts they created. Their text-making was surrounded by observations of the teacher, Sally, and her own reflective fieldnotes and action research, together with a wider ethnographic study of the effect of the artists upon the whole school. Small-scale micro interaction, was thus placed in a wider context, and analysed in relation to the more macro concerns of the Creative Partnerships initiative. The participants of the research were as follows:

1   The artists. I spent time with the artists at their staff development day, interviewed them during and at the end of the project and watched them in action.
2   Teachers. I interviewed all the teachers at the school and then spent time discussing the research with Sally Bean, the teacher I worked with. I then involved Sally Bean in the research process itself. She also conducted her own action research project on her practice.
3   The children. I gave the children cameras and placed an audio recorder on the tables when they were making the boxes. I visited the classroom on a regular basis for the period of the box-making episodes two years consecutively.

4   The parents. I interviewed some of the parents about their children's involvement in the projects.

5   Community events, Junior school and additional follow up interviews with children and parents.

I was lucky enough to have access to the reflective materials that Sally collected as part of her own action research project in Year 1 (2006).

The data I discuss here were collected in two consecutive years. I visited the classroom in order to explore the processes and practices of the children's multimodal meaning making. As I used cameras in the research, I was able to document the way in which the boxes were made over time. I recorded interaction between children as they made the boxes and then interviewed the children at the end of the project. I also analysed my own role within the project and looked at what I brought with me into the classroom.

I analysed the data by focusing on the children's talk at the point of making the boxes and then tracing this in relation to the talk around the task and the classroom habitus. I used Wolcott's system of three columns to consider the links between description (transcript) interpretation (themes arising from the data) and analytic codes (Wolcott 1994). I placed emerging themes alongside the transcripts that I collected and placed the photographs taken by children of their boxes alongside the transcripts of what they said while they were making the boxes. I interviewed the children after they had made the boxes. I went back and traced certain linguistic

FIGURE 6.1 Example of a box

themes, which were echoed across the dataset, for example, the phrase 'we decided that' and 'good effect'. This required detailed linguistic analysis of both the children's transcripts and the transcripts taken of Sally's discussion. I also drew on Sally's own fieldnotes and her transcripts taken during the first year of the project. The analysis then involved looking at the policy and research documents produced by Creative Partnerships in order to situate the dataset within the thinking generated by CP at the time of writing the article.

Year 1 – Creative Problem Solving in The Material World

The children were encouraged to work in small groups to create boxes that represented a particular environment, such as the Arctic, the ocean, the jungle or the desert. They were encouraged to choose their environments, research these using books or the internet, and create animals and plants to go in the environments. Shoe boxes were used to create dioramas that represented the animal habitats. As Sally wrote:

> The children were given the brief: to design and make a model of an environment using a shoe box. They had spent some time, during the Spring Term, learning about living things and the way they adapt to their habitat and found out about a large variety of living things and both local and global environments.
>
> (From SB's fieldnotes Spring 06)

Here, I focus on some of the themes that emerged from analysing the Year 1 data. These can be divided into:

- we decided on;
- a good effect;
- the unexpected outcome;
- funds of knowledge.

The first two I could link back to expressions used by Sally and were then echoed in the children's talk, and could be identified as *emic* concepts, while the second two concepts I found in the data, and could be seen as more *etic* concepts (see Bloome and Street in this volume).

Theme 1: 'We Decided On'

When I started researching Sally's classroom, the initial focus of her work was on profiling learner agency (Burnard *et al.* 2006). She had found it helpful to watch the artists, Heads Together, when they worked in the school, and the way they let children decide what to do, as she described here in an interview I conducted with her:

It was a big eye opener for me, that they were so capable at deciding what they wanted to learn and what they wanted to do in that session and in that project.

(Sally Bean interview 20 March 06)

In initial discussions with the children, in the first year of the project, when I talked to the children about the boxes, I heard her voice echoed by the children in their discussions, particularly in the phrase 'we decided on':

TIMMY: We *decided on* the animals and the trees
KATE: And the trees?
TIMMY: and leaves folding down
CARL: and we tried to make it look like with the glue there, painting green.

Lefstein (2008) describes the term 'discourse genres' as being relatively stable ways of communicating and interacting, which serve both as resources for fashioning utterances and constraints upon the way these utterances are fashioned. When I analysed the data from Year 1, I realised that the phrase 'we decided that' was one Sally set store by as a discourse genre. For example, in the excerpt above, the children were echoing the rhetorical notion of 'we decided that', which I also recorded when listening to Sally speak in the classroom, and here in her fieldnotes of her own action research:

SB – that was a problem a pair had last year. When they came to make the rain drops. They cut out lots of little drops from clear plastic and threaded them onto cotton but they weren't happy with it in the end and they decided that they should have thought about it more.

(Sally's fieldnotes Year 1 2006)

Theme 2: 'A Good Effect'

Another kind of talk was talk that focused on the materialisation of the children's aims for what the boxes should look like, and the difference, in some cases, between what they would like to achieve, and what they did achieve. When I analysed the data from the children and from Sally, that both Sally and I collected, I could see that Sally's approach to creativity was focused on the realisation of the children's ideas within the material artefact, the shoe box. Sally singled out the group below for their ability to problem-solve in the material world and she highlighted their ability to come up with solutions to material problems. A group of girls were creating an ocean box. They talked about how it was going. This is Emma talking about her difficulties with the seaweed standing up;

EMMA: first we got a box and my partner was Sophie secondly we painted our box and then we added some things to it. My partner tried to make seaweed and we couldn't we tried everything we could think of and then teacher Mrs Bean had a bolt of lightning and she thought of something and we did it but we haven't tried it yet but I think it will work. I hope so.

(later in the discussion)

KATE: So why didn't it go well when it got to the seaweed?
SOPHIE: because we tried some see-through crunchy tissue paper, and that didn't work, we wanted it to stand up and it didn't.

(20 February 2006)

The children tried to make the seaweed stand up, but, finally, they put it at the back of the box, as they describe here:

EMMA: The seaweed's going um pretty well instead of putting it in the middle of the box we decided to put it in the back of the box. So, it's going all well but the problem with our animals is that they won't stand up. The dolphin will stand up on its front but it won't stand up right now but its standing up, but we got a dolphin an angel fish and a star fish and a crab and the crabs um ... um one of its pincer's come off and we are going to try and stick it back on but its taking a bit of time, and I don't think anything going to ... we have tried masking tape we have tried lots and lots of PVA glue on but its just not working.
SOPHIE: It looks like a good effect, the bubbles – all the fishes swimming here.

(20 February 2006)

Sally described what she observed from this episode in a later discussion:

I'd found them some green cellophane, it was the stuff that they wanted that they described, they just did not have the language for it, and they actually wanted the seaweed to stand up so the cellophane would have been floppy, they were finding ways of how they would have been able to strengthen cellophane, you know backing it onto paper and onto card, but they would have found that it wasn't transparent, and they toyed with all sorts of ideas, they tried a few types of paper and card and they weren't really getting the right effect, and then I just said to them, would you like me to give you an idea and I gave them some overhead projector transparency and I said they could paint on to it and mix some glue with it and it could stick and they tried it an found that it worked pretty well! It was thick enough to stand up and that idea of mixing the paint and the PVA they shared the information with other groups.

(Discussion September 2006)

Problem solving, difficulty and overcoming it were the focus of this group. The material world offered challenges that they wrestled with, before overcoming them

FIGURE 6.2 The researcher in the classroom, Year 2 taken by children

with new decisions and material solutions. While Sally's perception of her role was of an enabler and her focus on the children's decisions led her work, the children's perception of her was as a powerful instigator of change (a 'bolt of lightning'). Sally's view of the class was this:

> They have done tremendously well, with the amount of external things they have brought into this project, and they have overcome a lot of problems themselves, and a lot of difficulties, whether it has been testing out materials or trying something and it not working and I have just tried to be there as a facilitator.

> (SB March 2006)

A further 'discourse genre' as well as the phrase 'we decided that' was the phrase, 'a good effect'. Sally used it in her discussion above when she describes the green cellophane and how the children were not really getting the right effect. Sophie also mentions that the look of the box is a 'good effect'. I was interested in how this expression 'good effect' was linked to the material realisation of the boxes, as a sign of success, much as the expression 'good effect' was used in the programme 'Changing Rooms' which was then a current favourite on television, by which rooms were made over to the astonishment of their inhabitants. This 'discourse genre' which maybe has its roots in everyday creativity, could be perceived within the shards of discourse I analysed.

Theme 3: 'The Unexpected Outcome'

Many of the children followed the concept of the environmental box, and the objects inside the box were coherent with the environment (ocean, jungle, desert and Arctic). The boxes, however, also provided a space for other things to happen and for the children to enter the box as a play space. As I watched the groups, some decisions were more unusual than others;

ANDREW: about the path …
KATE: tell me about the path
TIMMY: we did it squiggly but then
ANDREW: we did it in a line but on our environment sheet it's all curvy so it's got bendy so we did it um so we did um when we looked in the (room) we thought of doing it curvy but then I thought of doing it that way, so it goes out and in
TIMMY: So you walking from there and you walk over that path – we could have put some shops in couldn't we?

(8 March 2006)

Timmy imagines himself walking over the path of his box and creates a new idea – the 'shops'. This brought an 'everyday' quality to his realisation. The notion of shops in the desert had not really struck me before, and this could be described as an 'unexpected outcome' in the creative process (Craft 2000, 2002).

Theme 4: 'Funds of Knowledge'

I began to see how the work with the children also referred to 'funds of knowledge' (Gonzalez *et al.* 2005) that enabled different kinds of discourses and realisations connected to everyday practices to take place. One child, Carl, who was originally from the Philippines, described his King Cobra:

CARL: We found a real cobra in the book over there.
KATE: Can you show me?
FRANCESCA: we need more red
KATE: Have you seen one on the tele?
CARL: I have seen one on the zoo. *I saw a real one in my cousin's house in the Philippines.* He has got a real King Cobra in his house he has got it locked up in his cage. He's in the Philippines.
KATE: What colours were it?
CARL: black at the top and steely and brown at the bottom.
KATE: Were you scared?
CARL: he went *ssss* like that.

(Taped interview 8 February 2006)

While the instruction for finding out about the animals to put in the boxes had been very much about looking on the internet and in books, the children's own 'funds of knowledge' (Gonzalez *et al.* 2005) also were brought into the field of the classroom when thinking about the qualities of the animals they were researching.

At the end of the first year of observations, I was able to identify two contrasting and competing definitions of creativity within Sally's classroom. One was about learner agency, as described by Burnard *et al.* (2006), in which the children were given the opportunity to decide for themselves what they did. However, the creative aspect of the classroom was also realised in the 'unexpected outcome' (Craft 2000, 2002), when home funds of knowledge, or different kinds of decisions, surfaced within the material quality of the boxes. The decision to have a man in the jungle, or place a King Cobra in the box, were imbued with different kinds of meanings, ones that drew on home 'funds of knowledge' (Gonzalez *et al.* 2005). These definitions, decisions, and meanings highlight the different relationships existing between myself the teacher and the pupils within the activity of the creativity project.

Year 2 Creativity as Being Instantiated in Narrative Talk

In Year 2, I revisited the class in the Spring Term of 2007. This was a new class of Year 2 children (aged 6–7) but with the same teacher (Sally Bean) and the same activity. I conducted the same project, visiting weekly when the children were doing their boxes and recording the process using cameras, tapes and fieldnotes. This year, Sally reported to me that she thought that the children were not as creative as last year, particularly with regard to the material quality of the boxes, in that they tended to copy the children's boxes from last year and not focus on innovative solutions to material problems. Sally focused on the same issues, that of creative problem solving in the material world:

> I would like you and your partner to make your own decisions. I will help you and your partner if you get incredibly stuck but if you have not had a go at solving the problem first you need to do that, these are your boxes.
>
> (13 March 2007 SB)

This year I found the following key themes in the analysis:

- the unexpected outcome;
- narrative connected to the boxes;
- material and narrative problem solving.

Year 2 Theme 1: 'The Unexpected Outcome'

I continued to watch the children make decisions about the boxes. These were sometimes unexpected, as here:

KATE: Is this the monkey in the trees? Where did you get the ideas from?
BOYS: We just thought of it.
KATE: Whose is this here?
CHRIS: Its a man but – Jon did you do that?
JON: No
CHRIS: I did both of them – Jon did that head though.

(Taped interaction 17 April 2007)

As with the shops in the desert, in Year 1, here, the box is enlivened by having real people in it – something Sally Bean had not envisaged in her conception of the boxes as inhabited by the creatures that lived in those environments.

Theme 2: Narrative Connected to The Boxes

In the final example, three girls, Savannah, Taylor and Coral, were creating an ocean environment. I watched the process from the initial making of the box, through to the decoration of the box, until the final moment when the box was placed on the side of the classroom for display.

One of the processes I watched was the slow construction of a hill at the back of the box, using masking tape. This hill was the subject of much debate and discussion:

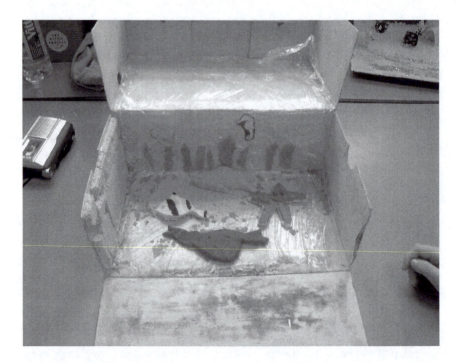

FIGURE 6.3 Image of a box

SAVANNAH: here we are going to paint over the masking tape so it makes it look like.

TAYLOR: We are going to put some fish in the seabed.

SAVANNAH: Yes, that's going to be – these are the seabed under here we are going to get some over there.

TAYLOR: we are going to wrap some of the dolphins under.

SAVANNAH: Yes we are going to try and get the dolphins to come in here so it looks like they are getting ready to jump up over the water!

(Taped interaction 13 March 2007)

As the hill was slowly built up, using paper, and then painted over, in a corner of the shoe box that was the box environment, the girls began to work out the hill's meaning:

SAVANNAH: We build the hill because that's going to be where every fish sleeps!

KATE: You said that about the dolphins peeking through, I like that.

SAVANNAH: Taylor, I am gonna put that shell there because it looks more nice in there I am going to bring this little light and I am going to stick it there because it can be light.

TAYLOR: Yes but the light will have to go there because it doesn't look as bright in there.

KATE: You have a little light.

SAVANNAH: We could put the dolphins we could put the dolphins.

TAYLOR: we could put the light in there because it makes it light.

SAVANNAH: Because the fish will swim into there anyway (higher pitch).

TAYLOR: No they could swim, the dolphins could be peeping through there couldn't they?

TAYLOR: Its gonna have to be ripped a bit like that.

SAVANNAH: No the dolphins sleep there, Taylor, it can't be like that.

TAYLOR: Yes that's where the dolphins sleeps.

(Discussion 13 March 2007)

The hill is a point of contestation until Taylor agrees that the hill can be a place where the dolphins sleep. This domestic role for the hill was explored further on in their discussions a couple of weeks later. As the box took shape, its making opened up a new world, in which the dolphins all acquired the role of mummies and babies and the children described a mini world in which the babies went to school, learnt and played within the environment,

SAVANNAH: That's the mummy dolphin and that's the baby dolphin!

KATE: Oh brilliant!

SAVANNAH: We put them together because the baby has to follow the mummy.

CORAL: We made it out of clay.

TAYLOR: Yeah.

KATE: Are you the ones that had a dolphin school?

FIGURE 6.4 Construction of the hill

GIRLS: yeah! A dolphin school.

CORAL: Because the mummy is going to take the baby to school.

KATE: I love this.

TAYLOR: Yes, that's right, it's really close. Because it only lives down here.

TAYLOR: We did the jellyfish, er one's the sister, one's the brother, one's the baby and one's the mum.

CORAL: that's the baby.

TAYLOR: yeah and that's the sister and that's the brother and that's the other big sister.

(Discussion 17 April 2007)

In this sequence of talk, which went on for some time, and takes up over two pages, as a transcription, the girls describe how the school is made up of a number of children, in an actively imagined space, where children learn using shells for pencils and live an ordered 'play school' environment:

SAVANNAH: The daddy's died.

TAYLOR: We made some children because there is no point making the school if there aint gonna be no children to go in.

(17 April 2007)

The children used the box to re-create their space, the space of the classroom and they focused on how the 'space of school' could be recreated using the 'space of the ocean' at the same time:

SAVANNAH: We did some shells so then they can pretend they are paper and pencils.

TAYLOR: So they can write on it.

CORAL: We put big shells and little shells because the shells are going to move.

TAYLOR: The big shells are for writing on and the little ones are for the pencils.

KATE: For the pencils?

CORAL: There are 24 shells on there (starts counting 1 2 3 4 5 6 7 8 9 10 11 12 13).

(17 April 2007)

These extracts again highlight the relationship underpinning the structures set up between the child and the artistic object as mediated in a particular structural (relational) context. The narrative talk takes in sleeping dolphins, a dolphin school, a space where the babies stay at home, where the daddy dies and where the shells are used for writing. The school story that is enacted through the box has its origins in everyday life as well as in school experience. The narrative text occupies a hybrid space, across the domains of home and school and while the event (the talk spans both domains) the box also contains a number of references to home practices, such as sleeping and babies, as well as schooled practices such as paper and pencils – literacy materials.

FIGURE 6.5 Finished box

Theme 3: Material and Narrative Problem Solving Through the Boxes

The boxes were used as spaces where both material dilemmas and narrative concerns were raised, and represented, across the collaborative structures that Sally set up. In the case of the school it was the issue of the rock that became a door that determined the outcome, that of the environment as a dolphin school.

> Taylor: We did the school because um we just wanted to make, well we decided that we wanted it to be a rock, but then we changed us mind to put it to a school because there's a door.
>
> (17 April 2007)

The decision to make the rock into a door for the dolphins to emerge from then created the imaginary space of the dolphin school. Taylor articulates the reason for the school being located within the material world (we changed us mind because there is a door). In the earlier excerpt of talk, where there was a discussion about the dolphins sleeping, it was clear that the rip in the hill transformed the box both into a home (with a bedroom for sleeping) and a school (where you could line up). The materiality worked together with the narrative to open up new possibilities for meaning making.

However, while the focus of the teacher, Sally Bean, was on creativity as located in the *material problem* solving, I was interested in the *narrative talk* of the children, as they turned their boxes into an imaginary school, as well as an imaginary home. While Sally was focused on creativity as being about learner agency ('we decided that') and about the importance of craft activities as a space for this learner agency to be deployed, I was interested in the 'ordinary' culture of the children, in the world of the dolphin school, where the babies stay at home, and the siblings are described and the baby follows the mummy on the trip to school. Everyday life is brought to life in this sequence of talk which I found, like Steadman's girls' talk in *The Tidy House* (1983), to be an enactment of everyday life in a small Yorkshire town, its features of siblings, and walking to and from school and playing school. Culture, as 'ordinary' (Williams 1989) and creativity as being about the mix of everyday life with schooled symbolic repertoires could be linked to Willis' concept of the symbolic creativity that children bring to meaning making in everyday life (Willis 1998).

Discussion

This data was collected at the end of a Creative Partnerships project and focused on one teacher, not on the artists' role in the school. However, reflecting on the data, it can be linked back to Heads Together, (the artists) and their belief in children as agents in their own meaning making, which, in turn, can be traced back to the work of Burnard *et al.* (2006) in seeing creativity as being, above all, about profiling learner agency. Creativity as being a craft activity, an idea implicit in Sally's teaching and instantiated within the work of many creative practitioners who focused on the material as a space for children's agency to be realised (see Heath and Wolf 2004).

I was, by contrast, interested in the surfacing of the children's 'funds of knowledge' across the two datasets, and found much to perplex me in the data. Why was there a man in the desert? Why was the King Cobra so special to Carl? Children drew on local knowledge to flesh out information they had gathered from the internet about their environments. Many children drew on trips to the seaside to articulate how they saw their ocean environments. Everyday life seeped into the making of the boxes. I, therefore, as a researcher, was following the work of Willis (1998) and Williams (1989) in looking at everyday knowledge and a mixing of hybrid genres of meaning making surfacing within this activity. Sally was less interested in the narratives that emerged from the box making but on the processes and practices as described by the children as they made the boxes.

Sally's own location of her practice fits well both with the background of many of the children who attended the school, whose grandparents were miners or farmers, and for whom craft would be important, and also with the focus of the artists, who liked to create new kinds of texts from the children's drawings. As she said of herself,

> My personal interest in creativity started at an early age and has continued into my professional career as a teacher. Art and Design and Design Technology were always my favourite subjects at school and I continued with this when I took A-level Art and then Art as my specialist subject during my degree.
>
> (From Sally's own personal reflection March 2006)

In Pahl and Rowsell (2010) I wrote of my own personal interest in this field:

> I (Kate) learned from Raymond Williams (1958, 1989) that texts are part of culture, that they sit within social contexts that themselves are subject to deep and sometimes unexpressed structures of feeling.
>
> (Pahl and Rowsell 2010)

These accounts of creativity I then linked to the analysis of the policy documents from Creative Partnerships at the time of doing the project.

What can we gain from bringing in a Bourdieusian analysis to this? At one level, the pedagogic habitus, of letting in new experiences and allowing learner agency can be seen in the texts and practices that occurred in the classroom, such as the dolphin school, the men in the desert and the cobra that hissed at the boy. Sally's *pedagogic habitus* could be seen instantiated within the ability of the children to figure out how to make seaweed stand up using transparent plastic and glue mixed with paint. These small-scale multimodal events and practices, unearthed during classroom ethnography, could remain at that level. However, what happens if this analysis is expanded?

My version of creativity (the girls' narrative talk, echoing the everyday as culture) as opposed to Sally's (creative problem solving in the material world) could be seen within the choices of data we chose to discuss (me) and in the focus for her teaching and discussion (Sally). Jones argues that, 'Much current thinking about creative learning has an impulse towards the social and the cultural' (Jones 2009: 77). He cites authors such as Cochrane, Craft and Jeffrey who talk about 'surfacing the learner's experience' and the focus by Cochrane on being close to young people's experience. He also identifies this space as 'lonely' – as being not connected enough to the past, and other studies of working-class life and experience. Other studies, such as Steadman (1983) and Reay and Lucey (2000) on working-class children's experience of space and place, are important place to locate the narrative texts that I found in the classroom ethnography. Other studies, such as Sennett's (2008) book on craft, concur with Sally's view of creativity as a space of practice, where autonomy is exercised by problem solving in a material sense.

Sally also expressed the belief that letting children lead projects was a more effective way of teaching and learning to take place:

> Giving the children a sense of ownership towards their learning really impacted on my teaching and, as we have continued to develop our topics, projects and curriculum, I try to make projects more children-led than teacher-led.

Sally felt that the first year (Year 1) the children were able to instantiate her beliefs in autonomy and problem solving in craft forms through the meaning making, and she reflected that:

> Now I feel that much more of my personal interest in Art and my personality can be reflected through my teaching.
>
> (Personal reflection March 2006)

In Year 2, however, she felt frustrated that the children were not quite as focused as last year;

> This class don't seem to think logically! I have just been watching [not clear] who is pretty intelligent and she is painting a small animal with a huge brush and she is reaching across the table!

Sally's 'logic of practice', therefore was focused on how the children responded to the material conditions of their meaning making. I was interested in the unfolding stories that arose as the children made the boxes. Sally's pedagogic habitus could be traced back to her interest in art and craft and design technology as well as her experience of the artists, Heads Together. My objectified reflexivity was visible in my use of Williams (1989), and Steadman (1983) and narratives as instantiated within the talk of the children.

Conclusion

As noted in this chapter and elsewhere in the book, Bourdieu's 'logic of practice' needs to be understood as *relational* above all. Having a relational consideration of the data deepened my understanding of how Sally and I were enacting our views of creativity in our research and in the analytic framing we brought to the field of play. It was helpful to have Ken Jones' account of the background history of creativity (Jones 2009) and in particular, his account of culture as situated with the domain of everyday working-class experience. I could then join up my thinking with work on mining communities (Warwick and Littlejohn 1992) and rural literacies (Brooke 2003) with this dataset. I am not sure which 'view' of creativity, had most currency. While I have since written about the girls' talk (Pahl 2009) I am not sure my writing has changed policy. Creativity as material problem solving, in the focus on glue and sticking, on making things into 'a good effect' however, I could see located in another domain of practice, the 'Changing Rooms' culture of the television makeover series, (in which ordinary people's homes were also transformed by extensive cutting and sticking) which was, perhaps more powerful in the world outside Creative Partnerships. Writing this chapter has made me reflect on the things I find in the data, and what teachers see in data, and led me to a consideration of the role of the *pedagogic habitus* as artists and teachers try to find a common language across different domains of practice.

Note

1   With thanks to Sally Bean for helping me understand what she was doing.

7

ARTIFACTUAL ENGLISH

JENNIFER ROWSELL

Introduction

The three pictures that begin this chapter appear in digital stories about an odyssey of self. Caspian,[1] a student featured in the research reported here, launches his story by looking at the viewer as he leans out of a train window; Esme presents a map of Australia with a gradual encircling of her childhood home in Cairns, Australia; and Brian starts his film with a digital clock set at 6 a.m., the time he awoke every day in Israel, before he and his family relocated to the United States. Where one film captures a moment in time as an enduring memory, the other depicts a movement from one part of the world to another; and the final one, relives a past moment quite different from the present. These images express agencies and lived histories. The visual triptych embodies an argument put forth in the chapter that multimodality affords more complete expression of habitus (see Bourdieu, 1990a/1980: 55ff.) than mono-modality. Each image gives a viewer a slice of someone's life, what I call in this

FIGURE 7.1 Digital stories about an Odyssey

chapter *fractal habitus* – that is 'pieces' of habitus .Throughout Bourdieu's work, there is a constant dialogue about the ways in which habitus shifts during improvisation and cultural production. This chapter is an attempt to develop a language for the subtle shifts in habitus revealed during individual creative expression. Through gestures and movement in drama; through medium and colour saturation or de-saturation in painting; and through visuals accompanied with music in film these modal choices embody parts of self in artistic and creative work. In an attempt to use Bourdieu's notion of habitus as a means of viewing how meaning-makers represent their everyday in representation and production, the chapter documents a High School ethnography and the ways in which teenagers 'sediment' fractiles of habitus in their production of digital stories. The study combines ethnography with multimodality by looking at a community and a group of students who use multimodality to represent their lived histories, families, and dispositions in order to foster a greater understanding of a canonical text. These 'multimodal' readings of lived histories illustrate arguments put forth in the chapter: that inspiration for self-expression grows from transacting with the everyday; and, that modal choice offers more creativity and expression. In the research reported in the chapter, 'fractal habitus' is interpreted through choices made during the production of digital stories.

There is extant research that supports digital story production as a way of repositioning students within situations and settings (Rosenfield-Halverson *et al.*, 2009). Nelson *et al.*, 2008; Rogers, 2008). In such work, scholars demonstrate how multimodal composition offers greater motivation and greater connection to intended practices and understandings. Nelson, Hull, and Smith-Roche (2008) analyse in detail a youth's digital story, which they consider a 'multiplicatively more complicated matter to vividly realize and publicize an authorial intention' (2008: 415). Through their analysis of a youth's careful, deft choice of modes, Nelson *et al.* show how they create a powerful message about himself and his world through the production of a digital story. Similarly, Rosenfeld-Halverson *et al.*, (2009) explore a connection between youth concepts of identity and a production of films about youth media arts organizations. The authors analyse how producers and designers of new media foster and even shape the identity development process of youth. So too, in Theresa Rogers' research (2010), she interprets mediation and repositioning of identity by four youths in their production of short films. Rogers' work documents the sophistication of four teenagers' concepts of design and, more specifically, how they embed values within visual, audio, gestural and interactive modes of expression and representation. Combining an analysis of multimodal production with Bourdieu's notion of habitus chips away at bits, fractures of habitus sedimented into produced texts (see Rowsell and Pahl, 2007). I build on such work by focusing on not only *what* a group of teenagers produce, but also, *how* they produce multimodal compositions.

From twenty-four hours to fifteen years, each digital story carries with it messages about the producer. Habitus, with its adaptive quality that adjusts to internal and external shifts, helps me to interpret choices in how students design their stories. In past and present work (Rowsell, 2009; Rowsell and Pahl, 2007), I have explored ways in which individuals adjust, unconsciously and consciously, habitus when life changes happen. For instance, in a chapter about four artists and how they consciously improvise on habitus (dispositions and experience) during creative expression, I analyse how an artist expresses internal and external shifts in habitus in his art when he became a father. In the chapter, I look at a four-year study of ninth-grade secondary students taking a multimodal approach to the teaching of English and connect with Bourdieu's theory of practice in order to offer a theory of fractal habitus in their multimodal meaning-making that opens more space, more creativity, and ultimately, more learning of text content. Admittedly, the more constraints and conventions a context carries, the less freedom to improvise on their understanding of their life histories. The argument about the creation of digital stories and the use of multimodality for the project rests on a belief that participants are more motivated and have greater interest because the context and the product reinforce habitus. In the chapter, I present how students design their journey stories around their fractal habitus, and it is through the embedding of their everyday life histories that they reposition their identity in an English classroom.

Background

From January 2006 to the June 2010, I worked closely with an English teacher at a high school in Princeton, New Jersey. Participants involved in the study are ninth-grade students who take a support English class because they are not performing well in English and they need extra support as a supplement to their standard ninth-grade English class. I have written previously about this group of students (Rowsell, 2009; Pahl and Rowsell, 2010). What differentiates this chapter from previous writings is that I use Bourdieu's notion of habitus and the *sedimentation* of fractal habitus into multimodal texts to show how encouraging an active embedding of the everyday, personal experiences, dispositions opens up a space for creativity and innovation that doxa-ruled spaces like schooling obstructs. In this section, I profile the context, participants, reflexivity, and methodological approach.

Study Participants

Within suburban towns, social class is at times hidden in a landscape of generalized middle class. Princeton, New Jersey, for instance, is predominantly an affluent community situated between New York and Philadelphia with a cross-section of middle-class commuters and local residents whose socio-economic status is somewhat blurred and being economically disadvantaged in this university town is hidden in a landscape of privilege and upward mobility. Central to the community is the presence of Princeton University, where students come from around the world to take courses with such scholars as Toni Morrison or Paul Krugman (2008 Nobel Peace Prize in Economics winner). It is regarded as an intellectual epicentre in the United States. The local high school mirrors the values of the community and it takes pride in a tradition of academic and cultural achievements. Although the high school has many accolades for student achievement, there have been years when it has not made adequate yearly progress on the HSPA (High School Proficiency Assessment, a standardized test administered in all high schools in New Jersey). For a silent, insistent minority of students in this community, there is an on-going pattern of under-achievement, which is often attributed to a mismatch between the interests and predilections of students and the demands of the school curriculum.

In accordance with *No Child Left Behind* (2002), eighth-grade students are required to take the Grade Eight Proficiency Assessment (GEPA) test. Students who score below 200 on the language arts assessment are placed in a HSPA/ Basic Skills program. It is this program that is the focus of my research. It seemed unacceptable to both of us (the English teacher and me) that students who clearly have the capacity to do well in English were not doing well because they did not feel connected to their study of English literature. Exploring their stories and using their lived histories and their ruling passions as material to think and write with became a means to relocate them in the formal field of practice in their English classroom.

As I have noted before (Rowsell, 2009), there is no lack of skill and effort on the part of these students. They are talented, have ruling passions and make meaning from a variety of texts, yet they fail to reach their potential in school. What continues to impress me about these teenagers is that their interests are as diverse and eclectic as they are. Some like to cook, some like to sculpt, some write stories, others like what typical teenagers like, such as videogames and sports. What is more, there are talented and caring teachers at this high school, yet there continues to be a growing pattern of disinterest and apathy displayed by students. Typically, their complex communicational worlds are rendered invisible within more anachronistic, print-ruled pedagogical frameworks. As other researchers have documented (Alvermann and McLean, 2007; Kinloch, 2009; Hagood, 2009; Vasudevan, 2009), adolescents such as these ones do not recognize themselves in their learning, particularly their learning of classical literature.

The Project

So it is with this background that we decided to create a unit of study based on Homer's *The Odyssey* (1996), a unit on the production of a digital journey story paralleling Odysseus' journey back to Ithaca. We began the digital storytelling unit in October 2008, at the beginning of the second marking period. Each student participant received an outline of what they needed to do to complete the project. The assignment explanation read as follows:

An Odyssey of Self

Life is all about stories. Everyone has a story, either about something they have heard, seen, or only hope to see. We all remember stories that we were told as children and will tell many of those same stories to our own families one day. Stories reflect our past, present, and future and represent our heritage, beliefs, values, histories, family, and dreams.

In English class, you have read stories that others share with readers. Homer tells us the story of Telemachus, the son of great Odysseus, who in just a few weeks, must leave his boyhood behind and assume his place as 'the true son of Odysseus.' He has much to learn before his journey ends. Odysseus, too, is on a journey. He must not only endure the physical journey of reaching home, but he must also take an emotional journey to reunite with his wife after 20 years.

This is your opportunity to tell your story … in your own voice.

Step One: Decide which part of your journey you will tell. Most importantly, think about your family, your heritage, and how these have contributed to your journey.

Step Two/Three: Think about pictures, sounds, movements that tell the story that you want to tell. Then, storyboard your short film to structure the content and design.

(Devised by Jackie Delaware in September 2008)

After being introduced to the project, student participants spent several weeks storyboarding their content, collecting multimodal assets (such as visuals, sounds, overall effects, transitions), writing and performing their voice-overs, and devoting hours in the studio/computer room to edit their films. During the final stages of production, I interviewed all of the participants about choices that they made during production, such as: What story did you decide to tell? How did you relate your story to Homer's *The Odyssey*? What modes/effects did you use? Why these modes and not other modes? Have they achieved the effect and mood that they wanted to create? If so, in what ways have they achieved this mood? Is there a dominant effect or mode in their digital stories? Along with interviews, Jennifer observed hours of studio time (i.e., class periods devoted to film production), noting such design practices as: selecting music for a film; choosing visuals and visual effects; the degree of collaborative work; the level of engagement in tasks; and, how much guidance each participant required during the design and production process.

There were some weaknesses and limitations to the research such as a lack of sufficient equipment and technology (e.g., we had a very small budget for equipment). In retrospect, another limitation to the study was the lack of critical framing about how equipment works and what such technical effects such as camera angles achieve and how and why certain modes afford more meaning in one instance than in others. In fact, the project would have strongly benefited from more critical framing about modes and modal effects (Sheridan and Rowsell, 2010), if the teacher-researcher and I adopted some design language. In the end, the unit dealt more with process than it did with product.

Student participants were assessed based on their multimodal competence as exhibited in their productions. The rubric that Jackie (the teacher-researcher) devised took account of how a student demonstrates a journey; choice in modal effects to give their story a mood and message; sequencing and transitioning content well; creativity and originality; and, multimodal salience and effect.

An Ecological Ethnography

The ethnographic approach to data collection and analysis reported in this chapter resembles what Judith Green and David Bloome (1990) call 'adopting an ethnographic perspective', which they describe as follows:

> by adopting an ethnographic perspective, we mean that it is possible to take a more focused approach (i.e., do less than a comprehensive ethnography) to study particular aspects of everyday life and cultural practices of a social group. Central to an ethnographic perspective is the use of theories of culture and inquiry practices derived from anthropology or sociology to guide the research.
>
> (p. 6)

Establishing a spectrum of ethnography helpfully separates extensive and comprehensive studies of a given culture from shorter ethnographies that take some account of cultural practice and an *emic* perspective of a context (see Chapters 2 and 3 in this volume).

To conduct this research in a ninth-grade classroom, I extend Bloome and Green's distinction between an ethnography and an ethnographic perspective by taking an *ecological* ethnographic perspective. While the research is ethnographic in nature in that it attempts to take an insider perspective of a particular community and group of teenagers taking a support English class, differentials and geographies of opportunity played a role in data analysis. This research is tied to another research study, which is also an ecological survey, this time of the Princeton community conducted with colleagues at the University of South Australia[2] (Nichols et al. 2009). In the research, the team asks such questions as: Are there socio-economic differentials in terms of access to information and networks of information within the geography of a particular community? If so, in what ways are communities sectioned off? What are some of the popular hubs of activity? Are there distinct networks and spatial hubs for specific individuals? Our study draws on a study by Neuman and Celano (2001), who conducted a comparative study of four neighbourhoods in Philadelphia in terms of the opportunities offered for children and their families to engage in literacy-related activities. Their method involved walking through a block of different neighbourhoods to systematically note different geographies and spatial features: stores and stands likely to sell reading materials, signs and their conditions (readability), public spaces where reading could be undertaken, and relevant institutional sites (libraries, child care centres, etc). Neuman and Celano found that neighbourhoods of different socio-economic status showed 'major and striking differences at almost all levels' in terms of access to literacy resources and opportunities (Neuman and Celano, 2001: 15). In this way, a neighbourhood's properties are broken apart and analysed, almost like looking at a habitat and analysing the inter-dependence and co-existence of animals, people, systems and properties. To collect data for the research, I observed, interviewed, and worked with students and their teacher on a digital storytelling project and I looked at the immediate community and its relationship to participants and to the high school. In so doing, I mapped out participant hubs in the town (or, in Bourdieusian terms, within their field of practice). I examined and discussed their valued artifacts, which they brought to school. Accounting for ecological dimensions of their community fosters analysis of how participants crossed fields of practice (Bourdieu, 1990a) from their home to school, and how these crossings effect habitus. For instance, mapping out their community (which for many of them is a series of streets in the centre of town) and relating these hubs to the ecology of their school is a way of breaking apart fractal habitus within a field of practice.

To situate the context and ecology of their classroom, Jackie (the participant teacher) and I combined assignments and canonical texts from their regular English class with the kinds of texts and practices that they engage in outside school. Also, I documented where students sit during studio time and with whom they interact and consult during digital story production.

Filming Researcher Fractal Habitus

To be active participants in the research, Jackie and I decided to produce our own digital stories. Jackie produced a digital story about being an English teacher for twenty-five years. I produced a digital story about another project on digital and new media producers.[3] It was 'epiphanic' to produce a film about a research study in that it made me appreciate that I lack the multimodal sensibilities that our students exhibit. For example, I chose a song by Leonard Cohen entitled *Famous Blue Raincoat*. What I failed to appreciate at the time is that a text producer cannot superimpose a mode because of preference, modes have to work in harmony and symbiotically with other modes and with the content of the story. In other words, the mere fact that I like the song is not a justification for its inclusion in the design. Modes affect meaning when they fit the meaning and, often they effect meaning differently when they are combined with other modes. Students in the study knew this. What is more, they had an intuitive sense about how to do it; the process appeared to be instinctual for them. Jackie and I did not have this same sense, at least we needed to hone our ability to choose the right mode to match the story that we wanted to tell. The experience of producing a digital story about another research project recalls Kress' insights in *Before Writing,* that 'cognition takes place in all modes, but differently so' (Kress, 1997: 42). That is, words and music by Leonard Cohen did not have the connective power nor did they evoke the details that a collage of voices captured. What I realize now that I did not recognize then is that my short film needed a powerful introductory piece as a segue to the content and spliced interview sound bites as a montage of voices was exactly the kind of trope I needed to create an arc for the film's narrative. Snippets from interviews threaded together gave my film an explanatory arc, where the song without a direct connection, on its own, did not achieve the same effect. In the end, I changed the first few slides in my story from words and bits of Leonard Cohen's song to a remix of voices from interviews that I had conducted as the title rolls across the screen. My short film needed a dominant mode and that mode had to mirror the message that modal affordances are the driving force behind content and design. Modes structure content and mirror the story, in much the same way that voice in writing is crafted through words and phrases. To conduct the research, I wanted to capture not only the process of making digital stories, but also to document how the blurring of institutional space into personal, expressive space fosters meaning making. In retrospect, I now appreciate how modes tell stories and how my own habitus was improvised and, perhaps, even shifted during the process, therein illustrating a merging of Bourdieusian sociology with multimodality.

Bourdieu and Multimodality

As noted in Chapter 4, habitus exists at an unconscious level, as a product of history that impacts practice. It is an internalized second nature – the basis of perception and appreciation – that is constrained by fields. In the work of theorists such as Gunther Kress (1997), Anne Haas Dyson (1993), and Kate Pahl (2003; 2004), it is clear that there are different pathways into literacy and the more freedom of expression and representation an individual has, the more meaning that can be made. A meaning-maker left to his, or her, own devices will use the best possible materials, resources, and skills to get the job done. Here, I build on the argument that field contexts of practice, such as a ninth-grade English classroom, need to offer a space to improvise on personal experiences, histories, and the everyday – i.e., the habitus – to effectively and most productively make meaning. In this way, Bourdieu's logic of practice and multimodality work in harmony as an argument for optimal meaning-making in a field of practice. The reported study illustrates well the identity work and fractal habitus transacted during a production process.

Bourdieu argues that visual forms such as photography celebrate what is photographable and signal histories, hierarchies, and social class (Bourdieu *et al.*, 1990b: 86). As Rachel Hurdley (2006) notes in an article about the framing of material culture: 'He (Bourdieu) comments that, as a product, it (photography) occupies a middle ground between nobility and the masses, distinguishing it from paintings and mass-produced prints' (cited in Hurdley, 2006: 359). Bourdieu's acknowledgement of the multiple, embedded nature of photography, and by extension the visual, takes account of how producers find their way into a creative process. For instance, when a producer chooses a sound instead of a visual, it signals information not only about how the producer wants a text to be read, but also signals aspects of a producer's identity, which is improvised during the moment of production (and seen in chosen modes). Logically, it follows that if a producer is limited by resources, tools, and possible practices, meaning is obstructed. Hence, an optimum field in which to make meaning provides space for habitus and the embedding of more extensive materials, resources, and tools to produce a text. Multimodality throws improvised habitus into relief, and, by analysing modal choices made during production, a researcher is able to identify a deeper understanding of the producer's habitus. By speaking with a person, becoming acquainted with their story, then talking through why they chose music instead of visuals, it is possible to grasp an underlying message of a produced object. It also enables a researcher to get closer to what happens during multimodal production.

Improvising on Habitus

Bourdieu refers to an unconscious appropriation of rules, values, and dispositions as 'the habitus,' defining it as 'the durably installed generative principle of regulated improvisations which produce practices' (1990a: 108). He further claims that '*habitus* are spontaneously inclined to recognize all the expressions in which they recognize themselves, because they are spontaneously inclined to produce them'. In *The Logic of Practice* (1980), Bourdieu argues that:

> official representations, which as well as customary rules, include gnomic poems, sayings, proverbs, every kind of objectification of the schemes of perceptions and action in words, things or practices (that is, as much in the vocabulary of honour or kinship, with the model of marriage that it implies, as in ritual actors or objects), have a dialectical relationship with the dispositions that are expressed through them and which help to produce and reinforce them.
>
> (p. 108)

It is this 'dialectic' that I here document: the relationship between the producer and the produced object that informs not only an overall message but also how we read and transform a message ourselves. Fractal habitus, as a term and concept, helps me to identify parts of self in multimodal texts. To illustrate how artifacts such as works of art or digital stories improvise through habitus, I offer Figure 7.1. In Figure 7.1, habitus drives practice and the act of meaning making and multimodal composition of digital stories, which reinforces habitus within a more formalized and codified field context of a classroom. Each case study participant presented below is a meaning-maker who actively sediments parts of themselves (their everyday, values, dispositions) into their productions (Rowsell and Pahl, 2007). Such an improvisation of habitus in a schooling situation resuscitates marginalized meaning-makers into a field of practice (school). For participants involved in the study, at home and out in the community, habitus has more freedom and is less constrained by rules and procedures than it is in school.

In the next section, I explain the theory of fractal habitus and how it serves as a lens of analysis for the filmic narratives.

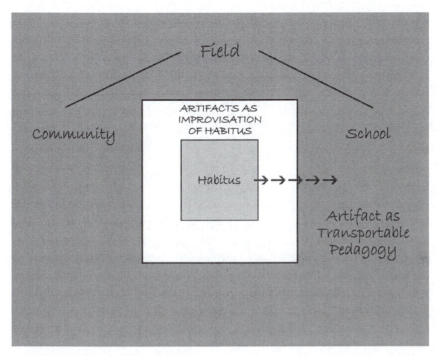

FIGURE 7.2   Depicting fractal habitus in artifacts

A Theory of Fractal Habitus

Bourdieu's work in Algeria provides an example of movements and tensions of habitus within fields. The Algerian peasants that Bourdieu observed in his fieldwork on the Kabyle had a less normalized structuring in that the Kabyle were regulated more by rules of honour than codified rules (Bourdieu, 1990a). The relative freedom that existed for the Kabyle provided an aperture to view habitus at work in context. It is Bourdieu's fine-grained analysis of habitus present in situations and contexts that helps me to analyse how students embed and sediment (Rowsell and Pahl, 2007) habitus into digital stories through fractal bits of habitus. That is, in creating a digital story in their English class, participants invented their own codified rules and protocols. Producing a digital story allowed more freedom of expression and subjectivity and hence, they served as an ideal forum in which to document fractal habitus in a multimodal text (through interviews and text analysis). Habitus remains habitus in situations that do not resist, but rather reinforce and even promote or endorse it. Certainly, students involved in making digital stories had very few structuring conditions and constraints, and their own ideas, values, histories, and dispositions could be fully improvised without critical challenges. In Bourdieu's words:

> Through the systematic 'choices' it makes among the places, events and people that might be frequented, the habitus tends to protect itself from crises and

critical challenges by providing itself with a milieu to which it is as pre-adapted as possible, that is, a relatively constant universe of situations tending to reinforce its dispositions by offering the market most favourable to its products.

(1990a: 61)

The notion of finding fractal habitus in digital texts devised by ninth-graders, opened up the field context of high school English for participants in the study. By interpreting their multimodal choices during the act of production and analysing how these choices materialize in a text and then one step further, speaking with them about their choices, fractal habitus is thrown into relief. Creating a favourable, equitable, safe environment, in which to make meaning, opens up creativity, innovation, meaning making to more properties of habitus.

Throughout his work Bourdieu has an abiding interest in what regulates practice and the ebb and flow of habitus in fields of practice. The field context here is an English classroom; the practice is creating a digital story; and habitus is an unfolding of student participant histories, dispositions, and values. A larger research question within the study and one that Bourdieu's approach helps to answer is: how can one take account of subjective action within settings while also accounting for structuring conditions that regulate practice? The answer lies in how identities mediate themselves in social reality. Social reality exists both inside and outside individuals and what Bourdieu's sociology elucidates is how individual dispositions are regulated by the constraints and affordances of situations and contexts.

As noted, the difference between the notion of 'fractal habitus' and my previous work with Kate Pahl on the notion of 'sedimented identity' (Rowsell and Pahl, 2007) is that for me fractal habitus represents the parts of self that students (subconsciously and perhaps even consciously) sediment into texts. I find fractal habitus is palpable in physical, material features in texts such as images, colours, camera angles that express habitus. Sedimented identity can be seen as the act of embedding layers of habitus into texts, where fractal habitus are the shards that do not necessarily represent the collective habitus but instead aspects, impressions of the everyday and innate dispositions that relate to the composition. Sedimented identity is the active layering of identity into texts; as our article describes it, 'we consider that this way of seeing texts is the instantiations of habitus' (Rowsell and Pahl, 2007: 394). Put simply, sedimentation is the process whilst fractal habitus is the product. To offer an example, in Caspian's film, rather than presenting all facets of his history and unfolding dispositions, he represents one key piece, valuing family and intergenerational presence in his life. Family and its foundational role in his character represent fractal habitus. As instantiations of habitus, sedimented identities are a process and practice, whereas fractal habitus are modes used to signal parts of habitus. Through multimodal composition and framing work around life histories, the artifactual and the everyday inspired participants to focus their story and choose fitting modes of expression. Any theorization of fractal habitus therefore rests on a belief that there is a tension between English and language arts curricula and multimodality.

Modes as Fractures of Habitus

What becomes clear in watching the participants' digital stories several times is that students chose *modes* to tell their story. This seems fairly obvious but the point is that students can communicate more powerfully when multiple forms of representation and expression are introduced into their learning. Relying on Kress and Van Leeuwen's work on the grammar of visual design (Kress and Van Leeuwen, 1996), there are two types of images: narrative images tell stories by having actors and goals, with actors doing something with these goals; whilst conceptual images depict timeless, stable meanings and the subject of a picture is often, almost always, seen frontally.

Many of the students such as Caspian and Esme took advantage of a strategy of 'framing through distances'. There were intimate distances where an image indicates a close distance between the viewer and the image. Caspian exploits intimate distances to represent the closeness that he feels with his family so that the viewer identifies closely with and connects to the story. Social distance frames narratives in such a way as to depict the viewer and the subjects in the image. Brian, another of the case studies profiled below, uses framing to create social distance between the viewer of his digital story and his quotidian world in Tel Aviv.

Students also use angles in their stories to force the viewer to look up or down on subjects in an image. Caspian, for instance, looks straight at the viewer to connect with the viewer. Upper and lower angles create power dynamics with the viewer – looking up at a subject implies that a viewer is deferring power to the subject, whereas, looking down at a subject implies that a viewer has more power. Manuel takes advantage of angles by presenting Cyclops having eye contact with the viewer – as a confrontation. This is shown in Figure 7.3.

Spatial arrangements indicate salience in images. The centre of a picture is the heart of the picture – where Patsy puts her rick-rack dresses or where Caspian puts his Grandpa. So too, eye contact indicates a relationship, almost a beckoning to the viewer. Kress and Van Leeuwen (1996) talk about a demand when a subject gazes at the viewer as in Manuel's digital story when he threads in the story of Odysseus and the obstacles that he faces head-on during his journey. In contrast, there are images that offer engagement with a viewer – the viewer maintains an almost god-like power of observing subjects as in Brian's presentation of parts of Tel Aviv. Differing modes are used to create an atmosphere and they draw out fractal habitus, and through looks, image placement, etc. The case studies presented below show a marked competence with choosing the right mode to express a meaning and to signal fractal habitus.

FIGURE 7.3 Confronting Cyclops

Case Studies of Fractal Habitus

My approach to case studies derives, in part, from the ethnographic tradition described by Clyde Mitchell (1984); that is, rather than 'enumerative induction' to generalize or to establish 'representativeness,' I adapt what Mitchell describes as 'a case study to support an argument … to show how general principles deriving from some theoretical orientation manifest themselves in some given particular circumstance' (Mitchell, 1984: 239). In this case, I support my argument through five students' productions of digital stories as evidence of fractal habitus within texts. In addition, I adopt Dyson and Genishi's definition of case studies as examples of 'the meaning people make of their lives in very particular contexts' (Dyson and Genishi, 2005: 35). Certainly, within the research, students privilege their local worlds (their home, their family, their community) as signifiers of self, as their values, beliefs, and dispositions. All of the participants are in the age range of fourteen to fifteen years old.

Case Study 1: Journeys Make Me Learn About Myself and My Family

Caspian embedded parts of habitus through his touching tribute to his family trip to Niagara Falls. Shy about showcasing his digital story at our screening event, Caspian produced a highly personal account of what a trip to Canada taught him about himself and his family and what his family means to him. What strikes me as I watch Caspian's film is the intergenerational and cultural piece of his filmic narrative. Caspian takes time to present every member of his family and depicts their characters through camera angles and photographs. In this way, habitus materializes in a sedimenting of family relations in the digital text and connecting with family in new, different ways through a journey.

FIGURE 7.4 The end of the rainbow

Beginning with Caspian leaning out of a train window, we are then introduced to members of his family: his Mum and sister, his Grandpa, his Dad and brother, his Grandmother, and the whole family together. After introductions, the viewer moves into the trip and highlights of seeing Niagara Falls and the end of a rainbow. The rainbow is the symbol of his digital story and gives the story a metaphorical arc as seen in Figure 7.4, because it appears at the beginning and end of his digital story.

To me, the most touching part of the film happens at the end when Caspian says, 'What I love most is coming home with more appreciation of my family.' With that line in mind, Caspian's digital story is potentially the most powerful example of how fractures of habitus, childhood and family infuse inspiration into a creative process. In the span of four minutes, a viewer develops a keen sense of Caspian and his familial roots sedimented (Rowsell and Pahl, 2007) into the film as a text. When I asked Caspian about how he composed his film, he said: 'My themes were trips that I took with my family because family is a big part of my life. I really enjoyed our trip to Canada and when we went to Niagara Falls'.

Caspian produced a film that is very much an ode to his family, depicted through visuals, camera angles, and symbols, such as the end of a rainbow. An epiphany that Caspian experienced after producing his digital story is to appreciate his voice. He did not expect to like his voice on the voice-over but, in the end, it worked for him. His voice-over was a way of navigating the story as an accompaniment to the strengths of his visual narrative.

Case Study 2: Memories Keep You Grounded

Esme's story charts her move from Cairns, Australia, all the way to Princeton, New Jersey. Esme created a digital story that looks back at her childhood home in

Australia and then at her present-day world: her friends, her high school, and her daily routines. Esme has difficulty focusing on tasks and is frequently distracted by texting and Facebook. She claims that she does not feel like a writer, yet, she had an immediate sense of how she would produce her digital story. Materialized in her digital story through movement in visuals, Esme embeds her everyday life, her habitus, into her journey. She uses Google Earth as a rhetorical device to show the thread between the local – Cairns, Australia to the global – to Google Earth and back to the local in Princeton, NJ. Like Brian featured later, Esme situates two quite different pictures of embodied self by contrasting her two homes.

There are hints or fractures of Esme's everyday embedded in her digital story as a text from her interest in fashion to her strong connections with friends. Unlike Caspian, there is less privileging of family and more privileging of friends and daily rites. There is a sense of the struggles that she had moving to the United States and in accepting a new identity. In our interview, Esme describes her compositional process: 'the story is about my life growing up in Australia and moving to America and meeting new people and staying with them for a few years and them helping me through moving. It showed the new friends I met when I moved'. Esme wanted to have a different spin on the notion of making a decision. In her interview, she points out that in *The Odyssey*, Odysseus 'chose between the whirlpool, and he made the decision to lose all of his crew and go into whirlpool'. Decision-making became a leitmotif in her film, in her words: 'it shows that I made decisions, well, my family did, with moving from Australia to America.' Throughout the year, Esme was critical of her work, but had to admit that the final version worked, there was cohesion through symbolism and she had grounded her film in her everyday.

Case Study 3: Every Day Is A Fashion Show and The World is Your Runway

Patsy is one of the most visually attuned and design-savvy students I have ever worked with. Once given an assignment, Patsy knows exactly what she is going to do and sets to work immediately on the design. Not only does she visualize quickly, but also, she wastes no time in finding visuals. She is focused and creative and has strong multimodal sensibilities. Early on in her production and design of her digital story, Patsy envisioned a sequence of her own fractal habitus within a rich tapestry of images from the fashion world. Like other case study participants, she is not inspired by her English classes, yet she exhibits comprehension skills, metacognition, and an understanding of figurative devices. She is Guatemalan-American and aspires to be a fashion designer one day and live in New York City – all three of these descriptors are foregrounded in her digital story. Patsy's short film moves from her childhood interest in dresses and fancy clothes to her present, abiding interest in fashion, trends, popular culture, and iconic designers such as Coco Chanel and Valentino. What amazes me about Patsy's film is the sheer number of images she combines to match her voice-over. As a multimodal composition, Patsy's film exhibits both proficiency with image selection and image sequencing, and technical skills by matching images

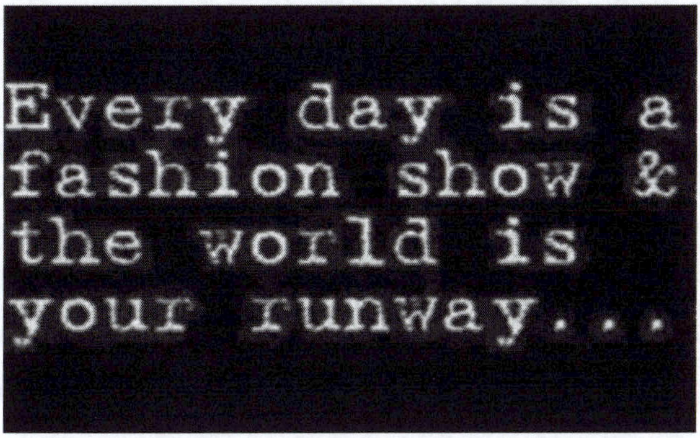

FIGURE 7.5   Patsy's first slide

with a spoken voice-over. Patsy's first screen throws into relief fractal habitus. After the first slide, Patsy foregrounds fractures of her childhood through a series of rick-rack dresses that her Mum (a seamstress) made for her. Each dress has been carefully chosen for its colour and connection to phases of her childhood. After featuring images of her fractal habitus, she presents a succession of images of designers and fashion models threaded in with personal photographs of her and her friends and their own distinct fashion sensibilities. In this way, Patsy's film moves from the global world of high fashion to her local high school world. Patsy concludes her digital story by circling back to the present-day and her own journey to New York, as a fashion designer. If graded on direct connections to *The Odyssey,* the assignment would fall short when compared with other students' work. However, the sophistication of her editing and her merging of modes alone gave her high grades. Patsy had lots of technology issues in the production of her story, but in the end she was impressed with the result.

Patsy's film is so effective because there are meaningful, salient pieces of her and her innate dispositions combined with well-known people and popular culture images. In her words, 'Well, I thought of some ideas that had to do with an odyssey and adventure stood out to me. I thought about fashion because that's an adventure to me. Some people may not take it seriously, but I do.' Patsy had an intensity about multimodal composition that helped her find a place in the English Plus classroom during the digital storytelling semester.

Case Study 4: Journeys of Success and Failure

Manuel is a tall and athletic young man, who can write well and contribute in English class when he is interested and feels confident about his understanding. When introduced to the digital storytelling unit, Manuel could not think of a strategy until I sat with him and brainstormed ideas. As soon as we talked about moving from struggles to success as an example of a journey story, he identified sports as a journey motif in his life. In charting developing skills in three of his core sports – soccer, basketball and football – he was probably more focused than any other student. Sports and his trials and tribulations with sports and bullies, sedimented fractal habitus that came out strongest in his voice-over.

He opened his story about soccer with Lionel Messi of Argentina and how he is an inspiration to him. Manuel used expressive language and humour to describe how he performs in soccer and then moved into basketball, a sport that he did not feel as confident in, admitting that 'at first I was horrible at it…no one wanted to play with me.' Manuel then talked about getting better at dribbling and how he is now on the high school freshman team. The final sport was football. Here, he used Kevin Curtis of the Eagles as an inspiration in football. Of all the students who completed digital stories, Manuel was the most adept at connecting his story to *The Odyssey* by linking a story about how his brother helped him do better in sports: 'I think that the Athena in my life was my brother – he boosted my chances of reaching my goal, just like Athena did for Odysseus, even though Odysseus and I are different we are similar people'. In our interview, Manuel claims: 'when I thought about the digital story, I thought about sports because I like to play sports all the time and sports are a big part of my life'. Manuel proceeded to talk about how he structured and sequenced content: 'I have three main sports that I play which are basketball, football and soccer and there are eighteen slides in my digital story and that means six slides for each sport'. Manuel applied effective multimodal compositional practices along with written compositional practices in crafting his filmic narrative. Of all the participants, Manuel stands out for me because he found such success in digitally, multimodally replicating the story of Odysseus, which noticeably repositioned him among his peers.

Case Study 5: This is My Typical Day in Israel

Like Manuel, of all of the participant students, Brian stands out because he found such success in digitally and multimodally inter-relating the story of Odysseus with his own story. Brian is fourteen-years-old and moved to the United States from Israel in 2006. Brian is quiet, thoughtful, and usually wears a hat to the side, just above his eyes. At first, I figured that Brian was quiet because his first language is Hebrew, but I soon realized that Brian can speak English perfectly well and is an eloquent writer, he simply tends to be quiet. The voice-over that he composed is detailed and breaks down every moment in an average day in Israel. Interestingly, as detailed as his voice-over is, he opted to say only the first line of the digital story and let pictures and written text tell the story, which, to my mind, aligns with his quiet demeanour. Scenes in Tel Aviv coupled with visuals of statues in ancient Greece signal his design sensibilities.

Brian sits beside and chats with the least likely person in the group, Ted, who is the most talkative student in the class. Brian is well-liked by his peers and is seen as someone who is creative. When I interviewed Brian about the production of his digital story, he talked about his choices in modes: 'I used simple pictures of Israel and then I found places in Israel but I got more specific and found the places where I lived and know exactly where they are.' Brian used Google Maps to locate particular places and spaces and, like Esme, Google Maps served as a rhetorical device to depict the distance between Tel Aviv and Princeton.

Brian's film begins with his voice saying, 'Hello, this is my typical day in Israel' and that is the only voice-over in the film. From there, he moves from his daily bus journey as seen in Figure 7.6 to hanging out with friends before school (using actual photographs of his friends).

What Brian claims he wanted his viewers to experience most of all is 'that there are a lot of interesting places in Israel and just knowing the culture is different.' As a viewer, I sensed his desire to represent the distinctive character of Tel Aviv in images of bus scenes and of the shawarma he often purchased from street vendors, as seen in Figure 7.7

As a producer, Brian likes to combine literal images like Bus 157 with figurative images. For example, to express the boredom he felt while waiting with friends for buses and trains, he presented a statue of a yawning man. Fractures and fragments of Brian's habitus can be seen in images of bus lines that he took and in childhood hubs and familiar scenes such as the local shawarma stand. It was a twist on the story of Odysseus and his epic journey that allowed Brian to reflect on his own epic move from Israel to the United States and how and what he carries with him in a new, foreign context.

In Table 7.1, I feature each participant with examples of ways in which they sediment fractal habitus and what fractal habitus is elucidated in terms of literacy practices.

FIGURE 7.6   Bus 157 in Tel Aviv

when we get off line 20 we always buy Shawarma

FIGURE 7.7 Shawarma off Line 20

Looking at the case studies, Table 7.1 displays fractal habituses that I found in digital stories and literacy skills that these material properties exhibit.

The table shows the relationship between fractal habitus, bits of every day, and literacy practices prominently displayed in students' multimodal compositions. By offering examples of fractal habitus, it is a way of demonstrating how their creativity and innovation led to a composition (and new compositional skills). As seen in the table, there are contrasts in how students sediment fractal habitus. Caspian focuses on agents in photographs through camera angles and figurative devices, whereas Patsy applies visual and technical effects through a fusillade of personal and pop culture images, and Manuel is more literal with pictures of sports figures, juxtaposed with actual characters in *The Odyssey* – relying on audio to connect effects. Not all participants in the larger study succeeded in completing their digital story. Students such as Daniel, who has been retained in ninth grade, began his digital story with keen interest, focusing on the role of dance in his life, but the final text never came to fruition. Daniel's story of incompletion of the digital story has as much to do with technology constraints as it does with an incommensurable gap between a doxa-ruled pedagogy *and* fractal habitus. That is, Daniel found it hard to surmount a gap between his own interests and an interest in canonical texts and expository writing. The study is therefore not utopian in its findings because there were students who were not interested in the project and some that did not even finish. Yet, the five student compositions represented below are telling examples of how multimodality opens a space for more sedimenting of fractal habitus.

TABLE 7.1   Fractal habitus and literacy practices

Name	Fractal habitus (evidence of student's dispositions)	Literacy practices
Caspian	Collage of family photos; use of symbols with the end of the rainbow; captures emotions in images such as photo of his Dad making a funny face or his grandmother smiling.	Structured story well with opening, logical sequence, and concluding structure; awareness of figurative devices; and, salience of journey motif.
Esme	Uses technical and rhetorical skills such as Google Earth to locate her childhood home; uses colour to signal mood; her visuals are sequenced well with her voice-over; displays her tie to friends through childhood and present-day photographs.	Voice-over is well written and executed; ability to interweave her own story with Odysseus' story; she thinks in terms of design.
Patsy	Begins with a succession of childhood rick-rack dresses; embeds the story of her own 'sweet fifteen'; features her best friends; talks about her Mum; relates her world to New York high fashion and moves from local to global with photos of her friends in high school and photos of Coco Chanel and Valentino.	Voice-over is well written and executed; has a sense of layering the story and sequencing it well with a beginning, middle, and ending. She is adept at choosing and threading together photos.
Brian	Constantly goes back to the bus he took in Tel Aviv; uses symbols and images to express mood; uses camera angles to set a mood and characterize his friends' personality.	Has a strong sense of story sequence; relates his story well and consistently to Odysseus' story.
Manuel	Effectively relates his story with Odysseus' story; features his favourite sports heroes such as Lionel Messi and Kevin Curtis; talks about his brother; uses colour to express meaning.	Strongest example of relating his own journey into sports in relation to challenges that Odysseus faced during his epic journey; exhibits a sense of story structure and story tropes.

Fractured Habitus and Classroom Ethnography

Caspian, Esme, Patsy, Manuel, and Brian let me see them in ways that I could not possibly have seen them through alphabetic print. Whether it is a lack of competence on their part or a lack of acknowledgement of their other, complex competencies, we could not reach them through a more traditional route, so we worked on multimodal properties that provided them with more comfort and confidence and ultimately, more choices for expression. What can be said in light of the research is that each case study student found success in their assignment.

Looking across case studies, not everyone responded to the assignment, and some did not even complete it. Some had technological difficulties and lost their work, while others lost inspiration mid-way through the process. For those who completed their digital stories, certain participants were natural, tacit multimodal meaning-makers. On the whole, more meaning, relevance, motivation, and understanding arose from digital storytelling than not. Admittedly, there were some limitations to the study: we did not have proper equipment; we lost files; some students did not complete their assignments, and some students did not find success in the assignment, but the intensity of their work during the six weeks of production spoke volumes to me and the teacher-researcher.

Producing digital stories gave students an opportunity to reposition self because they could relate their own stories with Odysseus' story of his long journey back home to Ithaca. Whether it is Manuel's touching description of his brother being like Athena in his life or Brian taking us back in time to the bus that he took around Tel Aviv – these are imprints, fractures, shards of habitus. In the end, the introduction of multiple modes increases achievement for some students; and a more democratic, two-way, flattened hierarchical teaching approach and pedagogy breeds success. Allowing students to experiment and improvise with audio, visual, interactive texts made them naturally more engaged. Working alongside students and having them relay feedback and permit peer involvement lessens a power dynamic in classrooms and supports them in conveying who they see themselves to be; that is, reveals their habitus, at least in part.

In Conclusion

In 2001, a year before his death, Bourdieu wrote a response to what he regarded as capitalist globalization or, in his words, 'the European social movement that is currently forming' (Bourdieu, 2001: 11) in *Firing Back: Against the Tyranny of the Market*. In this compilation of writings and public talks, he addresses two issues that correspond well with findings from my modest study of respositioning identities through multimodal compositions. The first issue Bourdieu raises is that multimodal communication and information technology are for the dominant and for the privileged, 'the modal information technology user is a thirty-five-year-old highly educated English-speaking urban male with a high income' (Bourdieu, 2001: 32). This 'modal information technology user' is the elite, young, savvy professional and not, necessarily, what he calls 'the under-paid, under-skilled worker' often cut off from multimodal composition. The germane point to my study is the paradox of observing how five teenagers learn best through alternate modes, yet they are cut off from them, maybe even penalized for their understandings of and practices with them, because they cannot succeed with more traditional, mono-modal texts and practices. By alternate modes, I am referring here to effects such as camera angles, use of photographs, sounds in audio clips, to remixed texts. The larger point here that relates to Bourdieu's discussion of the young elite is that there is an unequal distribution of *cultural capital*, and it starts early, through events and practices like studying mono-modal, canonical texts and an over-emphasis on the expository essay.

The second issue that Bourdieu raises did not feature as prominently as it might have in this digital story-telling project and that is: critiquing multiple genres of texts. What would strengthen our study would be, as educators, to teach students to frame, conjecture, analyse, and critique multimodal texts and designs so that students have a language and meta-awareness of how modes represent and express meanings. As Bourdieu contends:

> The intellectual world must engage in a permanent critique of all the abuses of power or authority committed in the name of intellectual authority or, if you prefer, in a relentless critique of the use of intellectual authority as a political weapon with the intellectual field.
>
> (2001:19)

It is not enough to ask students to create a digital story about a journey tied to their study of *The Odyssey*, they also need language and epistemic models for thinking about designs and modal choices (Sheridan and Rowsell, 2010). Students involved in the research already know what story to tell and maybe even how to tell it, but they need to know how to improve the text and how to think about it in relation to more traditional forms of communication. I hope I have shown that opening the teaching of literature to multimodality is one way of recognizing and redistributing such cultural capital.

Notes

1 Pseudonyms are used throughout the chapter to protect the identity of student and teacher participants involved in the study.
2 The research study alluded to is a longitudinal, ethnographic, ecological research study conducted with Sue Nichols, Helen Nixon, and Sophia Rainbird of the University of South Australia on *Parents' Networks of Information about Literacy and Children's Development*. The research is funded by an Australia Research Council Discovery Grant.
3 The research reported here is a study of 30 producers of new and digital media with Mary P. Sheridan (Sheridan and Rowsell, 2010).

8

"ALL THAT JAZZ"

CLASSROOM READING AS INTERTEXTUAL PRACTICE

DAVID BLOOME AND AYANNA BROWN

Introduction

We have two goals in this chapter. The first is to construct a dialectic between Bourdieu's sociology as applied to education and literacy (see Chapter 4; Bourdieu and Passeron, 1977a; Grenfell, 2009; Grenfell and James, 1998), the New Literacy Studies (see Chapter 3; Street 1984, 1995, 1997), and classroom ethnography (see Chapter 2). The field-based data collected for this study were of a seventh-grade language arts classroom. Inherent in the construction of this dialectic are two assumptions: first, that theory guides the conduct and interpretation of empirical research[1] while simultaneously the conduct and interpretation of empirical research challenges, revises, and builds theory (cf., Bloome *et al.*, 2005); second, that in any social event there is a tension between stability and change (what Bakhtin, 1935/1981, termed *centripetal* and *centrifugal* forces) defined by the event itself. As an aside, we note that both classroom lessons and academic research (including the activity of theorizing) are social events in which people are continuously engaged, explicitly or implicitly, in theorizing the event itself and the world in which the event is embedded; as such, teaching and researching are both inherently reflexive processes embedded in social contexts (see Schon, 1983; Bourdieu and Wacquant, 1992b).

A second related goal in this chapter is to develop an understanding and articulation of how literacy curriculum and pedagogy in classrooms might promote the development of students who, to borrow from Freire (2000; Freire and Macedo, 1987), simultaneously read the word and the world, and who are "actors" and not "objects"; that is, there is a close, reciprocal connection between theorizing classroom events through empirical research and the articulation of curriculum and pedagogy linking literacy and personhood (cf. Egan-Robertson, 1998).

Methodology, Theory, and Ideology

Inherent in the dialectics described above is the assumption that any pedagogic action (any pedagogic communication and any pedagogic work) is associated with membership in the broader class of institutional and ideological relations of pedagogic actions defined by the relationship of the dominant classes/groups to non-dominant ones. While, at the same time, the particularities and organic nature of pedagogic action is embedded in specific events and histories that both "reflect" and "refract" (cf. Bakhtin, 1935/1981; Bloome *et al.*, 2005; Volosinov, 1929/1973) the relationships of the dominant classes / groups to non-dominant ones.

Underlying this methodology is a presupposition that educational theories, including theories of literacy in education, are always theories in and of action; that is, theory(ies) is embedded in and defined by the actions (which are primarily communicative ones) of people in interaction with each other. These people may be engaged at the level of face-to-face interactions or they may be engaged with each other over a distance and over time, or they may be located in different social institutions. Yet, as people act and react to each other they construct social theory(ies), not as a thing held in any individual mind or as an intersubjectivity, but as an evolving social accomplishment, which gives meaning to their actions (including defining personhood) within a field of cultural production. Another consequence is the structures of the power relations among themselves and among social institutions. Given such a presupposition, theory does not stand separately from ideology and the actions of scholars do not stand outside engagement in the events being "studied." More simply stated, in our view, theory does not exist in an academic text on a bookshelf waiting for a scholar to read it and, at a safe and detached distance, apply it to a corpus of data only to be reported in academic journals and papers to inform and enlighten others and to guide government policy. To theorize is to act, to act is to theorize; there is no theory outside action.

Context

The context for this study was Ms. Wilson's seventh-grade language arts classroom, which was located in a large school that only housed seventh and eighth grade students. The school served the local neighborhoods of primarily working-class African-American families. The school had a reputation for low academic achievement, which was reflected in published test scores. On the same campus as the school was a grade 6 through 12 academic magnet school (admission through a lottery process). Although many of the students in the magnet school lived in the local neighborhoods, a significant number of its white students did not.

Ms. Wilson was a young, African-American woman, who had received her undergraduate degree from a historically Black university. She had recently moved into the area in which the school was located. Ms. Wilson had a background in culturally relevant pedagogy and in the theories and pedagogy of Freire (2000). She also had a deep knowledge of African-American literature, African-American history, sociolinguistics (with an emphasis on language variation), and the educational theories of African-American scholars (e.g. Dubois, 1903/2000, 2001; Woodson, 1933/2000).

Ms. Wilson[2] began the school year by challenging her 30 seventh-grade students in her third period language arts class to read two novels simultaneously. She had carefully selected the novels, *The Lottery Rose* (1976) and *The Outsiders* (Hinton, 1967), because she knew they were popular among 12- and 13-year-old students, and because the adolescent protagonist of each novel had to address difficult circumstances. In the first book, Georgie had to address the abuse he suffered from his parents and the anger and disruptive behavior that were part of the consequences. In *The Outsiders,* Ponyboy has to address the violence that surrounds his life, being raised by his brothers (no parents), and the marginalization that accompanies being a working-class teenager.

The decision to challenge the students to read two novels simultaneously derived from a collaborative research program with a local university. Ms Wilson and another teacher had spent the summer with a small group of university researchers; they were all interested in how the construct of "intertextuality" might be used to create powerful reading and writing practices (see Goldman and Bloome, 2005). Each teacher had independently designed their curriculum based on the summer seminars and collaboratively they would study what happened in their classrooms.

A Classroom Conversation

In this chapter, we focus on one lesson that occurred early in the instructional unit, which lasted for nine weeks. Although we focus on just one lesson, we recognize that the lesson does not stand outside a history of previous and future lessons as well as a history of the various communities and social institutions of which the teacher and students are members. We also recognize that the lesson exists in a nexus of other institutions, each of which has an "interest" in imposing itself with various "cultural arbitraries" and with various claims of authority (cf. Bourdieu and Passeron, 1977a/1970) upon the interactions of the teacher and students in the lesson. The lesson stands within the ideological conflict that defines the relationship among histories, communities, and social institutions; yet, neither the classroom nor the lesson is simply reflections of that ideological conflict but active participants in it. The methodological warrant (which is also the theoretical warrant) is to capture and articulate that ideological conflict including how the teacher and students take it up, since how we "capture" and "articulate" that ideological conflict is part of the conflict itself.

Two long excerpts from the classroom discourse follow. We return to these excerpts throughout the chapter. The classroom is crowded, too many desks and students for its size, it is hard to walk around the classroom. On the particular day of the lesson, it is hot but the air conditioner is loud and must be turned off during instructional conversations. After the students entered the classroom and the bell rang, Ms. Wilson began the lesson with her third period class as follows:[3]

101. T: Here we go
102. T: This is where I started
103. T: During first period I asked the class
104. T: What do we know about Lottery Rose
105. T: Like we did for the Outsiders
106. T: This is what we know about the Outsiders
107. T: Wrote that on the board
108. T: Ok
109. T: Then I went to first period and I said what do we know about Lottery Rose
110. T: They gave me some ideas
111. T: Then I asked second period the same thing
112. T: They gave me some ideas
113. T: Now the list may be a little complete now
114. T: But just in case it isn't
115. T: We need to add on
116. T: Ok
117. T: Let's go down and see what ummm / first and second period said
118. T: Ok
119. T: First thing was my comment and read
120. T: that the (read from the white board) <u>main character was Georgie Burgess</u>
121. T: Ok that was my two points for the day
122. T: Alright the next thing
123. T: (read from the white board) <u>Georgie is abused by his mother and her boyfriend</u>
124. T: What's the boyfriend's name?
125. SS: Steve
126. T: Ok
127. T: Next thing
128. T: (read from the white board) He said Ms. Preston car caught on fire
129. T: Who's the he in that sentence?
130. SS: Georgie
131. T: Georgie
132. T: *Anybody know why?*
133. T: Why did he set xxxxxx
134. T: Carl
135. C: xxxxx
136. T: Why
137. C: Because he doesn't like her
138. T: *That a reason to set someone's xxxx on fire?*
139. SS: No
140. T: She said No
141. T: That was his reason his reason
142. T: His response
143. T: Alright

144. T: Just for the sake of my own sanity
145. T: Let's leave the highlighters alone
146. T: The tops and popping them on
147. SS; xxxxxxxxxxxxxxxxxx
148. T: OK next thing
149. T: (read from white board) <u>Georgie tried to steal a book about flowers from the library</u>
150. T: *True or untrue?*
151. SS: True
152. T: *Did he really try to steal it?*
153. SX: No
154. SS: Nooo
155. T: *Ok so help me out*
156. T: *Let's clarify this*
157. T: Who can explain the situation
158. T: What really happened with the
159. SX: He didn't xxxxxx
160. T: Hold on
161. T: Antonio
162. A: He checked out the book
163. A: He said he gave it to a girl
164. A: xxxxxxxxxxxxxxxxxxxxxxxxxxxxxxxxxxxxxxxxxx
165. T: Ok
166. T: So he checked
167. T: Who check out the book
168. T: He checked out the book or the girl checked out the book
169. A: Georgie
170. T: Georgie checked out the book
171. T: And he said he loaned it to
172. T: Someone else
173. A: xxxxxxxxxxxx
174. T: *Help me aaaa just a little bit just a*
175. T: *Jessica what happened*
176. J: He told the librarian that he lost the book
177. T: Ok
178. T: Why did he tell the librarian that he lost the book
179. SS: xxxxxxxxxxxxxxxxxxxxxxx
180. T: Ok I heard two things
181. T: I heard Josh say xxxxxxxxxx cause he let somebody else borrow it and hadn't got it back yet
182. T: Then I heard somebody else say because he wanted to keep it
183. SS: Xxxxxxxxxxxx
184. T: *Now which one*
185. T: Where are we

186. SS: xxxxxxxxxxxxxxxxxxxx
187. T: Ok
188. T: What did how did the librarian respond
189. T: Did she say
190. T: *You know Georgie you know that's awful he have a fine of two dollars*
191. T: *Bring the book back and you will never check out again*
192. T: How did the librarian respond to
193. T: Georgie's story
194. T: Let's just call it that
195. T: Sonia
196. S: She said check xxxxxxxxxxxxxxxxxxxxxxxxxxxxxxx
197. T: Ok
198. T: So rather than ummmm being angry with him and expressing that anger she said
199. T: Why don't you bring the book out bring the book back
200. T: You can check it out all over again and we'll go from there
201. T: How many of you felt that was a good response from the librarian
202. T: Why was that a good response
203. T: *I mean isn't the rule that you*
204. T: *check out the book /the book is late /you get a fine / you return the book*
205. T: Why was this good for Georgie?
206. T: That …
207. SS: xxxxxxxxxxxxxxx
208. T: *Whoa whoa whoa whoa whoa*
209. T: Why was it good for Georgie that she was more understanding

Ms. Wilson and the students continued discussing *The Lottery Rose* in a similar manner until 40 minutes into the 60 minute lesson. Then, the lesson shifts and Ms. Wilson focuses on the homework from the previous night. This is discussed with a further extract later in the chapter.

As the instructional unit continued over the next eight weeks, the students continued to read both books, compare the situations and personalities of the two protagonists, share their responses to what they read, and discussed the social issues raised in the novels. Toward the later phases of the instructional unit, the teacher engaged the students in identifying a contemporary social issue, researching it, and discussing ways of addressing it.

Production and Reproduction

Underlying lines 101 to 111 is the not-so-hidden acknowledgment that the students are batch produced. Ms. Wilson teaches five classes each day of 25 to 35 students; each seventh-grade class is subject to the same official curriculum and requirements. Lines 106 through 115 might be interpreted by the third period students as getting the "leftovers" from the earlier classes (reinforcing the condition of being "batch produced"); and the students' docile acceptance of this situation speaks to how naturalized such circumstances have become.

This particular school consists of more than a thousand seventh- and eighth-grade students, almost all of whom come from nearby working-class African-American neighborhoods. Although the students are not tracked by classroom sections, they are more generally tracked by the school in which they are enrolled. The school has the reputation of low academic performance, and its place in an academic hierarchy of schools is made starkly visible by the presence of an academic magnet school located less than 50 yards away.

The prescribed academic knowledge and skills for Ms. Wilson's class, for the school, and public schools more generally, are explicitly designed to prepare students to be productive members of the workforce and of society more generally (cf., Hirsch *et al.*, 2002; Hirsch, 2006). Informed by various national "research" reports sponsored by the state and the business community (e.g., Anderson *et al.* 1985; National Commission on Excellence in Education, 1983), *the* official curriculum, pedagogy, and the assessment of students are regulated by the state and geared to insure that the students have *the* requisite skills needed to find a place in the workforce.

We have emphasized "the" in the previous sentence to highlight that the curriculum, pedagogy, and assessments demanded are presented by the state not as ideological but as "scientific." This provides a warrant for the state to claim that the mandated curriculum and pedagogy is ideologically neutral and simply the application of science to the teaching and learning. As such, any critique of the curriculum, pedagogy, assessments, or any claim that research is ideological, and hence implicated in reproducing power relations among classes and groups, is positioned as unscientific, unreasonable, against the interests of the students, and parochial (cf. Bloome and Carter, 2001).

The use of science to authorize *the* reading and literacy curriculum and pedagogy is consistent with what Street (1984, 1995) would call an "autonomous" model of literacy (discussed earlier in Chapter 3). This literacy model is invoked by the standardized reading tests which all seventh-grade students have to take, by the presence of a special class to reinforce reading skills, and another one for students with reading difficulties. It is also referenced in the instructional conversation: lines 106 through 130 make public what information the students should have comprehended from their reading (what might be called from cognitive science the *situation* model, cf. Kintsch, 1994).

From the perspective of the New Literacy Studies, what is being learned with regard to reading is not just a set of generic skills, but rather a particular set of social and intellectual practices for comprehending and using written language that take the guise of defining reading universally; what might be labeled a school reading practice (see Street and Street, 1991, for a discussion of pedagogized literacy). The nature and ideological constitution of school reading practice is highlighted by Bloome (1983) in a study of how two African-American students (from another school) responded to a standardized test item. Here, one of them, Michael, gave an incorrect answer, used his background knowledge of how people act in the world to answer the question. On the other hand, Samantha, whose answer was correct, made a distinction between what she knew from her background experience and what answers were expected by the test makers. When Samantha was asked about the validity of Michael's answer she indicated that although his answers made sense and were true, she knew it was not the answer that the test makers wanted.

The attention given to the school reading practice on a nearly daily basis from grades kindergarten through twelve, and the frequent assessments of this practice, exemplify Bourdieu and Passeron's (1977a/1970) proposition that pedagogic action

> must last long enough to produce durable training, i.e. a habitus, the product of internalization of the principles of a cultural arbitrary capable of perpetuating itself after [Pedagogic Action] has ceased and thereby of perpetuating in practices the principles of the internalized arbitrary.
>
> (p. 31)

The adoption of the school reading practice is not simply about acquiring a set of cognitive and linguistic skills, but is also about accepting that practice as *the* reading practice (or at least so presenting oneself in official educational settings). It is in this sense that learning to read in school is also about adopting a cultural ideology including how one defines who one is and who others are. Some students will develop a double-consciousness (cf. Dubois, 1903); they will "read" in a particular way in school and in related institutional settings, but will be conscious that such reading is for school contexts and may employ other ways of reading elsewhere as culturally appropriate.

The Complexity of Historical Footing

Although most scholarship and professional texts on reading curriculum and pedagogy omit discussion of race (except perhaps to note the achievement gap between white and Black students) (Brown, 2008), race is a ubiquitous presence in Ms. Wilson' classroom and in the school. Not only Ms. Wilson, but most of her students, and the students in the school, are African-American. Ms Wilson has decorated the classroom with posters of famous African-American authors, and she was the faculty sponsor of the school drill team (an activity closely associated with African-American schools). Even if Standard English is used in the classroom, the hallways are filled with the use of African-American language. The racialization of Ms. Wilson's students' education is further highlighted by the contrast between the racial composition of their school and that of the mostly white academic magnet school just 50 yards away.

The dominant narratives about race and education in the United States are one context for Ms. Wilson' classroom – although they are rarely viewed as narratives or ideologies, but rather as scientific:

> Education is the great "leveler"; race is not a factor in academic achievement (education is color-blind); all children can succeed if they have highly qualified teachers who hold high expectations for their students and if the students apply themselves to their schoolwork.

This dominant narrative continues by noting that in some cases, either because of deficits or differences in culture, language or intelligence or because of economic factors, some African-American students do not achieve at the same level as their white counterparts. Education, therefore, needs to compensate for those deficits and differences. Within this dominant narrative, pedagogical models such as culturally relevant pedagogy (e.g. Ladson-Billings, 1994; Gay and Banks, 2000) and cultural modeling (e.g., Lee, 2001; Lee *et al.*, 2003) are viewed as ways to compensate for the students' inability to engage with the requisite curriculum and to help them bridge to it; although such is not the view of the scholars who generated these pedagogical models. As such, these pedagogical models become part of the process of reproduction rather than being challenges to and critiques of *that* curriculum.

As we reflected upon Ms. Wilson's classroom and the history of African-Americans in public schools in the United States, a complex picture emerges that challenges the dominant narrative above. The enslavement, segregation, murder, degradation, and denial of personhood and education to people of African descent in the United States are part of the historical context of Ms. Wilson's classroom. But so, too, are histories of struggle against such conditions; the building of community locally, nationally, and globally among people of African descent; the evolution of an African-American language; the generation of an African-American literature; the evolution of African-American aesthetics in music, dance, and visual arts; the building of African-American institutions of higher education, medicine, and science; among other similar histories. Yet, the default histories and narratives that contextualize teaching and learning in Ms. Wilson's classroom are not based on these oppositional, historical developments, but on the dominant ahistorical narratives described earlier.

That default, dominant history and narrative presents African-American students with a double bind. If they do well in school and acquire school reading practices and the values and ideologies of the school, they encounter the ideological model of white supremacy and Black inferiority; however, in so doing they must acquire (or look like they are acquiring) the cultural capital and habitus associated with the dominant ideological group and consequently appear to distance themselves from their own cultural history and communities.

Such a situation has not gone unnoticed by African-American educators and others (e.g., Woodson; 1933, Dubois, 1903/2000, 2001; hooks, 1994; Lomotey, 1990, 1992; Hilliard, 1978, 1999/2000) who have called for an education for African-American students that is specific to their historical circumstances and to their agendas as members of the African-American community, while also providing them with access to participation in the broader society. In brief, these theories can be viewed as actions to transform the ideological field in a way that eschews deficit models and the dualism of community versus academic success supplanted by a repositioning of African-American teachers and students as actors creating (recreating) the world in which they live grounded in a history of community building and struggle against the denial of personhood.

Some educators and teachers, such as Ms. Wilson, have explicitly taken up that call and have viewed their educational practice as taking up the dominant ideologies of the school and refracting them. In terms of the New Literacy Studies, as Street (1993) argues it is not enough to ask how people adopt a particular literacy practice but rather how do they take it up? How do they adapt it? How do they make it serve their social, cultural, political and economic agendas rather than those of the state and the literacy sponsors authorized by dominant groups and institutions?

Refraction: From Reproduction to Cultural Production

As teachers like Ms. Wilson take up and refract the dominant ideologies of school practices such as school reading, what they are doing no longer seems well characterized as reproduction. Consider lines 132 through 209. On the surface, Ms. Wilson appears to be reviewing the text-based situation model described in the book. However, she subtly changes the reading practice in line 132 by asking the students, "Anybody know why?" Her question is uttered in a different style, and a different intonation pattern than her previous talk. Carl responds with a surface level reason, and he is challenged by Ms. Wilson – "*That a reason to set someone's xxxx on fire?*" (line 138) also rendered in style distinct from her formal classroom style. On the surface, the question in line 132 appears to be a call for an expected moral response; but given the subsequent conversational patterns that follow and that permeate this lesson and Ms. Wilson's instructional conversations in many of her lessons across the nine weeks, we suspect that something more is going on. We suspect that Ms. Wilson is beginning to challenge the students' school reading practices – their habitus for reading events in school – and beginning to socialize them into using literature reading as a way to explore the diversity of what it means to be human (personhood) and as a way to deconstruct and reconstruct the worlds in which they live.

For example, consider the discussion of the lost library book that begins on line 149. Ms. Wilson reads the item contributed from an earlier class and written on the white board and asks if it is true (line 150). The question in 150 is also rendered in that informal, intonation style and perhaps seemed to the students to have an obvious answer, after all it was written on the white board (a location of authority). But the question is a "set-up" as Ms. Wilson challenges their answer (line 152 *Did he really try to steal it?*) and some of the students respond by giving her an answer they may believe she is seeking (see lines 153 and 154). She pushes the challenge further in lines 155 through 158, beginning by shifting again into more informal style.

Additionally, she embeds African-American language into her communicative discourse, appropriating it as useful for engaging in classroom discussions. This is reflected in the discussion sequence lines 132 through 138. The use of African-American language within academic instruction functions to connect with her students' various uses of language but also operates a tool of refraction. While

K-12 schools continue to wrestle with how to honor students' rights to their own language (Scott, Straker, and Katz, 2008) and teach students how to use academic literacy in oral and written forms, Ms. Wilson seamlessly shifts between African-American language and academic discourse during instruction. The discourse shifts validate African-American language as an appropriate form of communication and allows her students to hear African-American language dismantling the deficit beliefs about non-standard forms of language in schools. (See Williams (2006) and Brown (2008, 2010) on how African-American teachers validate African-American language and academic discourse within classroom instruction.)

Dixson and Bloome (2007), who also conducted an analysis of this bit of Ms. Wilson's instructional conversation, argue that Ms. Wilson shifts in and out of a conversational style that has deep roots in the African-American community. They describe it as "jazz" because it involves both a rhythmic pattern associated with jazz as well as an interactional organizational pattern found in some jazz performances combining convention and improvisation (see also Dixson, 2005, 2006). Building on the work of Meacham (2001), Dixson and Bloome argue that:

> Jazz is not a set of abstract structures removed from a historical or cultural context. Rather, jazz is both an epistemology and a performative process of cultural production.... Meacham asserts that reading comprehension between and among students of color is an improvisatory cultural process.
>
> (Dixson and Bloome, 2007: 30)

What is at issue is not whether Ms. Wilson's style is or is not jazz, but rather the context (or field) that it indexes and the consequences of that context for teaching and learning. Ms. Wilson's stylizations may be indexing a continuity between the students' home cultural contexts and her classroom, a historical context, and/or an invitation to engage in reading as an improvisational meaning-making practice.

In brief, rather than view Ms. Wilson and her students solely within the framework of education and reproduction, it may be useful to also view them as agents within a field of cultural production. In an essay on art and literature, Bourdieu (1993a), writes:

> The literary or artistic field is a *field of forces*, but it is also a *field of struggles* tending to transform or conserve this field of forces. ... Every position-taking is defined in relation to the *space of possibilities* which is objectively realized as a *problematic* in the form of the actual or potential position-takings corresponding to the different positions; and it receives its distinctive *value* from its negative relationship with the coexistent position-takings to which it is objectively related and which determine it by delimiting it. It follows from this, for example, that a position-taking changes, even when the position remains identical, whenever there is a change in the universe of options that are simultaneously offered for producers and consumers to choose from.
>
> (p. 30, original emphases)

Rather than view Ms. Wilson and her students as consumers of art and literature whose understanding and valuing of art and literature, in this case of reading, are produced by the educational system, they can be viewed analogously as artists and authors, social agents whose position-takings are defined by the "problematic" generated from a field of struggles over race, education, and history. What is at issue is not how Ms. Wilson and the students understand and value the literary works, the books they are reading, but how these experiences shape the ways they author the narratives of their lives and how they construct (transform) the universe of options that are simultaneously offered for producers and consumers to choose from (from above). In this sense, Ms. Wilson might be viewed as analogous to a jazz musician who has her own style of improvisation, teaching novices to play jazz themselves each with his or her own style of improvisation within the constraints of a field of possibilities while simultaneously challenging the monolithic nature of that field of possibilities. The *cultural capital* at stake for Ms. Wilson and her students, however, is not music but language and literacy.

In line 157, Ms. Wilson shifts back into the regular school style and asks for a description of the situation model, which is provided in lines 162 through 173. Then, in line 174 she shifts back into "jazz" style but more dramatically than in previous shifts. The students provide two different answers, both of which are correct; but the correctness of the answers does not seem to be at issue. Rather, Ms. Wilson focuses on the reaction of the librarian (lines 188–94). She renders part of the question in "jazz" style and part in regular school style, simulating an imagined utterance of the librarian (line 191).

Sonia gives a surface level answer that Ms. Wilson builds on to ask the students if it is a good response (line 201). Many of the students non-verbally indicate it was a good response, which from the syntax of the question and the proposition rendered in line 198, would appear to be the answer Ms. Wilson was looking for. But it is another set-up. In line 203 she again shifts into "jazz" style and asks the students about whether or not rules should be broken. The students begin to respond without raising their hands even as Ms. Wilson attempts to focus their attention on why the librarian's response was a good one (lines 205 and 209). Ms. Wilson's challenge to the library rules can be interpreted as asking the students to question the relationship of institutional rules and human needs. Ms. Wilson's challenge also raises the issue of personhood. The librarian is more than an institutional dupe following rules; she provides another model of what it means to be human.

The Cultural Production of Being "Not Georgie"

We now return to the lesson where 40 minutes into the 60 minute lesson, Ms. Wilson begins to review the students' homework by asking Bonnie to read aloud the passage she had highlighted. For homework Ms. Wilson had asked the students to mark passages in *The Lottery Rose* that they found interesting or important. Ms. Wilson told the students to get out their copies of the book and then asked Bonnie, one of the students, to read one of the passages she had marked:

401. B: (reading from the passage she highlighted in her book): <u>Miss Preston didn't</u>
<u>like Georgie much / she got mad at him for not doing his work/ she pointed</u>
<u>to / the work she pointed to / when she wrote a long list on / the blackboard</u>
<u>she especial she got mad / especially /</u>

402. SX: *she got especially*

403. B: *she got especially mad at Georgie because he played hooky and lied* <u>xxxxx</u>

404. T: Ok

405. T: Why was that / important enough for you to highlight or make note of

406. B: Because she didn't get that mad at the students but just at Georgie

407. B: She got real mad at him

408. T: So you think she singled Georgie out

409. T: She displayed more anger toward him than she does the other kids

410. B: (nods head in agreement)

411. T: Ok Johnny

412. J: She's mad because she she plays hooky and

413. J: talks bad and stuff and then xxxxxx he can't read

414. (1 second silence)

415. T: Ok

416. T: Have any of you ever been the Georgie

417. T: In this

418. T: I'm not talking about the abuse part

419. SX: Oh

420. T: *But the being in class and not doing the work or not understanding and acting out*
and said

421. T: *You said here are your damn X's and xxxxx up xxxxxx* (makes big X in the air
with her hand)

422. SS: (Laughter overlaps hands gestures near end of the previous line)

423. T: Ok

424. T: have any of you ever been the Georgie and mad at the rest of the world

425. T: *Can I ask you a question?*

426. T: *this this is just for my own personal professional development*

427. T: *How did you move out of the Georgie phase?*

428. T: *How did you move away from the / being angry and / not doing the work and /*
move into the /

429. T: *phase you're in now?*

430. SX: who

431. T: Whomever

432. T: *Who was once*

433. T: Ok

434. T: Johnny

435. T: How did you progress from being Georgie into being Johnny?

436. J: St<u>op play<u>ing</u> hoo<u>ky</u></u>

437. T: Ok so your first step was to stop playing hooky
438. T: Ok
439. T: Anybody else
440. T: *I was once Georgie now I'm Helen*
441. H: I xxxxxxxxxx if I didn't do my work and stuff xxxxxxxxxxxxx
442. SS: (laughter overlaps last half of previous line)
443. T: So you are arguing that if you did not do the work then you would be
444. H: Yeah xxxxxxxxx
445. T: Ok
446. T: Terry
447. (1 second silence)
448. SS: (soft laughter overlapping the previous two lines)
449. T: You <u>learned</u> <u>Helen</u> that if you did not do the work you would be a bad person.
450. T: *Defiine a bad person*
451. T: What's a bad person?
452. H: a person who doesn't listen
453. H: Has no goal in life doesn't want to make anything of themselves
454. T: Ok a person who has no goal and doesn't want to make anything
455. T: So that's your definition of a bad person.
456. H: Yes
457. T: Ok a guy with no goals
458. T: *I was once Georgie and now I am Steven*
459. S: I said if I don't start doing my work I am not going to get no anywhere
460. T: Ok if I don't start doing my work I am not going to get anywhere in life
461. T: If you ...
462. T: I'm sorry Brian
463. T: *I was once Georgie and now I am Brian*
464. BR: Ahhhh
465. BR: When I a when I was in the second grade and my momma told me that if I if I didn't start doing my work then
466. BR: there was going to be something something and I xxxxxxx
467. T: Ok so she might have said you know if you don't get that work done / *I'm gonna get something else done*
468. SX: ooooo (softly rendered, overlaps juncture between "done" and "I'm" in previous line)
469. SS: (a few students laugh)
470. BR: It wasn't a whupping though
471. T: Ok it was something enough for you to get kick in gear and all right
472. T: Ok
473. T: *Somebody help me understand cause cause I I grew up in the kind of family where*
474. T: *You didn't do what you were supposed to do and you got a spanking*

In line 401, Bonnie reads and an unknown student helps her correctly render the text (line 402) in a move reminiscent of elementary school reading instruction practices and their emphasis on accurate word-by-word rendering. In response to Ms. Wilson's question of why she highlighted that particular passage (line 405), Bonnie and Johnny note Georgie's problem behaviors and that he can't read (line 413). These are provided as a rationale for why the teacher, Miss Preston, gets mad at Georgie. Ms. Wilson does not challenge the students' rationale and its implied moral justification, but shifts the focus of the instructional conversation from Georgie to the students themselves. She asks, "Have any of you ever been the Georgie?" (line 416) and "How did you move out of the Georgie phase?" (line 427).

From field work in previous classes Ms. Wilson taught, we know she believes that it is important for students to put themselves into the comments they make. The previous year she had told a class at the end of a heated discussion:

> think about yourself in relationship to your comments … a lot of you are making excellent comments but they are devoid of you as a person. It's very easy to make generalizations about people or about other people when you're able to take yourself out of it. But when you put yourself back into your statements put yourself in relationship to your comments you're making and then see if the comment still works.

Ms. Wilson's question about being the Georgie is, in part, a reflection of her philosophy about putting "yourself back into your statements" and avoiding clichés and generalizations. She is pushing students to think more deeply and empathetically about what it means to be human. But we believe that there is something more happening in this section of the instructional conversation.

By asking the students how they moved out of the Georgie "phase" she provides them with a developmental narrative within which to frame a part of their lives and she positions them as "not Georgie." The students associate being Georgie with playing hooky (line 437), not doing their school work (lines 441, 459) and being a bad person (line 449). A bad person is someone who doesn't listen (line 452) and has no goal in life (line 453). From lines 465 to 471, Brian employs the narrative structure Ms. Wilson provided to tell a story of how he changed. Each of the narratives told or suggested by the students characterizes their earlier selves as "bad" and then having been saved by their actions or the actions of their family. Part of what is accomplished through this segment of the instructional conversation is that the students are positioned (and position themselves) as having evolved and who they are now is someone who is serious about their education and about who they are becoming, and not "bad." This is also signaled within the word phase (lines 427 and 429). We find this word significant to this analysis because it connotes transition and development. As a "phase," the characterizations the students offer about themselves are positioned as stages, which are active and continual rather than static characterizations of one's personality. The students' presentation of their own experiences do not relegate them as unsuccessful in Ms. Wilson's class because she positions the students' present day identities as a new phase. Consider the refrain she uses, "was once Georgie and now I am 'x.'." The students are able to identify their present day identities as "new" or potentially "transformed" from past experiences – even if they have yet to resolve "bad" choices. In one respect, Ms. Wilson acknowledges that several of her students have had negative experiences within school and their communities. Rather than assuming these experiences are unresolved, she allows her students to "name them" thereby rendering them resolved.

Naming one's own identity and telling one's own story is a central aspect of Critical Race Theory (e.g., Dixson and Rousseau, 2006; Ladson-Billings, 1999; Solorzano and Yasso, 2001), which is both a theoretical frame and a research methodology that serves to refract and challenge dominant discourses within the institutional structures that rely on dominance as means of authority and control. In Ms. Wilson's class, the students' naming their own identities provides a space for self-reflection and ownership.

There is another relevant aspect of the refrain in the significance of the Black Church and the discourse of redemption and change. One of the pillars within the Black Church is its call for a congregation to acknowledge and respond to once being "lost" and now "being found." This discourse is present is several spiritual songs like "Amazing Grace" and "Precious Lord" where peril precedes glory and redemption. Yet, within the Black Church, the sociopolitical and cultural relationship of Black people within the United States is often used as an anchor and social context for Christian living. More simply stated, praise and rejoicing about everlasting life leaving "this old world behind," include the acts of remembering the status of people of African descent in the United States and the rejoicing that comes when that status or positionality changes. We offer this spiritual context because it is used as a foundation for the direction of Ms. Wilson's lesson. While she does not actively discuss Christian principles or the perspectives of the Black Church in her lessons, she uses "I once was Georgie [lost], but now I am 'x' [found]" as a direct reference from Christianity. She asks the students in the beginning of this discussion (line 427), "How did you move out of the Georgie phase?" This question functions in two interesting ways. First, it allows the teacher to gain insight into how to support her students in the future based on their own admissions. Our data supports the notion that Ms. Wilson sees her role as multifaceted where her students' academic success also hinges upon her ability to connect with her students outside the classroom.

The second aspect of Ms. Wilson's question we identify as important is allowing the students to "think out-loud" about the conscious choices they've made in the past to own their own success. By asking them to think about their own personal changes in this context, she encourages them to reflect on their roles as actors in their lives. Because this lesson happens within the first few weeks in her class, the hidden agenda may be to cultivate an environment where students can make choices and author their own success.

Yet, Ms. Wilson does not appear to be satisfied with the student responses as she challenges them in lines 473 and 474 to move beyond the simplistic narrative of being motivated by threats of punishment. She is pushing them to see themselves as being able to act on themselves and on the world in which they live; and to do so not simply because they might otherwise be punished, but rather because it is their own chosen agenda.

In Conclusion: Reading Practice as "Jazz" – Dialectics of Continuity and Change

Like a jazz musician who employs the constraints of the music's meter and key and the traditions of jazz in creating a new interpretation and set of meanings, Ms. Wilson challenges and pushes her students' reading practices. It is not enough to accurately render the text, describe the situation model or use simplistic generalizations and moral codes to make meaning with text. Rather, Ms. Wilson challenges her students to employ those constraints as they improvise ways to read the world and to define themselves and what it means to be human.

The close examination of Ms. Wilson's and her students' pedagogic action and, in particular, their instructional conversations around literary texts, accompanied by recognition of the various historical and institutional contexts in which they acted, suggest new ways of conceptualizing reading and literacy curriculum and pedagogy. It is not just that there are a variety of diverse reading and literacy practices or that some practices are more appropriate in some settings than others. Nor is it just that reading and literacy education are part of the process of cultural reproduction of extant relationships and hierarchies among dominant and non-dominant classes and groups. The reading and literacy practices Ms. Wilson is pushing her students toward are not scripted nor predetermined; but rather are spaces for improvisational practices as they learn to address the cultural politics of personhood and of being actors in the world (as opposed to just being acted upon). Their engagement in such spaces can be viewed as analogous to jazz practices; and, similarly so, the description and interpretation of those spaces is also a "jazz practice."

Notes

1 We define "empirical research" as any field-based research intervention, regardless of methodology and paradigm, seeking to capture and describe what is happening, how, when, where and by whom.
2 All names are pseudonyms.
3 The transcript was generated using procedures described by Green and Wallat (1981) and Bloome *et al.* (2005). Transcript conventions: T = teacher, Sx = unidentifiable student, SS = many students, xxxxxxx = undecipherable; *text in italics* = pronounced change in communicative style from the usual teacher communicative style of talk, underlined text = text read aloud from a book, / = slight pause.

PART III

Working at the Intersections – In Theory and Practice

This book can, in one sense, be seen as a dialogue between issues of theory and practice in language in education and literacy. Part I included chapters which gave accounts of the principles of practice of Ethnography, New Literacy Studies, and Bourdieu. Part II then showed such principles in practice in a range of empirical research setting. Crudely, we went from theory to practice; although many aspects of each were included across both parts. Our objective in Part III is to develop this dialogue. We aim now to take the practical examples and experiences from Part II and reconsider them in the light of the methodological principles, theoretical relations, and practical engagement set out in Part I and, in so doing, develop the implications of our approach explicitly in terms of classroom language research methodology. Chapter 9 does this by exploring issues of theory and practice in terms of different types of theory, their salient characteristics, and the contexts from which they arise. We see here how 'theory' has a much wider range of uses and interpretations than is commonly acknowledged, and that 'educational practice' can be central to its formulation and application. The chapter applies this perspective to the practice of language classrooms, conducting research and, indeed, the knowledge and understanding of the researcher her/himself. The points raised are amply exemplified with reference to the practical case examples included in the book; commonalities and differences are compared and contrasted. In one sense, we are building theory and practice on the backs of Parts I and II. The final chapter further extends the development of the synthesis of ethnography, NLS and Bourdieu by using the latter more explicitly to begin to constitute a version of classroom language research as a Bourdieusian theory of practice. In other words, we further develop our thinking about the underlying theoretical principles of classroom language and the implications they have for research practice into it. Central to this discussion are concepts which have guided much of our thinking throughout the book: context and field, agency and habitus, cultural capital, and reflexivity. Further reference is made to the practical experiences included in the reports from Part II as a way of offering a methodological framework for the type of classroom language ethnography that has been at the core of this book.

9

NEW LITERACY STUDIES AND BOURDIEU

WORKING AT THE INTERSECTIONS OF THEORY AND PRACTICE

CHERYL HARDY

Introduction

In the first part of this book, three main strands were set out which would guide us through it; namely, Ethnography, New Literacy Studies and Bourdieu's theory of practice. The principal tenet of our argument has been that research practice seen from the perspectives of NLS and Bourdieu's work brings fresh insights into classroom language ethnography. The second part of the book then offered a series of practical case examples of classroom practice with a focus on the way language featured in different ways in pedagogic discourse. The aim has been to offer a range of theoretical viewpoints and practical exemplifications. However, such viewpoints and examples should not be seen as relative, as simply another way of looking at pupils, teaching and learning, but as providing a basis for a possible synthesis of the three approaches. At its inception, the book was conceived as an integrated text, rather than as an edited volume and, in this respect, the theoretical and practical chapters converge on a common position. In the two chapters of the present part, that common position is explored.

The sub-title of this chapter is 'Working at the intersections of theory and practice'. This title was chosen in order to highlight the relationship between the practical contexts in which we are interested and the generalisable statements that may be made about them – and how, why, and in what terms? However, in the course of the chapter, a whole range of other intersections are examined: between pupil/ student and teacher; language and literacy; linguistics and ethnography; Bourdieu and New Literacy Studies; and teaching and learning. Suffice it to say that each of these intersections raises issues of theory and practice, but the contention here is that they often converge on the same methodological and epistemological questions. This present chapter takes further just what can be understood when the case examples presented in Chapters 5 to 8 are considered from a theoretical perspective. The next chapter will develop an approach to classroom language ethnography based around Pierre Bourdieu's theory of practice, both in technical and philosophical terms. However, first we take a step back and reconsider the theoretical background of taking an ethnographic view in educational research.

Becoming Ethnographic and the Study of Classrooms

Chapter 2 showed just what a multi-faceted approach ethnography can be. Taking its name from anthropological practices in the social sciences, this methodological practice is rooted in a tradition which sets out to examine social phenomena in their natural (naturalistic) environment. In the past, this often involved the study of exotic cultures where religious and social practices were very different from those commonly known in the Western world, for example, Margaret Mead's cultural ethnography of growing up in New Guinea (Mead 2001/1930).

The intention here was to understand such cultures *in their own terms* from the point of view of an insider as well as to make sense of them from our own world views. Nevertheless, it remains difficult to find a precise definition of ethnography; such definitions vary from the holistic, but vague to the systematic, but prescriptive. For example, Boyle (1994) reports Werner and Schoepfle (1987: 42) as describing ethnography as little more than 'what ethnographers do', 'or as a description of folk'. In contrast, for Hammersley and Atkinson (1993) it arises from the researchers' participation in people's daily live (p. 2). For Hughes (1992) also, it is the study of a 'localised group of people', sharing similar social and cultural characteristics, and should be viewed as both 'process and product'. Boyle (op. cit.) stresses its holistic and contextual nature, as well as the reflexive element necessary to its practice. These general characteristics can be related to the theoretical perspectives offered in Part I. Moreover, the practical examples in Part II also reflect these descriptors. But, why is such a perspective appropriate for educational contexts, particularly classrooms, and where does language feature in it?

As mentioned in Chapter 4, Bourdieu himself was concerned to understand cultural phenomenon 'in their own terms' – that is, ethnographically – but always argued for what he called a 'socio-genetic' reading of work; one which offered a way of understanding the historical and cultural forces that gave rise to, and shaped the phenomenon studied. With this is mind, it is worth taking a little time to consider ethnography's relation to educational research in general, and how it emerged as a dominant approach to understanding classroom practice. This discussion will tease out issues of theory and practice on which our own classroom language ethnography can be built. How so?

A Historical Perspective on Educational Research

As mentioned in the Introduction to this book, until the mid-1960s, educational research was dominated by a positivist paradigm. In effect, such educational research as was carried out arose from psychology, and showed a marked preoccupation with measurement and standardisation of both pupils and pedagogy. The dominant language learning theory was based on behaviourism, and on the belief that education was all about induction into the right way of thinking and doing things. The nature and role of theory in education were primary issues. As we saw in Chapter 8, this view of educational research reinforces and reproduces the values and practices of those most dominant in a society. O'Connor's view (1958) of educational theory in the 1950s, such as it was, amounted to seeing it in terms of the dominant normative scientific paradigm: hence as a way of forming, evaluating, and connecting hypotheses which would explain particular educational phenomena. For him, 'educational theory' should be judged by the same standards as 'scientific theory'.

The leading exponent of 'scientific theory' was, of course, the Austrian Karl Popper (1967), who argued that the strength and the descriptive power of any theoretical statement lay not so much in proving it to be 'correct' but by the degree to which it could be 'falsified'; in other words, that it could generate statements that could be shown to be wrong. Everything else was supposition or worse, myth. Here, knowledge advanced as hypotheses were falsified, leading to further refined hypotheses. But what did this look like for education? Clearly, little in a functioning classroom has any degree of certainty or uncertainty that would satisfy the scientific Popperian criteria since what occurs there rarely has descriptive rigour against which underlying processes can be assessed; rarely is it predictive with any degree of confidence.

The philosopher Paul Hirst (1967) noticed this in the mid-1960s and, in his subsequent arguments, laid the basis of what we now know as the 'foundation disciplines' in education: its history, sociology, psychology and philosophy. Since a cultural understanding of educational contexts must surely include something of the social, historical, mental, and philosophical – not to mention other underlying political dimensions – such foundation disciplines would each feature in any ethnographic perspective. In this way, an ethnographic approach could be seen to have operated symbiotically across the foundation disciplines.

As early as 1967, the anthropologist Del Hymes had given us the idea of a 'linguistic event' and saw, in contradiction to Chomskyan linguistics, that there were 'rules of use without which the rules of grammar would be useless' (Hymes 1967). This view implied a socio-cultural reorientation to language and language learning. It is not surprising therefore that the 'new' sociology of education referred to in Chapter 4 focused on how language functioned as a means to construct classroom knowledge rather than simply on the measurement of performance, intelligence, etc. A similar historical reorientation led to the recognition and inclusion of local perspectives, individual biography, and personal trajectories in the contextualisation of the objects of study in educational research. Meanwhile, philosophy increasingly took on 'the Post-modern Condition' with its heightened sense of reflexivity, relativity, and understanding of linguistic signs and signifiers as arbitrary in nature. For ethnographers such as Clifford and Marcus (1986), anthropologies were to be 'read' in terms of 'politics and poetics'; and, moreover, this was to apply not simply of those being studied, but to the researcher themselves. Even psychology took on a social constructivist temperament via the existential applications of such writers as R.D. Laing (Laing 1966 and 1971). This thumbnail sketch shows the qualitative leanings that educational research adopted for much of the last quarter of the twentieth century; in other words, educational research became ethnographic in one form or another.

Language Ethnography or Language Psychology?

As noted above, the philosophy of man in the twentieth century in many ways became the philosophy of language; linguistics metaphors such as 'discourse' and 'signs' were used increasingly to describe socio-cultural phenomena. However, this convergence disguises a fundamental opposition at the heart of these trends: that which existed between the social and the psychological. This tension can be found everywhere across the social sciences. Even in the work of Ferdinand de Saussure (1966/1916), we detect a paradox: on the one hand, Saussure's work served as grounding principles for modern linguistics, with their focus on psychological process; on the other hand, philosophers adopted the very same Saussurian principles in their development of postmodernism as the guiding principles for a contemporary philosophy of man.

A similar tension was present in classroom language research where, during the 1960s and 1970s, there was a collision, in language terms, between a structural-grammar approach to language learning, and thinking dominated by behaviourism where educational research and practice focused on classroom linguistic events. For first language learning (L1), this amounted to a continuing preoccupation with literacy interpreted as skills and techniques, especially in reading and writing. For second language learning (L2), a grammar translation methodology dominated pedagogy. During the 1960s, two things impacted on this opposition, so that a blurring of the boundaries between the social and the psychological occurred, but in a way that left the tensions between the two unresolved and, to some extent, implicit. The first was the Chomskyan revolution (Chomsky 1968), and with it the notion that language was not only an innate property of the brain – physiologically based – but that there existed a natural Language Acquisition Device that could be access through pedagogy. The second was the socio-cultural reorientation that was taking place in the social sciences, and with it the rise of naturalistic methods of investigating educational contexts. Hymes' restatement (op. cit.) of Chomskyan *competence* as *communicative competence* is a good example of attempts to socialise the psychological. This point has serious ramifications for the theoretical perspectives, which subsequently guided classroom language ethnographies. The work of researchers such as Barnes *et al.* (1969), referred to in Chapter 4, still sought to find answers to questions of language and learning in the structure and form of language itself. Open and closed questions, Flanders' teacher talk law of two-thirds (Flanders 1965) and the 'I-R-F' sequences of Sinclair and Coulthard (1975) are, *essentially*, about language and its use. In this sense, and despite being rooted in real classroom contexts, an internalist view of language was adopted rather than attempting to construct language learning as a series of socio-cultural events, with all that implies in terms of agency and context. This tradition continues to this day in all studies, which explore classroom discourse in terms of the structure of language itself without considering it in relationship to its social and cultural provenance including both teachers and pupils. Even where a more socio-cultural perspective on classroom discourse was taken – for example, in the chapters in *Knowledge and Control,* referred to in Chapter 4 – the focus was on the language event itself. For example, Keddie (1971) was interested in the way that teachers' pre-formed views of pupils' abilities shaped interactions between them to the extent that they could be transcended. She argued that the language classroom, and language in the classroom, were thus prone to a kind of miscommunication that could be eradicated by a more informed approach on the part of teachers, and which could lead to the restructuring of subsequent pedagogic discourse.

A similar substantive intent, albeit implicit, underlies a more social constructivist approach to language learning, for example, in the perspectives adopted from the Soviet psycholinguist, Lev Vygotsky (see Vygotsky 1962, 1978). As noted in Chapter 4, Vygotsky developed a 'dialectical' approach to the tension between the social and the psychological in which nothing appeared in the internal, without first appearing in the external. The limit of how far this could take place was regulated by the notion of the 'Zone of Proximal Development': the position where optimal teaching and learning could take place. Indeed, it was the responsibility of the teacher to pitch a lesson appropriately within a child's ZPD. Thought and language were intimately connected with the primary cognitive act, where the child engages with the world – both socially and materially. *Control* was a key feature of this developing engagement: control of self, others and objects. A seminal text, *Common Knowledge* (Edwards and Mercer, 1987), was intent on taking this further by highlighting the meta-structures of language events in the classroom, as the way in which knowledge and understanding are shared between teachers and pupils, and pupils with each other. In later work, and under the influence of Bruner (1986), the teaching within the ZPD was 're-invented' as 'scaffolding'. This analytic metaphor itself conjures up the image of support and structure, and was interpreted as such. Mercer (1981) himself emphasises the way that pupils are supported through scaffolding provided by the teacher, and even 'brought back on line' when they stray.

Such social constructivist approaches are no less 'normative' than the structural-grammar methods of the previous decades. Essentially language events, and the way they mediate teaching and learning, are interpreted from a normative functionalist point of view which, no less than classical functionalism, sees them in terms of prescribed ways of thinking and doing things with words. Standard values and norms in language are therefore the order of the day, all of which are seen as necessary skills and prerequisites for the (linguistic) health of society. This is what Street (1984) was implicitly criticising with his call to New Literacy Studies (NLS): contra literacy as an autonomous realm into which pupils need to be inducted, and promoting an understanding of literacy as a socio-historical construction constituted through language events played out by specific individuals in particular learning contexts . Much of the rest of this book is about the realisation of this understanding of literacy.

So, NLS was important because it broke away from a view of literacy as a series of independent technical skills and developed researchers' understanding of it as an ideological construct, as one that was contingent on historical practices. However, such an ideological approach cannot be without a theoretical foundation and guiding principle, and thus conceptual tools to guide practice. Such tools imply and impose their own narrative, which have important ramifications for what we think, indeed, what we can think, about literacy events. Heller (2008: 51), for example, is not alone in arguing that there is a paradox at the heart of NLS – one met earlier in this chapter. On the one hand, it wishes to avoid any view of literacy as socially and cognitively developmental because, as a term, it runs the risk of universalising its subject and of falling into a kind of social neo-Darwinism akin to the normative functionalism described above. On the other hand, NLS seems no less wedded to a form of Vygotskyan social constructivism which focuses on the interplay between an individual and their context, the psychological and the social, purely in and through the mediation of language form. Language cannot – as in the autonomous approaches to literacy – be seen simply as a 'foundational mode' of thinking, rather, it is to be understood as historically located and embedded in actual social relations. It is in this respect that Bourdieu can be particularly useful. Indeed, it might be argued that, in contrast to many of the other chapters in *Knowledge and Control*, where Bourdieu focuses on academic discourse he is less interested in the phenomenology of classroom interactions. Rather, he sets out to highlight the need to analyse how classrooms, and thus pedagogic knowledge, is constructed as a previously given within and across fields. The accent here is not so much the actuality of classroom discourse, although this is needed as a practical exemplification of process, but on how it is shaped and formed by external conditions, which themselves are to be articulated as a 'social structuration' within existing relations of power. In effect, it can be argued that Bourdieu was more focussed on structural relations between individuals (pupils and teachers) and the fields that surrounded them, and on the consequences that these relations had for what is thought and how, than on the actuality of classroom discourse and its levels of (mis)communication (see Hardy 2010 for a recent example.) As we have stressed in this book, for Bourdieu, literacy can only be a question of *legitimate language*; that is, what is consecrated, who is sanctioned to speak – and how, at any particular place and time – and the values that mediate literacy events. In this, literacy is best understood in terms of the relational structures between individuals and the field itself.

This section has highlighted some of the tensions to be found at the intersections of the social and the cognitive, between teaching and learning, with NLS and Bourdieu's theory of practice. These oppositions are explored further, in both this chapter and in Chapter 10, in terms of the practical case examples given earlier in the book. Before this discussion, the way and extent to which theory features in these debates is reconsidered.

Educational Theory and Practice

In the previous section, I referred to the nature of theory and contrasted its 'scientific' and 'educational' forms. Behind my present discussion is the question: what is the form and role of theory in the perspectives under consideration? Is there a theory of New Literacy Studies? What are the 'theoretical' aspects of Bourdieu's 'theory of practice'? How does theory feature in ethnography? Most importantly, what are we to understand by 'theory' in our proposed 'classroom language ethnography'?

In a Popperian view of 'scientific theory', it was not just that theory should be judged in terms of the extent to which it can be falsified, but that what resulted from such an approach was seen as 'objective knowledge'; that is, 'knowledge without a knowing subject'. Popper argued for an understanding of our surroundings in terms of what he called three worlds: World 1 was the world of physical objects; World 2 that of subjective impressions, and, World 3 was the world of objective truth which was dependent neither on physical manifestation nor subjective assertion. For Popper, even if every living creature on the Earth disappeared, the boiling point of water would continue to be 100 degrees centigrade. Such objective reality was beyond observation or interpretation. As noted earlier, the view of early philosophers of education with respect to theory was not dissimilar; especially in a psychologically based paradigm which concentrated on psychometric measures. Here, there is a direct, linear and one-way relationship between theory and practice, as shown in Figure 9.1.

The simple relationship shown in Figure 9.1 was soon eclipsed by Hirst (1967) with his view that 'educational theory' occupied a special place between the science of the normative foundation disciplines (sociology, philosophy, psychology and history) and actual classroom practice. For Hirst, it was not so much that 'educational theory' could not match the criteria which were to be fulfilled to be recognised as 'scientific theory' but that the latter misrepresented and undervalued the place of theory in education. Educational theory according to Hirst could (and should) provide 'principles of practice' (pedagogy) for education through a deeper grasp of the nature of learning, the values which underpinned it, and the background context in which it took place. Just as physics and chemistry drew on mathematics to develop theoretical positions, so educational theory could draw on the disciplines of

Concrete
practice

Normative
scientific
theory

FIGURE 9.1 The direct relationship of theory to practice

psychology, philosophy, history and sociology to develop an understanding of what to do in practice. Thus, principles for educational action could be justified according to the findings and rationale of such foundation disciplines. In other words, theory's role was to tell practice what to do, or at least to provide a principled framework. When these inter-relationships are represented diagrammatically, 'justifying educational principles' provide mediation between the foundation disciplines and classroom practice (see Figure 9.2).

The autonomous view of literacy as generic skills and competences which was outlined earlier in this book, is an example of this type of educational theory; in that, a certain way of defining reading and writing, based on experimental tests, is used to conceptualise what it is to read and write in terms of certain skills and techniques, and to construct an appropriate classroom teaching methodology designed to make sure that pupils learn them. Here 'justifying educational principles' (JEP) about literacy skills and competence are used to 'tell teachers how to teach' literacy.

The relationship between behaviourism (theory) and audio-visual/lingual approaches (practice) to the teaching of modern foreign languages in the 1960s and 1970s offers another example of normative educational theory justified by foundation disciples. More recently, the National Literacy Strategy (DfES 1998) which was implemented as government policy in the UK in the 1990s and 2000s adopted a certain approach to reading – phonics as opposed to real books – which was predicated on a particular theoretical view of reading and how one should therefore be taught to read (See Figure 9.3). These examples illustrate two important features of this discussion: first, the contested nature of theory; second, the way it can operate in the field to determine actual classroom practice. Nonetheless, this form of theoretical knowledge is not the only type of knowledge operating in classrooms and educational contexts. A more complex, if highly abstract view of theory, that of the German social philosopher Jürgen Habermas, shows that this view

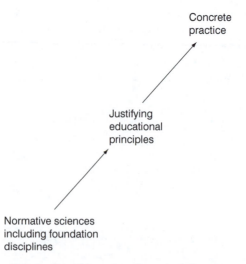

Concrete
practice

Justifying
educational
principles

Normative sciences
including foundation
disciplines

FIGURE 9.2 The mediation of justifying education principles

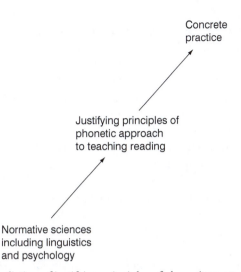

Concrete
practice

Justifying principles of
phonetic approach
to teaching reading

Normative sciences
including linguistics
and psychology

FIGURE 9.3 The mediation of justifying principles of phonetics on teaching of reading

of knowledge is only partial. For Habermas, one form of knowledge was indeed 'normative,' what he termed 'nomothetical' (see Habermas 1987, 1989). However, this form of knowledge was to be contrasted with other forms, such as the 'critical' and the 'hermeneutic' – the former revealed underlying socio-political processes whilst the latter took account of 'subjective knowledge'. A key point for Habermas was that one form of knowledge was not necessarily *better* than another, but that each disclosed different *interests*. So, whilst 'nomothetical' knowledge supported the formation of generalisable rules as its outcome, the 'critical' addressed the social and political potential of knowledge, and the 'hermeneutic' underpinned experiential and interpretative knowledge. Clearly, all of these may be applied in an educational context, where not all questions can or should be reduced to the instrumentality of teaching and learning from a technicist point of view. Here, it is no longer the case that theory simply 'tells practice what to do', but that 'practice' actively engages with theory from a critical perspective. Of course, teachers do operate in classrooms according to principles which themselves are based on theoretical perspectives, as shown in the Figure 9.2. However, the process depicted in Figure 9.2 omits an important aspect of educational practice: teachers' own rationale for their classroom actions which are most often generated from their own past (practical) experience. Much of this knowledge is fragmented, intuitive, affective, holistic and highly contextual. For this reason, it is termed 'tacit knowledge' (Polyani 1998/1958) – that practical 'horse-sense' that is the prerogative of the experienced practitioner.

It is probably worth pausing now to consider the nature of this 'tacit' knowledge from a theoretical perspective. Polyani writes that an 'act of knowing exercises a personal judgement in relating evidence to an external reality, an aspect of which (s)he is seeking to apprehend' (Polanyi 1998/1958: 24–5). As stated, such tacit knowledge is essentially intuitive and subjective. As it emerges from practice, it is also contingent on a practical context to be re-activated at a particular point in time.

In some respects, it is the very opposite to Popper's objective, or World 3, knowledge without a knowing subject, since it is, in fact, subjective, World 2, knowledge, with *only* a knowing subject. This type of knowledge could be seen as almost being 'pre-theoretical'. Such a statement implies a level of subjectivity that might seem unstable, hyper relative, and even arbitrary. However, this is not the case with tacit knowledge which is based on a practitioner's experience and, therefore, has an internal coherence based on an individual's classroom practice, but articulated to varying degrees. One way of elucidating this point is to return to the nature, or characteristics, of theory itself. So far, the predictive quality of theory has been stressed, but, that is not its only attribute. Theory must also be understood in terms of its other essential features. Theory is a reduction: it must express something complex in a simpler form. Theory is intended to be useful: neither a theory that expresses the obvious, nor one that is too obscure to be of much use in a practical context. Moreover, a theory must be expressible and readily articulated: it must not be just a hunch, because it must be communicated from one person to another. Finally, a theory must have some degree of coherence and regularity. In other words, it must pertain to more than a single event. Tacit knowledge, as I have described it, shares many of these characteristics; in that it is useful, generalisable, coherent and a reduction of complexity. In this respect, if tacit knowledge is not exactly 'theoretical' from a Popperian, scientific point of view, it does share many of the features of such theory. This type of theory, which reflects articulated tacit knowledge, will be referred to as 'fundamental educational theory' (see Vandenberg 1974), as shown in Figure 9.4.

It is 'fundamental' since it is still highly personal and contingent; 'educational' since it pertains to classroom practice; and 'theoretical' in that it shares the theoretical features outlined in the last paragraph. However, there is still one feature to examine more closely – the 'articulated' nature of theory: that theory can be expressed, communicated and therefore shared. Many of the statements made in the practical case examples in Part II of this book are examples of 'fundamental education theory' since they arise from practice; they are subjective in many cases, and yet they express issues of principle and practice which are of general relevance, and therefore, cannot be viewed as relative, arbitrary, and *sui generis*. Researchers working within a New Literacy Studies paradigm do make use of appropriate theoretical underpinnings from the foundation disciplines but what marks NLS as distinctive is the central position it gives to literacy as contextually defined practice. Since this approach sees literacies as socio-cultural practices, dependent on actual events, particular places, and on individuals' articulation of how to teach and learn literacy, the outcomes of NLS studies offer examples of 'fundamental educational theory'.

The next step in this investigation of educational knowledge is to consider these different types of theory in relationship to one another as a continuum.

Each theoretical area in Figure 9.5 is distinct but inter-related. In other words, the different types of knowledge under discussion are represented in terms of their relational rather than their substantive nature. In this respect, they are dependent on time and place and on specific interactions. The 'triangle' is a representation of the variety of relationships which exist between theory and practice. Since Bourdieu's

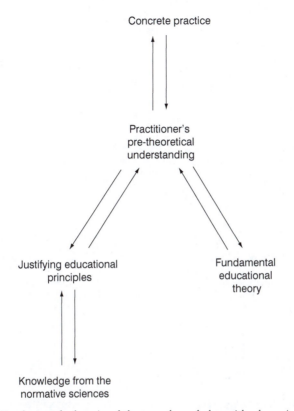

Concrete practice

Practitioner's
pre-theoretical
understanding

Justifying educational
principles

Fundamental
educational
theory

Knowledge from the
normative sciences

FIGURE 9.4 Fundamental educational theory – knowledge with a knowing subject

approach to research was predicated on a 'theory *of* practice', the area at the top of the triangle is particularly pertinent because, for him, any research undertaking must begin with a consideration of a practical, empirical context; any object of research must be studied in its practical environment (its *field context)* and at the same time, the activity of research itself is viewed as a practical engagement. Here, both the researched – teachers and their students – and the researchers themselves are implicated in the research activity and in how its findings are constructed. Hence, in Bourdieu's theory of practice, it would be necessary to see the triangle both in terms of the object of research and the practice of the researchers themselves.

On the right hand side of the triangle, a form of knowledge is represented which is predicated on an explicit expression of knowledge formed in practice – an articulation of tacit knowledge itself. The best way of describing and supporting such a process as theoretical is with recourse to philosophical resources based around phenomenology. Fundamental educational theory can therefore be understood in terms of an *imminent* reflection on practice where, in the terms used in Chapter 4, the *noema* is expressed through an engagement with an individual *noetic* event. This is what tells us what we know about such an event at that point in time. In contrast, if we look at the left hand side of the triangle, educational theory, or principles of

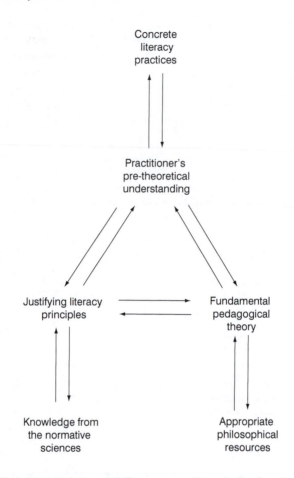

Concrete
literacy
practices

Practitioner's
pre-theoretical
understanding

Justifying literacy   Fundamental
principles   pedagogical
theory

Knowledge from   Appropriate
the normative   philosophical
sciences   resources

FIGURE 9.5 Relationships between different types of knowledge (based on Vandenberg 1974)

practice, provide a stable objectification of what we know about a particular research object – for example literacy. This knowledge itself is formed on the basis of the natural sciences, aspects of which are normative. It is 'theoretical' to the extent that it conforms to the type of characteristics outlined above: generalisability, articulated, useful, simplified and predictable. This knowledge source informs and is informed by practice. However, it is formed at some theoretical distance from practice and takes little account of tacit knowledge.

The completed triangle (Figure 9.5) demonstrates the inter-relationships between three distinctive types of knowledge – tacit knowledge, fundamental educational theory and justified educational principles and shows the theoretical underpinnings for each as justification for regarding theory and practice in this particular way. From a more ethnographic perspective, the sides of the triangle might be described as 'application' – left hand – and 'understanding' – right hand (see also Gitlin *et al.*, 1989). Further, the left and the right sides of the triangle respectively represent knowledge which mirrors Bourdieu's objective and subjective knowledge. They therefore conform to the type of structural understanding set out in Chapter 4, as being both 'structured' and 'structuring'. It is worth remembering that Bourdieusian science seeks to go beyond the opposition of these two to a synthesis, so that a new form of *praxeological* understanding can be constructed out of research activity. In this way, the horizontal arrowed lines provide links at the bottom of the triangle – between left and right; objective and subjective; nomothetical and phenomenological. These links are particularly important as it is here that the epistemological breaks of which Bourdieu writes, the synthesis to which he aspires, and the praxeological knowledge he is attempting to open up, are occurring (see Bourdieu 1977/1972: 1–2). In other words, nomothetical knowledge – justifying educational principles – must connect with fundamental educational knowledge, and vice versa, all whilst both of these take account of practice as represented by tacit knowledge. The triangle is, therefore, to be seen as dynamic which expresses both discrete items within the theory-practice continuum, and their constantly changing inter-relationships.

In its abstract form, the triangle represented in Figure 9.5 awaits practical application to the real world. Indeed, we might see this application as the 'return of the repressed' to the construction; namely the actuality of agency and context – the people and the places. To put this more succinctly and in Bourdieusian terms, the triangle must be articulated through the lens of habitus and field. This is particularly important at the practice end of the triangle where practice occurs in a field context that is both structuring and structured. The most obvious examples of this are the material spaces of classrooms, their physicality and ideational structures, for example, and the logic of practice enshrined in curricula and actualised in classroom pedagogy. A classroom is liable to a full field analysis and at the same time, the agents involved – teachers and pupils – who come with their own backgrounds, attitudes and experiences can be studied in terms of constituents of habitus at play. What happens in the classroom for teaching and learning happens at the interface of this habitus and this field context. The triangle can therefore be actualised socio-genetically. If we are exploring theory and practice in classroom language ethnography, we need to do it both in terms of theory and practice, as represented in different sites of activity, *and* in terms of the habitus-field interface being played out in those sites. For the top of the triangle, this may be actual classroom practice and teachers' and students' habitus. However, on the left side, activity is to be accounted for in terms of the structures of the academic field in question and the habitus of those involved in it – the researchers and academics. Acknowledgement of this amounts to a reflexive stance, about which more in the next chapter. Indeed, it is also possible to see the academic activity of research as the object researched. In this case, it would be possible to set this at the top of the triangle – as a practice – and therefore as a source of both objective principles formed within the established field and fundamental theory as an expression of personal tacit knowledge with respect to the academic object under study. Both of these forms of theory will necessarily reflect the *interests* of the field itself, and any consequent biases. For Bourdieu, all this would be articulated through a field analysis which would, *ipso facto*, include detail of the way that individuals' habitus supports particular position taking and differing degrees of dominance within the particular social environment.

With this view of the inter-relationships of different types of theory as a background, I now want to return to the practical examples presented in Part II of the book to consider in more detail how these are theorised. What features of field and habitus can be found there? And, to what extent do the studies offer us examples of the types of knowledge forms raised in the above discussion of theory and practice.

Practical Case Examples

The LETTER Project (Chapter 5)

The LETTER project is offered as an example of how research is undertaken within a NLS approach, but it can be viewed in different ways. It can be understood as a specific intervention by researchers interested in adult literacy into a specific field – that of female literacy in Uttar Pradesh. But, it is not research in a pure sense – 'research for research's sake' – since it arises out a practical need and reflects a very deliberate strategy of social engagement in overseas development. This approach itself defines a certain relationship to the object of research, and thus, a certain *modus operandi*, which itself must be understood in terms of the structured and structuring habitus of all those involved with the project. The researchers, the literacy trainers and the Dalit women each come with differing degrees of academic capital, and with particular epistemological orientations. For example, not only are the researchers amongst the originators of New Literacy Studies itself – and therefore occupying legitimated positions within the academic field – but they also have in common particular dispositions and methodological approaches. To acknowledge the existence of *multiple literacies*, to see them as a social construction and, as events susceptible to ideological infusion, the researchers have developed what is termed an 'ethnographic perspective', which they distinguish from 'straight' ethnography. For the researchers, their 'practice' in undertaking interventions in India is, therefore, guided by principles of practice derived from such an ethnographic perspective. This perspective can be objectified in terms of the human sciences as grounding principles for a particular theoretical orientation. The orientation would be placed on the left hand side of the triangle in Figure 9.5 as 'justifying educational principles'.

This research can also be seen as a study of how one field interacts intentionally with other national, regional and local fields. The researchers will also have their own personal as well as academic habitus and, their practice itself will be shaped by tacit knowledge developed from previous experience of similar projects. Their work takes place at the intersection of three distinctive fields: that of the study itself, the national field of adult education in India together with the international academic field of the researchers, and the local field of *Dalit* culture. This inter-relationship of fields is not uncommon in an academic field (and is not dissimilar to Bourdieu's own (see *The Algerians* 1962/1958)

The object of research, the rural Dalit women of Nirantir, exists in a state of 'empirical practice', apparently unencumbered by any engagement with objective principles or articulations of fundamental theory. From the perspective of the academic field, their habitus is that of the naïve, unreflexive state, subsumed by a common sense relation to the field that surrounds them. As Street states in Chapter 5: 'the women themselves were to a large extent unconscious of their distinctiveness'. The project focus is on training local teachers to discover more about these alternative ways of looking at the world, and about pre-existing Dalit literacies and numeracies. For NLS, this is an ethnographic study of the literacies practices of the Dalit. From a Bourdieusian perspective, this project is an investigation into the structures of the local Dalit field, what acts as capital, and how it engages with the broader social space.

As noted in Chapter 4, Bourdieu often began with a key observation. Here, the key observation is the fact that the local field is a great deal more sophisticated than first thought because these women have alternative ways of looking at the world. For example, they see rivers as animate objects in contrast to Western categories which define them as inanimate. This alternative way of interpreting the world is itself a question of legitimation: which is acceptable? Clearly, in principle, both can be adopted and, in their respective fields, probably are. However, 'improving literacy' may mean learning what would be acceptable as 'correct' within a Western literacy event.

There are three key points to make here. First, the women's practice is both unconscious and tacit. Moreover, they do not recognise that it is the very thinking structures derived from their surrounding local field – their habitus – which in part positions them as a highly dominated group within the broader social space. They are unaware of the symbolic power of this way of thinking, in a negative sense.

Second, an important aspect of the study was the way that adult education practitioners were trained in ethnographic style research, who then trained adult teachers to conduct research into their own learning groups. In other words, an indirect approach to the rural women was made through local trainers and facilitators. In this way, objective principles of practice where passed on which, in practice, could be used to explore tacit thinking and knowledge. They are trained 'to see' with a particular 'ethnographic eye'.

Third, this method itself discloses a different structural form to the researched in terms of the relation between the field of knowledge and those who are to be the object of instruction. As pointed out, normally, literacy is seen as a deficit. It is therefore assumed that the 'illiterate' must be instructed in what can be regarded as a legitimate way of speaking and writing. The resultant method is 'top-down' and one-way: from field to habitus, as the latter is brought back 'into line' with the dominant culture. However, the LETTER project began with what existed 'in the field' and the habitus of those involved, and worked outwards to construct a field of literacy informed both by local and national patterns. Such an approach is essentially dialogic in the same way as the theory-practice triangle suggests above, and is predicated on principles, logics, and norms found in habitus and field and their intersection.

To conclude this brief consideration of the LETTER Project, there are two further points I would like to stress. First, in these microanalyses of ethnographic context, quite a small amount of data can, if sufficiently analysed, render enormously important information on underlying generative structures, and the principles of practice which constitute them. Second, the focus of such analyses might begin with seemingly mundane artefacts and events: for example, calendars, routine statements, etc. Both may seem quite simple compared to the academic arsenal. However, both observations are consistent with Bourdieu's own practice.

A Different Eye (Chapter 6)

Similar issues of perspective can be identified in Chapter 6 on pupils' creativity. A distinctive feature of this chapter is the researcher objectifying her own generating principles and stating explicitly what she was interested in: the unfolding stories that children used when making boxes. A second key feature is the clear relationships she identifies with the broader national space through its policy for socio-economically deprived regions – Creative Partnership Funds. The context, that of 6- and 7-year-old children constructing objects out of classroom materials, is a relatively mundane one, but one with rich potential. In terms of the research itself, the researcher and the teacher are at least in part working at cross purposes. The 'pedagogic habitus' of the researcher has been shaped by academic readings – for example, texts by Williams (1989) and Steadman (1983). The 'pedagogic habitus' of the teacher, on the other hand, was predicated on her interest in art and craft, design technology, and her experience with artists in the classroom. Whose reality is real? At one point, Bourdieu writes about the 'scholastic fallacy' as *skholè* (Bourdieu, 2000/1997) defined in terms of leisure. This does not mean that researchers take it easy, but that they have a 'non-empirical' relationship to the part of the world they study. As soon as they adopt a semi-objective stance towards the world, their relationship to it changes. They do not live in this world in its everyday, sensual sense, as a naïve experience, since they have a different *interest* in it. The problem is then, when, and how scholastic interest imposes itself on their view of the world, with all its pre-formed interpretations and constructions. In other words, a certain – academic – view is imported into reality which is then used to describe it as *real*. The result is the re-integration, with its self-referential confirmation, of the scholastic view that is now passed on as a deeper truth than the thing itself – scholastic fallacy incarnate. What a 'different eye' demonstrates is one researcher beginning to create a reflexive space where such processes are objectified, as part of her research practice – an example of the articulation of 'fundamental educational theory' of research practice. This degree of reflexivity, however small, is significant since it is integrated into the object of research itself. This researcher's view is clearly identifiable in her discussion of the pupils' dialogues where what is sought is a deep understanding of the inherent structure of what is occurring. The author contrasts her interests with the teacher's focus on 'the progressive pedagogic space', on how the children respond and on what she is doing, for example when she says 'I try to make the projects more children-led …'.

What is reported appears as a simple classroom project, but one that is made up of a complex array of features, all intertwined in a fluid and dynamic way. Returning to the triangle, the teacher's own principles of practice, derived from her training and experience – her practice and tacit knowledge – motivate her to do what she does, but this time shaped by and through the educational principles made explicit in specific curricular initiatives – National Literacy Strategy and Creative Partnerships. These projects, which themselves were shaped and funded by governmental policy, set out to use artistic experience and creativity as vehicles for the social inclusion of economically deprived groups (here an ex-mining community in north-east England). The National Literacy Strategy was a key component in this mission. As such, Creative Partnerships were shaped by a certain rhetoric about what constitutes creativity and how it should unfold in the classroom.

By adopting a 'linguistic ethnographic' approach, the researcher was able to highlight aspects of creativity in the language of the classroom. What we see is a coming together of different languages of creativity: first, in the field context of this classroom, the language of the pupils in expressing what they are doing, interacts with that of the teacher coming from her own interests and pedagogic habitus; second, the language of the researcher, based on her own experience as teacher and researcher re-presents the broader perspectives of an academic field' and third, the language of the principles of practice of governmental policy is enshrined in curricular documents and actualised in aspects of classroom pedagogy. What we see is creativity as an individual and external event – a specific site context, a field, and a field within fields – all somehow being played out in the dynamic of pupil-pupil and pupil-teacher relations, to a greater or lesser extent. Moreover, we see such a dynamic as *sedimented* in literacy events, in the very language of discourse, its genres, and the knowledge bases drawn upon to express them. One might ask, then, what are the rules of creativity? And, how are they shaping these events? Bourdieu's theory of practice combines with our triangle of practice to allow us to navigate through the data in formulating a response to such questions.

The Fractal Habitus (Chapter 7)

Creativity is also the focus of the research reported in Chapter 7; although, here, the learners involved are perceived as underachieving in their literacy lessons. The rubric 'underachieving' is an explicit expression of an aspect of the logic of practice of education: the assumption of normality, legitimised as such by those most dominant in the field, and offering consecration to those who conform to it. These students have not yet gained this acknowledgement, even though one might argue that they are not wildly deviant from 'the norm'. Rowsell accepts their non-conformity. Their lack of achievement in more traditional English lessons is her starting point, which is to offer them creative opportunities through their film making, with whatever technical skills they are able to procure. In one way, the practice of the students (and of their teacher) is not directly informed by formal educational principles at all. Although it is possible to set their pedagogical activity in the context of official curricular requirements, it is innovative and therefore unorthodox and could also be read as in opposition to this doxa. The students' film-making practice has a product, which itself is seen as sedimentation of habitus, albeit partial, in other words, as containing slices of a particular form of life histories. The 'fractal habitus' of the title refers to these 'slices'.

Elsewhere, Rowsell (op cit.) has worked with artists' experience of 'fatherhood': an experience where, on becoming a father, individuals respond consciously and unconsciously by adjusting their life view and lifestyle (habitus) as a result of this dramatic change in their personal history. This chapter demonstrates the way similar adjustments are made by underachieving students who have experienced personal dislocations, for example, through family immigration from Israel or Australia or more simply, through a holiday to Niagara. These students, offered the model of Homer's account of Odysseus' journey home, expressed their own personal experiences of dislocation in artistic and linguistic practices, in this case, film. The focus of the work is both deeply psychological and phenomenological. The creative act itself can again be seen as a relation between *noema* and *noesis* as part of a dynamic and personal response within specific site contexts. Of necessity, this response entails a certain challenge to the self in the demands it puts upon the individual. Bourdieu writes of his own disrupted experiences – in rural south-west France and in Paris, for example – as resulting in a *cleft habitus* which he describes as a 'coincidence of contraries', one which 'helped to institute … an ambivalent and contradictory relationship to the academic institutions, combining rebellion and submission, rupture and expectation …' (Bourdieu 2007/2004: 100). To a lesser extent, fractal habitus, as exemplified by these students' films, is not dissimilar. Personal adaptation with respect to times of crisis and challenge is always a form of control over self, others, and the material world in which dispositions are reinforced, modified, or attenuated in the face of the situations presented to individuals. In this case, the challenge is the creative act into which 'bits' of the student self are expressed and sedimented as 'multimodal texts' in a way which parallels the process involved in the formation and articulation of fundamental educational theory. Through the external and internal shifts involved, we see the way that the identity of the self can be 'repositioned' by objectifiying the structural relations that surround it and the forces they exert on individual action.

The highly personal undertaking of film making can be compared to the more formal field setting of the English classroom in a way which makes explicit their relative positioning with respect to consecrated forms of literacy, literature and pedagogy. Literacy, in this case, takes on an unorthodox multimodal dimension, including both written and visual texts defining the producer and the product in terms of creativity (agency) and medium (context). A fractal habitus can also be seen to be a *fractured* habitus in the narratives emerging from this activity, as they juxtapose working with and against the 'rules of the games' set in formal pedagogic discourses.

It is important to see this research activity in terms of its framing. By adopting a specific 'ethnographic perspective' the researcher is using the approach both as a pedagogical principle, in setting up the classroom activity, and as a research approach to the collection and analysis of data arising from it. The researcher undertakes to make a film herself as a way of positioning herself reflexively both in the classroom and in the research. Central to both activities is the development of a language to talk about them. In a globalised world, we are used to acknowledging multimodal communications as alternative forms of discourse. However, it is not enough for the students in this case simply to express their ideas in their own terms; they also have to address the differences in relations between their own text and more traditional texts – here Homer's Odyssey. What this case finally offers is an opportunity to consider the valuation of texts in literature and in less doxic media in terms of the *cultural capital* at play and, in so doing, to understand its provenance and functioning in the literary field and in the broader cultural field. In this way, theory provides an underlying language of critique to shape the ethnographic perspective employed.

Classroom Reading (Chapter 8)

The sedimentation of theory into practical action can also be identified in the microanalysis of the lesson in the reading classroom case study. The focus here is on race and culture, in that the school context under consideration is predominantly an African-American one. There is then an explicit observable differentiation between the cultures dominant inside and outside the school. Of particular note here are the very evident structural relations between the dominant forms of pedagogy, as prescribed in official documents, and in the actual discourse of this classroom of African-American students. Moreover, such differences should not be seen simply in terms of linguistic morphology, but as consequences of the contrasting logics of practice from which they are constituted.

Bloome and Brown show how the state defines its official literacy pedagogy in terms of the requisite skills needed to be effective in the workplace, and that these 'justified educational principles' are supported by a series of 'national' research reports –normative science. State action is therefore legitimised and seen to be both neutral and scientific. Of course, that neutrality is itself an ideological position, that of the most dominant, and one that asserts a particular reading of literacy – autonomous – over a cultural one where literacy is seen as a social construction, and thus both arbitrary, and ultimately relative. For the *symbolic violence* of pedagogy (Bourdieu and Passeron 1977a/1970) to do its work, nothing further has to be done. The same is asked from all students (justified in terms of equity), all whilst knowing that the tasks are in fact highly differentiated so that not all can deliver the same. And, by being invisible, presented as neutral and scientific, the differential challenge is *misrecognised* and is all the more pernicious and effective for that.

Cultural difference – between two cultures (one of the school and one of the community) – has long been recognised. As the authors assert, such a difference has often led to policies of compensation and other less legitimated strategies of celebration and resistance. However, at base there is a paradox for the individuals involved: namely, what is required of them is a 'double consciousness', a kind of ambidexterity which requires a student to be competently operative in two totally distinct 'languages'. At the heart of that demand lies a paradox – named as a 'double bind' in Chapter 8. If the Africa-American students are to succeed, they have to acquire the literacy style and skills of the dominant white majority, which itself implies tacitly accepting Black 'inferiority'. Yet, if they do not do this, they remain as part of a dominated culture. This socio-cultural dilemma is not so different from that facing any bilingual student where languages (and their implicit cultures) are juxtaposed with all the questions of loyalty, identity, acknowledgement and distinction acutely posed.

At the heart of the empirical data in this case is an example of the tacit knowledge of an expert teacher in practice. We know next to nothing of her formal theorising, nor of the extent to which she can (or could) articulate this knowledge as a form of 'fundamental educational theory': this is one of the aims of the collaborative research project in which she is engaged. Neither is much known about her own pedagogical habitus or the methodological conventions of the pedagogy she was expected to employ. What we do see, however, is the way she is able to draw on two distinct styles of literacy – white and Black, majority and minority, dominant and inferior – in her own teaching in order to support her students in their task of developing this bicultural literacy. What she models for her students is a fluent ability to switch between language forms and cultures. Bloome and Brown refer to it as a 'jazz', itself an African-American vernacular, to describe its organisational patterns of interaction, response, improvisation, and rhythmic variation. What is brought together are the cultural experiences of the students involved and the text in question through the medium of the teacher's tacit knowledge, a knowledge which itself draws on actual cultural artefacts, their valuation, and the way they can be played against each other with a view to developing the 'seeing eye' of the students. Cultural sedimentation is present – for example, in the use of language resonant with well known negro spirituals – which is meshed (through questioning and answering) with the students' own world view and experience (habitus), and what they need to be able to say (and how) about the written text. As Bloome and Brown argue, what is presented here is 'theory' as something that is lived in a tacit way, not as a stand-alone separate entity waiting to be applied. The same might be said about our understanding of both pedagogic principles as set out in the triangle of practice above, and the way that Bourdieusian sociology furnishes us with a way of seeing the world – actively! These issues are extended in the next section.

The Practice of Theory

The final chapter will offer a synthesis of Bourdieu, Ethnography and New Literacy Studies as a way of defining a new perspective on classroom language ethnography, which is the *raison d'être* of the book. The next section is intended as a preparation for this discussion and seeks to highlight aspects of theory and its place in the approaches used so far.

The earlier sections of this book considered various relationships between theory and practice. A prime issue here was that theory never exists in a single form, and that it is possible to identify different types of theory – normative, educational, fundamental, and even 'pre-theoretical' – which all shared characteristics of classic definitions of theoretical statements. Each of these has been shown to have its place in educational contexts. The case studies illuminated this in practice: agents involved in learning and teaching contexts – researchers, teachers and students – operated from schema, state regulated curricula and from educational principles, all of these theoretical in nature when taken in terms of this broader definition. These theory-practice relationships were never simply one-way. Practice shapes theory as much as theory impacts on practice. The 'triangle of practice' outlined above must be seen in terms of constantly changing and fluid structures where two-way relationships continually anticipate further knowledge bases beyond immediate interactions. The triangle can be applied to an individual teacher's activity as it implies the present or absence of ways of knowing that underpin classroom practice. Actual classroom practice is so intense, it would be impossible to be active in situ whilst holding various other theoretical forms explicitly in mind. However, such lack of explicitness does not mean that they have no effect, as we have seen, tacit knowledge is itself a medium essential for the sedimentation and transmission of these other theoretical forms, and can be seen as 'dispositional' in Bourdieusian terms. The principal usefulness of Bourdieu's theory of practice is its demand that such activity be situated within the actuality of those involved in time and place. So, the teacher and their students are not treated as generalised, anonymous entities, bleached of biography, and background, but as individuals with particular habitus to be read in a generative structural sense and thus prone to pre-dispositions and changing dispositions. Moreover, the whole unfolds in a social space which is structured according to logics of practice enshrined in formal forms of pedagogy such as syllabi, curricular documents and teaching materials. The practical case examples have highlighted these relations between the literacy curriculum and those involved in working with it.

Ethnographic practice can itself be seen in terms of a similar 'triangle of practice', with its own theoretical positions – again normative, fundamental, tacit, and pre-theoretical – linking researchers with their object of research. A significant element of the practice of a language researcher is to work in the literacy classroom as part of their ethnographic field work, while bringing theoretical knowledge to bear on what goes on in practice and to examine its relationship to the literacy curriculum as an underlying rationale for what occurs. Such research activity can never be one-way, but rather involves dialectical relationships in both theory and practice, and between them.

We have seen that New Literacy Studies represented a significant break from the way that literacy was traditionally viewed: as a set of independent skills to be imparted to the learner in an instrumental way. For NLS, the classroom is seen as a social construction, and as a place where social and cultural factors play a crucial part in what occurs, and how. Such factors are attributable to ideological and political forces, as well as the personal trajectories of those involved in the classroom. But, here a dichotomy opens up: that between the social and the cognitive. NLS's affirmation that literacies are to be seen in socio-cultural terms, not simply a set of developmentally specific autonomous skills, is correct. However, insisting on literacy as a social construction runs the risk of being satisfied with a simple narrative assertion of the need to view literacy through a cultural lens, and to ignore any of the issues of cognition in the acquisition of literacy. As we have seen earlier in this book, structure needs to be understood as much as a cognitive act than a social one. In this sense, Bourdieu's theory of practice is both phenomenological and psychological. Literacy forms actively structure a social space which is already structured, and thus one which exhibits power relations as transmitted by pedagogic practice, based on national curricula, which are themselves informed by specific ways (logics) of seeing the world associated with the most dominant. We saw this above in the way a curriculum was presented as scientific and neutral, and thus encouraged misrecognition of the inherent cultural difference set up within its principles of practice. Bourdieu's approach is useful in examining the psychological beyond the social, and again in the use that can be made of habitus and field to tease out the specificity of theory and practice in actual literacy exchanges.

Yet, Bourdieu is still regarded as a macro- rather than a micro-theorist, and thus one with little to say about the detail of classroom exchanges (see Hardy, 2011), however, for a recent example which develops its potential in this direction with practical exemplification). Much of Bourdieu's best known work pertains to 'field analyses', of the relations between fields and the structures of field themselves with the importance of individual encounters underplayed. Thus his approach is recognised as useful for studying the relations of what is occurring between or outside a field, rather than 'within' it; whilst, on the other hand, educational researchers are often more preoccupied by the actuality of classroom discourse, teachers' and students lives, learning and teaching, etc. However, what the practical case examples have shown is that it is perfectly possible to construct ethnographies of classroom practice in a way which retains the links with generating structures constituted outside the classroom and, indeed, it is necessary to connect with them if we are to understand what is occurring at a micro level, and why.

The classroom is made up of certain fundamental constructs – teacher, pupil, teaching and learning, etc. The process of education leads to differential responses and outcomes. The autonomous view of literacy is predicated on a value-neutral notion of acquisition – one that classifies learners. Both NLS and Bourdieu's work are useful in revealing the processes of the construction of these constructions and the implicit differentials which result in cultural factors acting as determinants of the outcomes of literacy education. This occurs because, in Bourdieusian terms, legitimated knowledge is more accessible to some than others because of inherent patterns of cultural capital embodied in individual habitus. Consequently, the affinities set up by education match the socially and cognitively generating structures of some more than others. To this extent, it is falsely dichotomous to suppose that there are oppositions between 'mid' and 'high' levels of theory, or between 'mid' and 'high', and 'low' levels. Bourdieu makes explicit what is implicit in NLS; namely, that each of these can be connected by the same theory of practice.

An ethnographic approach to the literacy classroom from both an NLS and Bourdieusian perspective sometimes seems to result in a view of that what is occurring there is a kind of conspiracy, as it appears to suggest that the field is set up to deliberately favour some groups of pupils over others. However, the central tenet of Bourdieu's work is that such processes and products are most often unreflected, since they are simply inherent in the logic of practice of fields – that is what they do! Indeed, the effects are all the more powerful because their provenance is 'misrecognised' within public discourses which legitimise policy and practice in terms of equity and inclusion. Is there an escape from this seemingly fatalistic conclusion? Yes, since these are systems which are constantly changing and being changed by the struggles of individuals and between fields themselves, which are inherent in the logic of practice whenever explicit moves are taken to alter structural forms. The next chapter explores this dilemma further. In this context, I conclude by raising the question of the practical usefulness of researching from the combined theoretical perspective of NLS and Bourdieu's approach.

In its crudest form, we might argue that bad research produces bad science. The linkage between research and policy (and practice) is not without contentious questions about the way one informs the other. However, we can conclude that research outcomes from approaches that do not offer as truthful a representation as possible of the pedagogic processes under consideration will lead to poor decisions about literacy in policy and practice. Finally, the bifurcation between an autonomous or constructed view of literacy is not just about politics and ideology, but about life skills in an increasingly complex, skill-hungry age. NLS and Bourdieu's theory of practice certainly furnish us with new tools of research so that better research will lead to better science, which itself will better inform policy. In this respect, NLS and Bourdieu's approach have a utilitarian mission as much as an epistemological one. Chapter 10 now explores how a synthesis of these two approaches might be more formally expressed, and what implications this new perspective has for research theory and practice, and the product of these endeavours.

10

A FUTURE SYNTHESIS

BOURDIEU, ETHNOGRAPHY, AND NEW LITERACY STUDIES

MICHAEL GRENFELL

Introduction

The main title of this chapter refers to a 'future synthesis'. However, as the rest of this book has made clear, actually, it is a 'present' synthesis. The contributors to it have already begun to combine New Literacy Studies and Bourdieusian social theory to create a framework delineating a methodological space, which we have referred to as classroom language ethnography. Chapter 9 looked at issues relating to the relationship between theory and practice, and the scope that the type of synthesis we have been advocating opened up for research into literacy presented in a series of practical case examples. Furthermore, it considered the usefulness of this approach for our conceptualisation of the literacy curriculum and, ultimately, a range of literacy events between teachers and students within the classroom. The present chapter takes these accounts as a starting point for a more formal statement on what this synthesis looks like in terms of principles of research practice. At the core of the chapter is an account of the elements involved in such an approach: the construction of the research object; conceptualisation of the research field and what constituents it is necessary to include in such an analysis; and the centrality of reflexivity. These are offered as guiding principles of research practice. However, we begin with a reconsideration of the underlying perspective which has guided the approaches used in the research in this book – Ethnographic – and further explore what 'theory of practice' signifies in this context.

Classroom Language Ethnography

The term *Classroom Language Ethnography* is a title, which has haunted much of the discussion in this book. What do we mean by it? To understand it, we might take each of its three words in reverse. We have seen that the term 'ethnography' itself is by no means unproblematic and, as a research approach, it has itself fragmented into various hybrid forms: linguistic, critical, realist, virtual, etc. However, all of these place themselves within a qualitative, naturalistic paradigm which begins with an intention to understand social systems in terms of their cultural patterns and artefacts. Participant observation is one of its key methodological principles: in other words, the researcher researches their subject not only as an observer, but by actual involvement in the very culture under study. To add the second word in our title phrase, therefore, 'Language' ethnography presupposes ethnographic study, which focuses on the differentiated language use and language patterns of the culture. Language, of course, has always featured in anthropological studies, and we have noted writers such as Hymes, perhaps the founding father of linguistic ethnography, whose work dates back to the 1960s, with its insistence on understanding the 'speech event' in terms of the social conditions which surround it. We might also remind ourselves, *en passant*, that language and culture almost became synonymous terms in the twentieth century when the very philosophy of man was predicated on a linguistic analogy which employed terms such as signs, discourse, syntax, structures, etc. Our three part title, 'Classroom Language Ethnography', therefore implies a naturalistic, socio-cultural research approach to classroom activity with a special focus on language and literacy. Even so, the term leaves significant scope for choice by each individual researcher about what is most suitable for a particular investigation: What type of ethnography? What are its key principles and terms? Which model of language is to be used? What are the implications/limitations of such a model? How is the classroom defined? What features of it are we most interested in and why?

Chapter 4 referred to how interest in language in the classroom originally concentrated on the form of language itself. The work of writers such as Barnes, Sinclair and Coulthard did much to highlight the structure of classroom discourse in terms of patterns of dialogue, questioning and answering. Nevertheless, although there was a qualitative dimension to their findings about language, socio-cultural conditions were largely overlooked. We have noted how traditional views of literacy were also preoccupied with language as a set of techniques and skills which pupils had to acquire in the course of their schooling. It was the advent of New Literacy Studies which challenged both of these views and placed both speech acts and literacy skills in their social and cultural contexts. NLS did much to highlight literacy's cultural construction; that is, as an aspect of learning and teaching that should be understood in social, political and ideological terms as well as through the technical aspects of language. In this respect, literacy moved from being a single autonomous set of skills to be a culturally defined construct. However, even in its most constructivist mode – a position that has much in common with Vygotsky's socio-psychological constructivism – there remain tensions between the particularity of agency and context and the necessity of academic narratives based on acknowledged and legitimated areas of scholarship. In extreme forms, this has resulted in the culture of classroom language being expressed only in academic terms, using all the associated patterns of conventional research practice rather than in its own terms. It is therefore in recognition of both the profile of agency and context, and of researchers' interests, that a synthesis with Bourdieu's social theory becomes most significant and most useful.

Bourdieu's own academic epiphany – from philosophy to sociology – came about as a result of intense ethnographic experience in the Béarn and Algeria. This personal experience was to reverberate throughout Bourdieu's entire career. Such facts are not cited out of biographical interest alone, rather they raise questions of relationships, experience, and motivations in undertaking ethnographic research. On the one hand, there is the danger for the researcher of being subsumed in the primacy of experience and failing to keep an objectifying distance with regard to the object of research. On the other hand, there is the temptation to enter the field with preformed views and ideas, expressed in existing theories which frame all that is seen (and allows only that which fits within the frame to be seen). Ethnographic experience – in the field – can be highly personal. It is also time consuming. It is unlikely that a researcher will achieve an understanding of any culture through a brief encounter of just a few weeks, or simply by periodic sampling. Bourdieu's own view was that it took him many years to be able to see the world through the eyes of an Algerian peasant: to understand what such an individual saw, what was important to him, and what strategies he adopted to gain what he wanted. This illustration is not simply anecdotal, since it raises generic questions about the nature of understanding and what is needed for its formation. Furthermore, it highlights what can and cannot be seen: the 'eyes' of a Parisian academic are always likely to be a 'world away' from those of a rural peasant; and yet, the former must cultivate the eyes of the latter if he is to understand how his actions come about. We have consistently argued that ethnographic research practice cannot be atheoretical – the researcher does not enter the field theoretically blind, but with their own theoretical *habitus* that will shape both how the object is investigated and the resultant outcomes. More generally, ethnographic researchers must consider the relationship between the research practices they adopt and their direct experiences of the culture which is to be explored and understood because what data are collected and how, and what procedures are undertaken to analyse them, all feed into the construction of the research object.

Several distinct types of educational theory and ways of theorising about literacy were discussed in the previous chapter. However, we might ask, what is it to understand from these theoretical positions, and in what way might they guide policy and practice – perhaps by placing them on the triangle explored in the last chapter? Ethnographic research generally lies on the right hand side of the triangle (Figure 9.5) and is concerned with the links between 'practice' and 'tacit knowledge' and 'fundamental educational theory (FET)' that is largely phenomenological. Bourdieu himself referred to this type of theory as 'ethno-methodological' (Bourdieu 1977b/1972: 3). In contrast, theory which lies on the left hand side of the model – from 'normative science' to 'justifying education principles (JEP)' to 'practice' – prioritises theory over practice. When 'theory' is put first like this, its power lies in its apparent potential to offer 'universal claims' to guide policy and practice. The goal of such theorising is a set of conditionally universal (and clearly specified) claims of the basic form: 'Given certain conditions, if such and such a type of event (A) occurs, it will be followed (or accompanied) by an event of type B' (Hammersley 1990: 104). Hammersley offers an example of this type of theory-building based on ethnography, what he calls 'differentiation-polarisation theory, drawing on work from Lacey (1970), Ball (1981) and Hargreaves (1967). He articulates this theory as follows: 'that differentiation within school amplifies the effects of social class distribution of cultural resources, thereby increasing inequalities in school performances and life chances' (p.106). In other words, if pupils are differentiated by streaming in schools, or banding, their school performance (and eventual life chances) follow a similar structure: the higher differentiated groups achieving more at school and in life and the lower differentiated groups achieving less. It follows that increasing differentiation increasing inequalities, and decreasing differentiation decreases them. Ultimately, there is 'polarisation'. In many ways, these statements do indeed make for 'good scientific theory': they are clear, liable to falsification and prediction, and can be matched against empirical data. However, this and its associated 'theories', would seem to have virtually nothing to say about the culture of the classroom, the socio-cultural provenance of the teachers and students, the interaction between the social and the cognitive, the way that classroom conditions are shaped by local and national framing structures, nor the underlying principles of practice which constitute them. In other words, the clarity of a theory like 'differentiation-polarisation theory' is at the expense of the personal, subjective, particular or contextual – in short, practical – aspects of theory which are central elements of NLS and Bourdieu's theory of practice. But, in what way is Bourdieu theoretical?

Bourdieu, of course, famously argued that he never 'theorised' as such; a statement itself which might seem surprising for all who find the conceptualisation of his discussion both highly theoretical and obtuse. Moreover, the 'theory effect', where *how* something is described becomes 'more real' that *what* is described, is one of Bourdieu's major charges against the 'scholastic fallacy' of believing in your own intellectualist worldview. Nevertheless, at the heart of Bourdieu's work, as we saw in Chapter 4, is a *theory* of practice. How is this theory articulated and what are the implications of its use?

Bourdieu's approach to investigating the social world is essentially empirical, in which he saw its relational and dynamic nature. Here, at a particular time and place, the changing structures and institutions of the social world are analysed (an external objective reading) at the same time as the nature and extent of individuals' participation in it (an internal subjective reading). These two distinct social logics are inter-penetrating and mutually generating, giving rise to 'structured' and 'structuring structures' (Bourdieu and Passeron, 1977a/70). Indeed, Bourdieu distinguishes between a theorist's viewpoint and a researcher's viewpoint: a theorist is interested in developing hypotheses to account for the particularities and functioning of an object of study (a move from 'Practice' to Justifying Educational Principles on the left hand side of triangle), whereas a researcher collects empirical data and analyses it in order to obtain a picture of how the 'real world' is constituted (this represents a move from 'Practice' to Fundamental Educational Theory on the right). Either of these viewpoints gives only a partial view if used alone. Bourdieu's approach does both, and more. His approach to the study of a social object can be described most simply as an on-going and reflexive interplay between the two positions – empirical investigation and theoretical explanation. In place of continued separation between the two positions, mitigated only by intensified interactions, Bourdieu advocates the fusion of theoretical construction and practical research operations – a theory of practice which is at one and the same time a practice of theory. Bourdieu, however, goes still further, arguing against simply adopting a scholastic view (from a distance). He sees the necessity for a return to practice and to the social world. Here, modes of thinking are necessary to understanding an object of study in relation to its *field* context and to the interests and positioning of the researchers themselves. Perhaps, the clearest example of this practical orientation in Bourdieu's own work is to be found in his early studies on education which could be argued to have led directly to his leadership of government reforms to the education curriculum in 1980s (see Bourdieu, 2008a)).

As noted in the *Outline to a Theory of Practice* (1977b/1972), Bourdieu sets out his theory of practice in terms of a series of 'breaks': from empirical knowledge; from phenomenological knowledge; from structural knowledge; and from scholastic (theoretical) knowledge itself (pp. 1–2). These breaks should not be seen as a series of exclusions; rather each theoretical position is retained and integrated into an overarching theory. In effect, we might understand these breaks as implying the addition of a fourth type of theory – *structural knowledge* – to the three previously identified in the triangle above). These forms of knowledge are presented as a tetradic model in Figure 10.1: as different types of knowledge recognised in ethnographic practice.

The key to the integration of these theoretical breaks is the addition of *structural knowledge* in relationship to the phenomenological, scientific and practical in order to indicate their essential structural nature. Indeed, we might say of such structural knowledge that it arises from practical action – that is the empirical cognitive acts of individuals in pursuit of their aims. Such an engagement involves a social context and individual agency – in Bourdieusian terms, field and habitus. However, it is important to understand it as an essentially constructivist aspect of human praxis – and from birth. Several epistemological principles follow from this account:

- That the primary cognitive act (i.e. that of a newborn child) takes place in a social environment and is essentially structural as it sets up intentional (what phenomenologists refer to as intensional) relations between the social agent and the environment.
- That environment includes both material and ideational structures.
- That the primary cognitive act therefore needs to be understood in terms of a search for social-psychic equilibrium, or control over Self, Objects and Others.
- That such an act – and subsequent acts – do not establish themselves in a value-neutral vacuum, but in an environment saturated with values and ways of seeing the world.

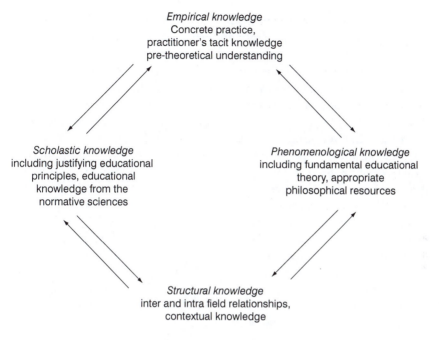

FIGURE 10.1 Bourdieu's epistemological breaks

- That such values and such ways constitute a preset orthodoxy into which agents are inducted.
- That such values and orthodoxies are dynamic and constantly evolving. However, their underlying logic of practice remains the same: they represent a certain way of seeing the world on the part of particular social factions of society.
- That way of seeing the world conditions and shapes the primary cognitive act in a dynamic relationship with individuals involved. In this way, individuals can be particular whilst all sharing commonalities with those immediately in their social environment.
- Both the particulars and the commonalities develop 'dispositions' to think and act in certain ways. The extent to which such dispositions are 'fired' depends on patterns of resonance and dissonance set up in the range of contexts in which individuals find themselves.
- The characteristics of orthodoxies, dispositions, and their underlying values are defined by the position particular social grouping hold in relation to other social groupings in the social space as a whole.
- That position is also structural and relational.
- Orthodoxies, values and dispositions express certain interests – those of the most dominant social groupings.
- In this way, there is a dialectical relationship between actual structures of social organisation and the structures of symbolic systems that arise from them.
- Nothing is pre-determined; everything is pre-disposed.

The world is infinitely complex. Any ethnographer struggles with representing that complexity. Faced with the multidimensionality, there seems to be a choice between two primary ways of tackling it. As noted above, the 'theoretical' approach held to be most robust and 'scientific' seeks to extract, simplify, and hypothesise on the basis of findings which can then be tested against further data analyses. However, a Bourdieusian approach to ethnography takes a different course; one which begins with the totality, accepts the complexity and seeks organising structures within it and their underlying generated principles. The logic of such principles is always to differentiate, but they do express themselves in different terms. In this way, the principles can be functionally operative at the same time as being misrecognised: if they were not, they would not be as effective. The whole of Bourdieu's conceptual universe – his theory of practice and the terms in which it is expressed (Habitus, Field, Capital, Disposition, Interest, Doxa, etc.), is predicated on this epistemological stance. However, it is a stance with practical implications. For example, social sciences sometimes use the concept of 'social class' as a primary classifier of social practice and outcomes. So, data is collected and similarities are grouped together under the social provenance of the individuals involved. A Bourdieusian approach is different in a way, one which is both more subtle and fundamental. In the common practice of sociology described, 'social class' becomes a pre-existing, independent variable. However, Bourdieu's intention was rather to construct a model of the *social space*, which accounts for a set of *practices* found there. These practices were to be seen as differentiating themselves according to observed differences based on the principles defining position in that social space. So, 'social classes' were a result of analyses. What is at issue here is not so much the *similarities* that classes share, but the *differences* between different classes. For Bourdieu, what we must do is 'construct social space in order to allow for the prediction of the largest possible number of differences' (1990d/1987: 3). What this results in therefore is less an account of 'social class' than a 'sociology of distinction' and differentiation, including its defining logic of practice and consequent social classification. A simple acknowledgement of 'distinction' as a basic human instinct is therefore not enough. Indeed, at one point Bourdieu takes exception with Veblen's view of 'conspicuous consumption'. For Bourdieu, it is not enough to understand consumers simply as needing to be conspicuous. Rather, it is necessary for individuals to be noticed in terms of specific signs of signification within a specific *field* at a particular place and time. In the same way, both in terms of the case examples of Part II of this book, and the example quoted above from Hammersley, it is not enough for those concerned just to distinguish themselves; they need to be distinct according to certain symbolic terms and values. Noticeably, students are often symbolically rich in their own terms whilst at the same seeming to be impoverished according to classroom language orthodoxies; as for example in the case of the African-American students in Chapter 8. As Bloome and Brown demonstrate, students are left with a dilemma: they either abandon their own base cultural values (with all that entails in terms of associated affinities) and embrace the 'new' orthodox values of literacy of the classroom; or, they assert their own heterodoxy and accept that it can only be valued from within. A third possibility may be developing a cultural ambidexterity which, as Chapter 8 showed, requires a special set of pedagogical conditions which can demonstrate the required linguistic and cultural improvisation.

I have used the example of social classes here, and have argued that, from a Bourdieusian perspective, they only exist to the extent to which they are acknowledged as such in practical contexts governed by the particular principles of their position in the social space. But, the same argument can be applied to any ethnographic classifier, including literacies. The purpose of this perspective is above all, perhaps, to indicate the processes and consequences of that acknowledgement. Anything else is indeed to confuse the 'things of logic with the logic of things' (Bourdieu, 1990d/1987: 117). Naming pupils in certain ways, without this view, is tantamount therefore to an insult as it acts as a form of *symbolic violence* in imposing a certain (scholastic) perspectivism.

In actually understanding the relationship between the ethnographic context and the social space as a whole – between social variation and differentiation – it is therefore necessary to draw a distinction between the *actual structure* of the social system in its *multidimensional* stratification, and the *symbolic products* which arise from it: 'In reality, the space of symbolic stances and the space of social positions are two independent, but homologous, spaces' (ibid.: 113). The consequent method, giving rise to structural knowledge, attempts to reconstruct the space of differences, or differential positions, and then to account for these positions as differential properties of the social space. For Bourdieu, such properties are valued and are consequently defined in terms of the types of *capital* outlined in Chapter 4; or what is symbolically valued within a particular *field* context. Regions of the field can be 'cut up' to see the functioning and positions of a range of *social groupings*. Again, in terms of the theory and practice set out in this book, such groupings may be of any kind – race, gender, academic achievement. Names and clusters resulting from classroom language activity can be defined in terms of criteria and affinities, and the way they are distributed across the total range of categories. Furthermore, the major 'primary' principles of differentiation – linguistic, cultural and social – can be attributed to both the *volume* and the particular *configuration* of (cultural, social and economic) *capital*. In other words, individuals and groups define themselves by how much *capital* they hold and the profile of *capital* types within that holding. In our present context, this is to be understood in terms of *linguistic capital*, *linguistic habitus*, and the way these are expressed and valued in particular *field* contexts. Differentiated social groupings 'on paper' can consequently be related to what exists 'in reality'. To the extent to which various individuals hold similar linguistic *capital* volumes and *capital* configurations (i.e. *habitus* and shared material conditions) in conjunction with others, they will constitute homogeneous, and thus identifiable, groups whilst remaining individually distinct as literacy students. Because they share a similar position in the overall structure of the *social space*, they share a similar *habitus*, which is identifiable in dispositional characteristics of literacy.

This four-fold approach has been referred to as 'a science of existential analytics', 'structural constructivism' (and 'constructive structuralism'), social philosophy, and reflexive sociology. A more accurate term might be 'structural phenomenological ethnography'. In the context of this book, for literacy and language, we have called this theoretical approach 'classroom language ethnography'. What is clear is that it requires certain ways of thinking and knowing. It produces theory that results not just from a simple piece of *declarative knowledge* – a theoretical statement that is falsifiable – but a declarative knowing that is also *procedural*, that holds within it the epistemological critique and synthesis that was necessary in order for it to be constituted in the first place – i.e. from the tensions between four distinct knowledge types. Hence, we might say that Bourdieu begins with a theory, which attacks theory. This way of knowing requires 'dialectical thinking', where more than one empirical and/or theoretical variable is held together at one and the same time; in the same way that a musician might need to hold more than one tone, tempo and rhythm together when playing a piece of music. The resultant knowledge may be contingent and temporary, and expressed as a sort of 'final vocabulary', to use a term employed by Richard Rorty to refer to 'the best we can do' at a particular point in time. However, this is a contingency which is not tentative, but rich, robust and critical – what Bourdieu refers to as 'radical doubt' and as:

> a temporary construct which takes shape for and by empirical work. Consequently, it has more to gain by confronting new objects than by engaging in theoretical polemics that do little more than fuel a perpetual, self-sustaining and too often vacuous metadiscourse around concepts treated as intellectual totems.
>
> (Bourdieu, 1989: 50)

In other words, Bourdieu's theory of practice holds in dynamic tension types of theory which struggle to 'fly apart'. It is therefore contingent, and temporally and spatially dependent. What it offers is a process which maintains the strengths of ethnography in terms of the subjective, particular and personal whilst also achieving characteristics of more scientific theory; in that it is objective, representational and generalisable.

In the Introduction to the *Invitation to a Reflexive Sociology* (1992) Wacquant draws attention to the 'fuzzy' nature of the resultant theory (pp. 19–26), noting that if Bourdieusian concepts are simply too 'blurred' and 'metaphorical' for some, one might respond with Wittgenstein's argument that when a concept 'depends on a pattern of life, then there must be some indefiniteness in it' (p. 23). In other words, if *habitus* is 'fuzzy', it is because life often presents itself in ways which are indefinite, incoherent, and even vague: its underlying differentiating logic of practice would not operate if it were not so. It is logical to the extent that it is practical. Such a view runs counter to those who wish to construct theories and concepts which are 'defined' and 'calibrated'. For Wacquant, the aim is consequently to 'produce a science of an imprecise, fuzzy, woolly reality' (p.23). However, as we have argued above, such a mission is far from being theoretically imprecise or epistemologically indeterminate. Rather, Bourdieu's theory emerges 'as a program of perception and of action, a scientific *habitus…*, which is disclosed only in the empirical work which actualises it' (1989: 50). This statement emphasises a point made elsewhere in this chapter about the significance of the researcher's own position with respect to and in the construction of the research.

I now turn to an explicit consideration of the essential features of approaching language classroom ethnography from a Bourdieusian perspective. There are three key aspects to this question: the construction of the research object; field analysis; and participant objectivation. There is a chronological element implicit in the order of these three aspects, because before undertaking a field analysis, attention needs to be given to the construction of the research object – participation in the research then raises questions of reflexivity. The three aspects might be understood as a series of consecutive research 'stages'. However, in another sense, they are each co-terminus, and must be seen as active at each stage as the research unfolds. Nevertheless, in the present context, and with this proviso in mind, the three key aspects are now discussed in turn.

The Construction of the Research Object

At one point, Bourdieu refers to the 'construction of the research object' as 'summum of the art' of social science research (1989: 51). A moment's reflection will reveal why this is so. As researchers, our choice of research topic is shaped by our own academic backgrounds and trajectories. To this extent, our research activity is a symbolic homology of the academic infrastructure with its various structural positions and groupings. I shall say more below about the effect of the academic field itself. For the moment, I want to focus on the research object itself. As has been noted on more than one occasion in this book, topics of research are not uncontested orthodoxies. Key aspects like 'learning' and 'teaching' are subject to intense argument about the terms of their representation. Of course, the same is true for 'classroom', 'language' and 'ethnography'. We have seen that 'ethnography' has also been conceptualised in different ways, as has the 'classroom' itself. Chapter 4 of this book showed the extent to which Bourdieu's theory of practice offered a major challenge to conventional approaches to language, literacy and linguistic study. Such approaches, concepts and terms themselves come articulated in words which seek to 'represent' them. This is why Bourdieu warns the would-be researcher to 'beware of words': Beware of them because words present themselves as if they are value-neutral, whilst in effect they are socio-historical constructions, taken-for-granted as expressions of 'common sense', but with specialist assumptions about their meanings and imbued with logically practical implications of such meanings. In practice, words are susceptible to a kind of 'double historicisation': first, a word is used to represent a certain phenomenon at a particular point in time – one which is often constructed and presented in a way which renders as transparent the social and historical aspects of its construction;

second, that dehistoricised form is then subject to further historicisation, as the original form is taken as the basis of fact from which further work and elaboration is operationalised. In this way, the most innocent word can carry within it a whole set of un-objectified assumptions, interests, and meanings which confuse the reality of representation with the representation of reality. Chapter 4 made the distinction between 'substantialist' and 'relational' thinking. In effect, it is so easy to (miss)take constructs as things in themselves rather than as sets of relations. To do one rather than the other – without knowing about it, still less acknowledging it – is to accept a whole epistemological matrix which has direct consequences for the way that an object of research is thought about, with the implications this error entails for the methodologies employed to collect and analyse data, and for the conclusions drawn as a consequence. Bourdieu offers the example of the word 'profession', making the point that as soon as it is taken as an *instrument*, rather than an *object* of analysis, a whole set of consequences follows. Moreover, such assumptions are not merely an innocent oversight, since one necessary modus operandi sets itself against another in a *field* competing for the limited *symbolic capital* that can be accrued from occupying a dominant position within it. This is no less true of the academic field. The word *literacy* can offer a further example. We saw in Part I how a traditional 'autonomous' concept of literacy – literacy as a set of technical skills – was opposed by the New Literacy Studies movement from the 1980s onwards; one which emphasised the social construction of literacy and, by implication, the ideological nature of the autonomous model. But, even NLS does not escape the challenge to objectify its own epistemological assumptions which reside in such key terms as 'ideology', 'social construction' and 'classroom discourse'. Indeed, each of the key concepts used in the analyses of the practical chapters of Part II might be similarly interrogated. As for the word *literacy* itself, it has become quite ubiquitous, and within the literature we can find reference to: *learning literacy, teaching literacy, emotional literacy, computer literacy, action literacy, reflection literacy, literacies* and others. All of which raises questions about the value, power and integrity of the word itself for representing both a product and process. Fuzzy indeed! But, with no epistemological bases on which to ground itself. We need to see such terms are employed by different factions of the academic field as an element in their struggles for dominant field positions. Many simply do not recognise the contested nature of 'literacy', and indeed do not want to recognise the use that the term has outside their own territory. To this extent, the 'construction of the research object' is often the most difficult methodological stage to undertake: first, because, its terms – the names of the game – are the product of history, and therefore which have developed a certain 'taken-for-granted' orthodoxy; second, because a whole set of specific interests are often co-terminous with seeing the world in this way. Bourdieu argues that to break from these risks 'relegating to the past' a whole set of thinking, hierarchically established by the history and consequent structure of the science field itself (Bourdieu, 1996/1992: 160). Jobs might literally be lost, careers ruined, etc.! There is often therefore resistance. What Bourdieu argues for is a combination of 'immense theoretical ambition' and 'extreme empirical modesty';

the constitution of 'socially insignificant objects' into 'scientific objects'; and the translation of 'very abstract problems' into 'concrete scientific operations' (1989: 51). His main method for doing this is through 'field analysis'.

Field Analysis (Classroom Language Ethnography)

As has been acknowledged at on more than one occasion in this book, the term 'ethnography' itself can be quite amorphous and ubiquitous. Very often it is used for any piece of qualitative research, or for research from a broadly socio-cultural orientation. Even established writers on ethnography are often unable to give a precise definition of just what it is or, somewhat paradoxically, are overly insistent on what does and does not constitute ethnographic research. Many of these dilemmas themselves issue from anthropology, which can be seen as a parent discipline to ethnography. It is worth pointing out that Bourdieu rarely used the 'ethnography' rubric, but did instead often did refer to 'ethnology'. The important distinction here is that if ethnography is concerned with the study of small groups and their contact with surrounding culture, ethnology aims more at cross-cultural comparisons, and the construction of a universal view of human history. Structural anthropology in general, and Lévi-Strauss's version in particular, would be good examples of this distinction. In a post-modern world, such a universalising mission has been heavily criticised, and consequently replaced with the alternatives – the cultural arbitrary and social relativity. In a sense, Bourdieu is equally critical of attempts to construct a totalising account of human action (in the way that Lévi-Strauss seems to do), all whilst paradoxically constructing a theory that does have 'an interest in the universal'. At the same time, Bourdieu's theory of practice needs to be seen as offering a stability against the apparent nihilistic reflexivity of the 'post-modern condition', albeit saturated with notions of 'radical doubt' and practical realism.

As noted above, even when educational research into language learning turned away from psychometric testing from the 1960s onwards, the alternative 'naturalistic' methods often did not take account of socio-cultural contexts, except in the broadest, general, background sense. As a result, so-called ethnographic research into language classrooms often amounts to little more that a narrative account of what is observed in situ with little underlying theory of research practice. Indeed, as in the case of 'grounded theory', there is still a sense that generalities can and should be generated from such localised contexts which 'speak for themselves'. Where language has been the main focus for analysis, the broader socio-cultural context of language discourse is often ignored or avoided. The structure of language – as for example, in Sinclair and Coulthard's work (op cit.) – is similarly allowed to speak for itself, as if the language in question did not occur in and in response to a particular pedagogical context, with all this entails in terms of socio-cultural conditions. The intent in using Bourdieu's theory of practice is to provide an approach which is as valid in the construction of the research project, as it is in carrying it out, and in analysis of resultant data. The same principles, the same theory of practice, orientate the researcher and the researched, the methodology and the resultant findings. But, how is it operationalised in practice?

It is perfectly possible to 'rethink' educational methodologies in terms of a Bourdieusian approach, for example, as with case studies that are common in educational and language research. Traditionally, case studies are used when 'how?' and 'why?' questions are being posed, when 'the investigator has little control over events, and when the focus is on contemporary phenomena within some real-life context' (see Yin, 1984: 13). These factors apply when there is an interest in *process* rather than *product*, and where authenticity of representation takes precedence over outcome. In an apparent echo of my earlier point about Bourdieu and research into real-life language education contexts, Bassey (1999) writes of 'fuzzy generalisations' as the end result of case study research, and as a way of highlighting the need to keep a balance between the particular and general significance in presenting research findings. Whilst case study research can, in some hands, be a recipe for a methodological free-for-all, there is no reason why it cannot also be guided by recognised schemes of analysis and recognised classificatory systems. Such formal/generic concepts can indeed be used for both explanatory and comparative purposes. The question is then which concepts and why? Clearly, from a Bourdieusian perspective, what is most important, both in constructing and analysing case studies, are the relational structures to be found within them; the logic of practice which generates and underlies them; and the symbolic products through which such relations are mediated. Such a research practice provides validity not so much in terms of traits or general commonalities, but through offering identifiable configurations within and between cases together with accounts of how these are formed and reproduced over time. In fact, Bourdieu's method is perfectly congruent with writers of the phenomenological-hermeneutic tradition, such as Dilthey (1988/1923), who argued that it was possible to discover general universals through the study of many particulars. Indeed, Bourdieu himself argued that a well constructed case ceases to be particular. We might even go so far as to describe Bourdieu's approach as 'structural phenomenology' of case; in other words, to see relational configurations as subjectively constituted in practice, but objectively 'constant'. So, whilst the manifestations of a process are constantly in flux, their underlying logic remains the same.

Such an approach must be understood as being both methodologically and epistemologically distinct. As similarly noted by Mitchell (1984), a *positivistic inference* (for example, statistics) involves conclusions drawn about the existence and frequency of two or more characteristics in a wider population from some sample of that population; whilst, on the other hand, a process where the analysis draws conclusions about the essential linkage between two or more characteristics in terms of a distinct systematic explanatory schema must be understood as a *logical inference*. The distinction between substantialist and relational thinking is also critically important here. In the first case, conclusions are drawn about the whole population from a sample of that population, whilst in the second it is the structure of the entire population that is most significant. Generalisation is then defined in terms of an underlying theory, and its unfolding nature, to which the case study is related; rather than the case study being seen as a discrete case, which may confirm or refute established 'truths' expressed in theory regarded as scientific within the academic field.

If we are to regard the case examples which interest us in terms of their field contexts, and thus, involving sites and agents which are to be understood as being constituted by structures which are both structured and structuring, we might broaden the perspective to the very construction of the case study itself. Thus, in creating a case study we are, in the process, *structuring a structure*, the structure of which can then be analysed in relational terms – as a *structured structure*. There is an epistemological homology between the *field* context and its representation. This is why, as part of the research process, it is so important to objectify the construction of the research object (which the researcher brings to the analysis) and indeed the consequent scientific *habitus* of the researchers themselves. Once this is understood, almost any data or locally present artefacts can be employed to create the case.

Clearly, a fully developed account of Bourdieu's methodological techniques and procedures are beyond the scope of this book, and would include a wide range of approaches to ethnographic and documentary material as well as the deployment of a number of statistical methods such as *Multiple Correspondence Analysis* (see LeRoux and Rouanet, 2010 for example). Indeed, it might be argued that Bourdieu was almost certainly the most empirical of the world leading generation of French intellectuals that included Foucault, Derrida, Barthes, Deleuze, Lacan, Althusser and Lyotard. There are a number of points that can be made about empirical research and data collection.

There is, in practice, a limit to what data can be collected. One can ask people something – in an interview or questionnaire; give them something to do and observe what happens; simply observe and record; or collect documents, photographs and artefacts and analyse them. There are examples of each of these in the chapters in Part II. It is also worth noting that ethnographic and naturalistic research seldom relies on only one form of data collection; instead accounts are built up from a range of triangulated sources. Today, we might use 'multimodal' approaches, where the same empirical source is looked at from a range of data perspectives. Such research does not preclude the use of statistics – Bourdieu used them extensively himself, as noted. For example, in his work on the peasant farmers of the Béarn, education, and culture, Bourdieu's discussions frequently include statistical analyses alongside first-hand accounts from individuals involved in the *field*. From this very earliest work, Bourdieu was insistent that one should not see quantitative and qualitative approaches as oppositional; all whilst recognising that 'statistics' are often used as a strategy to 'crush one's rivals' so to speak (see 1963) with the weight of objective 'fact'.

The key question for observational (ethnographic) methods is 'to observe *in what terms*'? This question relates to how the research object is constructed, the language of this construction, and the underlying principles and assumptions that construction which can easily be overlooked. Bourdieu at one point refers to the predicative statement used by logicians: 'The King of France is bald' (see for example, 1991: 250). The point is that by engaging in debate about whether or not the king is bald, one has implicitly accepted that there is indeed a king. By extension, to debate any attribute of the 'working class' is to have already taken on board the assumption that there is indeed 'a' *working class*, and further, that we are all agreed what it is and how it is represented. As referred to earlier, it was therefore no wonder that when a group of *lycéens* wrote to Bourdieu for support in their struggles against the then current educational reforms, he warns them against speaking of themselves in terms of *lycéens* in general, because this overlooks a whole social differentiation in actual social existence (2008b/2002: 181). His warning is similarly against those who speak *on* their behalf as much as those who would speak *of* them.

Language is slippery; all the more so when it is used to construct survey and interview questions. Bourdieu is interested in creating the 'conditions for the elaboration of truth' (2001/1982: 46); something that can only happen where everything in the research process is equally subject to 'objectification'. This is not the norm in conventional research practice. As a further example of the elusive nature of language, Bourdieu argues that the term 'public opinion' is a kind of auto-logical construction of the *habitus* of those constructing survey questions (1993/1984: 149–57). It does this by assuming that an opinion on something is available to all; that all opinions are of equal value; and that the questions themselves are valid ones. It does not therefore exist in reality. In reality, these are issues of competence, of consensus and of authenticity. So, questions such as 'Should teachers be allowed to go on strike?', or 'Should the curriculum be changed?', are more about the mobilisation of a pre-constructed opinion (and that pre-construction is never without *interest*!), often of those conducting the survey. Indeed the questions may be quite contrary to reality and should be better understood more as a series of *dispositions*. It is not only that 'public opinion does not exist', but that very often it is mistaken for what is taken as the 'truth' by the very groups being researched. 'By putting a microphone in front of a miner', Bourdieu argues 'many think that what you are going to get is the truth about miners' (2001/1982: 46), whilst, in reality, what is obtained is a representation of the union discourse of the previous thirty years! Similar misrepresentations can be found across a range of social groupings. For Bourdieu, this phenomenon amounts to a kind of 'dramatic auto-mystification' – that there is a source of social truth in the world that can be uncovered as a place of origin without reference to the prior conditions of enquiry. This is a kind of intellectual indulgence for Bourdieu. For him, the sociologist, or language researcher, must always be 'practically involved': they listen, enquire, and get interviewees to speak, all whilst putting everything under a critical discourse. This engagement itself implies a certain *modus operandi*. In effect, the sociologist can only re-present a particular point of view (of their object of research) by being capable of:

> taking account of all possible points of view ('to live all lives', as Flaubert said)…
> (to do this) to the extent that they are capable of objectifying themselves so
> that they can…understand that, in their place, they would be and think just
> like the objects of their research.

(Bourdieu, 1991: 5)

Such an ethnographic approach is exemplified by Bourdieu and his team in *The Weight of the World* (1999/1993). Here, Bourdieu warns against the type of conversational analysis which reads into each interview the contingent structure of a transaction (I-R-F, for example). Instead, he argues for an analysis of 'invisible structures', namely, the structure of the social space that organises it, the social space in which they are situated, and the past trajectories of those involved. It is necessary above all to ensure that an ethnographer does not project their own academic 'alter ego' into the interview and the objects of their analysis. As a consequence, in this study (op cit.), members of the investigation team were allowed to choose their own respondents from amongst and around the people they knew, because social proximity and familiarity help to reduce the symbolic violence implied by an interview when the interviewer is clearly coming from outside the field of experience of the interviewed. For Bourdieu, this helps to create the conditions of 'non-violent communication' (p. 608) between the investigator and the investigated. The end result is, contrary to normal ethnographic representations, a kind of 'realist construction' in which the authenticity of the primary empirical experience of the objects of research is clearly the source of the immanent generating structures found within it.

The aim is a 'constant improvisation of pertinent questions, genuine hypotheses based on a provisional, intuitive representation of the generative formula specific to the interviewee, in order to push that formula toward revealing itself more fully' (p. 613). However, Bourdieu also refers to the process of research as a 'spiritual exercise' since it also allows for the possibility of 'an induced and accomplished self-analysis'. He gives the example of a teacher who, after being interviewed, found consolation by understanding more about the social forces which acted upon her and rendered her life difficult (p. 470). It is well to note that the sort of ethnography we are discussing here is both a lengthy and delicate process. Moreover, such a process requires a constant return to past analyses in order to objectify them further in a way that is iterative. Such can be seen in the way that Bourdieu returned again and again to his own ethnographic analyses of the Béarnais peasants – 1962, 1972, 1989 (but see 2008a/2002) – in order to reconsider the structures immanent in what was observed there. But, what sort of structures?

So far, in this methodological discussion, we have considered issues about ethnographic data collection such as the terms of any observations, and the language of questionnaire and interview techniques. Of course, a Bourdieusian approach can employ any form of data or analysis in order to demonstrate underlying relational structures. As we have noted, statistical data can be as valid as qualitative data. A range of artefacts might also be employed as data sources. For example, Bourdieu refers to the way in which he has used Illness, Invalidity and Schooling Certificates in order to study the effects of the monopoly of state power (1989: 51). In Chapter 5, photographs of participants in the LETTER project are used; whereas in Chapter 6 the 3-D boxes made by pupils are included as part of the analysis. Nonetheless, we need some way to navigate through the various data sources which might be used in studying the structures underlying our objects of research.

'Field' is a primary analytical concept for Bourdieu; so much so, that 'field analysis' increasingly represented his main approach to research method. When asked by Loïc Wacquant (Bourdieu and Wacquant, 1992b: 104) what constituted such a 'field analysis' and how to proceed, Bourdieu described a relational methodology with three necessary steps. Put briefly these are:

> First, one must undertake an analysis of the position of the field vis-à-vis the field of power by considering particular events, institutions rather than through pre-existing historical narratives.
>
> Second, one must construct a mapping of the field itself, which shows it as the site of the objective structure of the relations between the positions occupied by agents who compete for legitimate forms of specific authority (*capital*).
>
> Third, one must analyse the habitus of agents in the field to identify the system of dispositions they have acquired by internalising a deterministic type of social and economic condition.

It should be noted that while the order, scale and emphasis of this general method varies, each of the three steps is essential. The precise application of this method in a *field* analysis is, of course, dependent on the research objects and on the particular times and places to which it is applied. Practical examples of such *field* analyses can be found elsewhere. See Grenfell (1996) and Hardy (2011) for applications to language based contexts, and Grenfell and Hardy (2007) for applications to artistic and cultural *fields*. These three inter-related steps can in fact be understood as the criteria for the 'structural knowledge' which was presented in Figure 10.1, and which acts as mediator between the subjectivity of Fundamental Educational Theory and the objectivity of Justifying Educational Principles.

Clearly, it is debatable as to what extent Bourdieu himself presented *field* analyses with each of these three elements represented equally; although invariably his empirical studies did include elements of all three. For classroom language ethnography, the first analysis really refers to the relationship between the literacy *field*, the pedagogical field and the field of state power. In our present case, this would specifically concern the way government language policy shapes what happens in schools and classrooms, for example, through official curricular documents, syllabuses, etc. Chapter 8 offers an example of this level of *field* structure, where the school curriculum and the expectations of literacy are set directly by state legislation and which, the author tells us, result in teaching methods which reflect the dominant values of a white majority. Such curricular documents define what is 'legitimate' in the *field*, which itself implies an underlying logic of differentiating practice against which schools, teachers and students can be judged. It is again worth noting that the latter must be seen in terms of relationships connected with particular positions in the knowledge *field*; for example, the varying status of school disciplines and acceptable pedagogies, what is and is not to be valued within the field. In Chapter 8, mastery of particular forms of literacy and literature are shown to be greatly valued in Princeton high schools as indicators of educational success. For

African-American students, whose cultural context prefers alternative literary forms and who have proved resistant to adopting these doxic forms, the literacy forms that the state legitimated curriculum presented an insurmountable, but necessary building block for any future achievement. Similarly, it is internationally recognised forms of literacy which are valuable to the Dalit women in Chapter 5 because they offer access to less dominated positions in the national *field*.

Field analyses are relational and the relations are ideationally constituted. However, the first step of an analysis also must include actual organisational structures, for example, by studying intermediary agencies between governments (ministries of education, for instance) and school/colleges. Such agencies may include examination boards, inspection services, and local education and teacher education authorities. In our present case, the point of focus here would be on language in education in policy and practice. Such an institutional 'mapping of the field' provides important information about the way that the local ethnographies are constructed.

A second step deals with these local ethnographies themselves, as they are concerned with functioning and structure of the *field* site itself. We have described the way that ethnographies are constructed as 'naturalistic accounts' of context. However, from a Bourdieusian perspective, the study of actual structural relations are always necessary. As noted, these relations arise in both structural organisations, and in the way ideas (curricular principles for examples) are expressed in practice through agents who occupy significant positions within the *field*. In Chapter 8, Bloome and Brown give such an account of how some African-American students are situated within a complex set of *field* relationships: between their school and other schools in the locality; between their teacher, the school literacy syllabus and the state-regulated curriculum; and between and within the participants in a collaborative research project about the practical construction of intertexuality in classrooms. Although the teacher acts in a particular classroom, in each individual exchange, there is expressed a whole institutional ethos originating from a particular language department, school, and the way the latter have interpreted state and national policies (doxa). What occurs in the classroom occurs in a value laden *social space* in which both material artefacts and linguistic discourse are immersed in a *field* where their particular forms are valued as cultural capital; for example, differentiated forms of literacy and other language practices. Rather than simply describing such a language classroom, or analysing the language to be found there in itself, a Bourdieusian approach therefore looks for structural relations within such a setting and the way these might be homologous to relations with agents outside the classroom. In this way, it is possible to locate the exact match and mis-match between what is and is not acceptable in linguistic terms, and the consequences for teacher, learner and the school.

In the final (third) step of a Bourdieusian approach, the *habitus* of the agents involved is analysed in terms of their own dispositions, identifiable in the particular capital they hold and the way this is expressed. Such expression might be found in an entire socio-cultural ethos, or in the particular pedagogy that they are applying. One illustration of this is to be found in the 'jazzy' language use of the teacher in Chapter 8 set against the dual cultural histories of her students. A further example can be found in Grenfell (1996) where *field* analysis shows how language teachers from a particular era of training exhibit different classroom practices in their approach to pupils as a result and, how these differences can be identified in actual questioning techniques. In other words, teachers have a certain 'pedagogical *habitus*' (which shapes what they do and why). In a similar manner, Pahl, in Chapter 6, explicitly examines the good match between the teacher's *habitus* – whose grandparents were miners and who claims to have loved art and design from an early age – and that of her seven-year-old pupils, the children of ex-miners who work enthusiastically and creatively at designing boxes. In each of these examples, *habitus* is dispositional, is valued according to dominant pedagogic capital, and is actualised in practice in classroom teaching. There are then relations of dominance derived from the *habitus* between the teacher, department and school (itself implying relations to state power), and the *habitus* of pupils themselves. Pupils come with a certain socio-cultural background – their own dispositional *habitus*. Rowsell, in Chapter 7, writes in a similar manner about how the outcomes of schooling for her students will be dependent on the way the ideational logic underpinning their own *habitus* resonates, or not, with the principles incarnate in the ethos of the school and the methods and content of the literacy curriculum. This system of convergence or divergence needs to be understood in terms of 'elective affinities', or dis-affinities, between schools and pupils, teachers and learners. The intention of classroom language ethnography is that these relations can be studied and identified in the language of classrooms by analysing them in terms of these three steps.

In a way, the three-step approach that Bourdieu suggested may appear to be overly schematic. However, it is worth emphasising that, although for analytical purposes it may be useful to keep the three steps separate, any ethnographic account will be constructed in a way which integrates the three of them to a greater or lesser extent. That being said, it is also worth emphasising that, and even though any one research project may focus on one step more than another, all three are necessary. Very often classroom ethnographies undertake only the second step of a full *field* analysis – omitting the broader socio-political *field*, and any analysis of individuals' inter-relationships within the *field*. Moreover, classroom ethnographies do not always focus on structures and relations within the classroom, nor take sufficient account either of external structuring influences or the individual, personal and professional *habitus* of those involved. Or, the focus becomes too biographical, where individual life histories go unanalysed and are expected to speak for themselves in a kind of affirmation of social uniqueness, and thus potential, instead of the researcher interpreting what occurs in terms of the interaction between generalities of socio-cultural and institutional context. Nonetheless, the scope for methodological improvisation is still enormous within these set parameters.

A Reflexive Approach?

In a sense, the main conviction behind a Bourdieusian approach to classroom language ethnography is not simply that in our normal operative state the world (in this case the language classroom) is not so much more complicated than we think, but that it is *more* complicated than we *can* think. The thinking tools that Bourdieu's method provides are intended as a way of opening up that complexity in order to provide new insights. However, it would be a mistake to consider the deployment of terms like *habitus*, *field* and *capital* as an end in itself, or that simply expressing data analysis with these words was a sufficient route to understanding and explanation. At its extreme, such an approach can result in little more than a *metaphorising* of data with Bourdieusian language. The three-level approach to data analysis outlined above is intended to be a key to avoiding such a reification of conceptual terms. However, there is a third vital ingredient for Bourdieu: reflexivity. We find it everywhere in his writing, but what are its practical implications for classroom language ethnography?

The whole focus on the construction of the research object we have discussed here is that it is partly an attempt to break with the 'pre-given' of the world, especially the academic one, and to rethink language and language pedagogy in a new way. As part of this process, reflexivity is more than a pragmatic option; it is rather an epistemological necessity. As we saw above, what Bourdieu is proposing is to break from 'scholastic knowledge' itself! In other words, the scholastic world of theory about language teaching and learning needs to be seen as being just as prone as the empirical world of language classrooms to acting on the basis of presuppositions created historically; so much so that there is indeed the danger of research knowledge becoming a kind of 'scholastic fallacy', where what is offered in the name of scientific knowledge is in actuality simply the reproduction of a certain scholastic relation to the world, and one indeed imbibed with its own interests. Bourdieu writes of three presuppositions which are key dangers in this potential 'misrepresentation' (see Bourdieu, 2000/1997: 10). First, there is the presupposition associated with a particular position in the social space; in other words, the particular habitus (including gender) as constituted by a particular life trajectory, and thus the cognitive structures which orientate thought and practice. Second, there is the orthodoxy of the particular site of the *field of language pedagogy itself* – its *doxa* – with its imperative to think (only!) in these terms, as they are the only ones acknowledged as legitimate in the *field*. Third, there is the whole relation to the social world implied by scholastic *skholè* itself; in other words, to see the former as substantive, given, and an object of contemplation rather than relationally – praxeologically – and existentially dynamic. Finally, therefore, in order to break from scholastic reason itself, it is, for Bourdieu, not sufficient simply to be aware through some form of return of thought to thought itself. Such actions are for him a part of the same scholastic fantasy that believes that thought can transcend thought and, in so doing, escape from all the socio-culturally constructed presuppositions listed above. Because these presuppositions are unconscious, implied and occluded in the very nature of thought itself, it is necessary to find another means to escape from them than the type of reflexivity commonly accepted by social scientists (for example, Alvin Gouldner). For Bourdieu, the necessary alternative is through a process of 'participant objectivation', or the 'objectification of the objectifying subject':

> I mean by that the one that dispossesses the knowing subject of the privilege it normally grants itself and that deploys all available instruments of objectification…in order to bring to light the presuppositions it owes to its inclusion in the object of knowledge.

(ibid.)

Social scientists, language researchers or classroom ethnographers are called on to apply the same methods of analysis to themselves as to their object of research. What this means, in effect, is to see their own research *field* in terms of *habitus*, *field* and *capital*, and to objectify their own position within it. Bourdieu attempted such a procedure himself in books such as *Homo Academicus* (1988/1984) and *Sketch for a Self-analysis* (2004). However, one point is crucially clear: although this undertaking can be attempted on an individual basis, and is partly necessitated by a personal epistemological imperative, what is even more important is that participants in a particular academic field, here language education, commit themselves to a similar process of reflexivity as a way of showing up the limits of its own science. Bourdieu is perfectly aware that such an activity runs counter to the conventional underlying logic of practice of the scientific *field*, with its interest in asserting its own worldview in competing for a dominant position in the academic *field* overall. As a result of the latter, there is often a reluctance on the part of academics to recognise and acknowledge the limits of thinking that a truly reflexive process would reveal. For Bourdieu, it is the particular mission of sociology – or at least his version of sociology – to insist on this reflexive stance. Indeed, anything else is a kind of ultimate act of scholastic bad faith.

It is possible to return this call to the *fields* of literacy and classroom language ethnography. We have noted that the term 'literacy' is itself open to a range of interpretations, each of which might be seen in terms of positions spread out across the academic *field*. The *autonomous* versus *ideological* versions of literacy are one possible opposition, but we have seen that there are other conceptualisations of literacy competing for recognition and *field* dominance. Here, New Literacy Studies can be seen to exist in a form which is bounded by specific principled relations to a range of epistemological and practical orthodoxies. Such conceptual boundaries define possibilities and limitations; for example, in terms of integrating the social and cognitive within an authentic socio-cultural framework. An example is provided for us by one branch of language research, linguistic ethnography, which has become a prominent methodological approach in recent years, and used in Part II; one which needs to be understood as a hybrid academic force situated somewhere between linguistics and ethnography. Here, the conviction is that 'ethnography opens linguistics up…and linguistics ties ethnography down' (Rampton 2007: 8). In many ways, this strand of language research can be seen to be a welcome synthesis of quantitative and qualitative approaches, the objective and subjective, one which parallels the move we are advocating towards a relational and structural classroom language ethnography. However, even here, it is necessary to 'objectify' both 'linguistic ethnography' in terms of its own epistemological and institutional structures. Such a *reflexion* (sic) shows up organisational and epistemological relations with real consequences in terms of method and resultant knowledge outcomes (see Grenfell 2010 for further discussion). The same would be no less true for classroom language ethnography.

In Conclusion

Bourdieu makes its clear that an undertaking based on his theory of practice may result in a downplaying of attributable research significance: 'to pay a higher price for truth while accepting a lower profit of distinction' (1991: 34). But, then adds 'the truth is that truth is at stake' and, to this extent, there is no authentic alternative but to follow its own logic. As has been argued here, such truth is only possible after a certain break from both the practical and theoretical worlds which are conventionally on offer through the addition of a knowledge form concerned with relationships and with structure. The result must be seen in terms of a new way of knowing – a *metanoia* or 'reflexive objectivity'. This itself involves a conversion to a new type of scientific *habitus*, characterised by what has been called praxeological knowledge. Such a conversion needs to be understood as both being dispositional and collective, rather than simply oppositional and individualistic. What is called for then is a revolution of an entire way of thinking within the community of language and literacy researchers. For Bourdieu, such a revolution is not simply a question of changing minds but changing the conditions in which minds are formed, which itself involves different intellectual environmental conditions: 'To change the world, one has to change the ways of world-making, that is, the vision of the world and the practical operations by which groups are produced and reproduced' (1989: 23). A Bourdieusian epistemology of practice provides the concepts for such a change in world making. In this respect, it is not simply the way of thinking that must change but the way that way of thinking is constructed that must also change. When applied to the language classroom, the result is what we have been developing as 'classroom language ethnography'.

As we have shown in this and earlier chapters, classroom language ethnography in Bourdieusian terms entails a series of specific characteristics. First, it must be empirical and be specific to a particular time and place. Second, it must be reflexive to the extent that it takes account of the researchers' own interests and experience in relation to the language classroom in order to 'objectify the objectifying subject'. Third, it should be iterative and cyclic, so that outcomes remain open to revision in the light of future investigations. But, the most significant defining characteristic of classroom language ethnography is that the analysis must be a relational one. The process of investigation must therefore necessarily include three distinct types of relationships, each of which should themselves be considered in relation to each other, that is:

- the relationships between the large scale economic, cultural and political contexts and the language pedagogy events studied in order to show how the one influences and shapes the functioning of the language classroom (the relationship between the *field* of language education and the *field* of power);
- the inter-relationships between key educational organisations and state institutions, and, the individuals who are engaged in the particular social and pedagogical language activity (the relationships between agents and *field* institutions);
- the relationships of similarity and difference between the characteristics of individual *field* participants, including the most dominant (categorisation of the *habitus* of a range of individuals).

Such an analysis offers a procedure for examining the practical functioning of literacies in their real-life socio-cultural settings, a process which shows clear relationships between subjective experience and objective understanding. This approach promotes a way of working in which structural knowledge derived from it contributes to a form of theoretical knowledge, that is now truly based on the actuality of practice. The theoretical (praxeological) knowledge arising from such an undertaking can then be seen as forming part of a knowledge base which itself adds to our pool of understanding of literacy and the classroom as constituted by the normative sciences.

11

CONCLUSION

MICHAEL GRENFELL

This book began by describing its content as a kind a journey, one that brought together classrooms, language and ethnography to create a new perspective on literacy. Language in education in general, and literacy in particular, have been at the core of our concerns in producing it. In the Introduction, we acknowledged the long history of research and scholarship into education *and* language, and language *in* education. We also recognised the shift in research perspectives in each of these fields that took place from the mid-century point, and the impact that this orientation had on methodology, theory and practice. There is little doubt that classroom based research increasingly took on qualitative approaches from this time; ones which looked at the 'culture' of classrooms. Yet, so-called 'naturalistic' research had less impact on language research in general, and language in education specifically, preoccupied as it often was with the form of pedagogic discourse and the structure of utterances. The rise of New Literacy Studies was an early acknowledgement of the necessity to view language in education through a socio-historic lens. In order to do so, some kind of anthropological approach was necessitated, and has indeed been realised in various attempts at classroom language ethnographies. However, such ethnographic perspectives raise issues of theory, practice and method. Ultimately, the aim of this book has been to develop these aspects of literacy research from both a NLS and Bourdieusian perspective.

Therefore, as well as a journey, the book can in some respects also be understood as a kind of 'meeting point' – of different traditions, perspectives and approaches. Part I presented three of these: Ethnography, New Literacy Studies and Bourdieu's sociology. The first chapter on ethnography offered an account of many of its basic tenets, and the way language needed to be seen as central to its concerns. However, the chapter also highlighted the complexity of issues involved and the scope for individual interpretation and adoption. As noted at different parts of the book, this breadth of approach has occasionally led to diametrically opposed visions of just what it is to be 'ethnographic', with certain of its defining principles openly contested by those working in the *field*. The second chapter on New Literacy Studies considered just where it came from, its *raison d'être*, and why it was needed. We have seen the contrast that needs to be drawn between an 'autonomous' view of literacy and a more socio-culturally sensitive one. It has been noted that there is in fact no such thing as 'literacy' in the singular, but multiple forms of literacy, each of which has their own *field* of practice. It is in understanding such 'fields of practice' that ethnographic approaches have shown themselves most useful. However, and partly because of its polyvalent nature, ethnography can lead to an overly personalised approach to language in education; one which makes use of a range of narrative material – poetics, politics, fiction, visuals, personal accounts, and classroom realia – in its accounts. Such different perspectives and methods can lead to fragmentation of research practice, and the basic principles of science underpinning it. The use of Bourdieu has therefore partly been to provide a surer epistemological base: one with a more explicit theoretical underpinning and established research practice. The consequent aims are two-fold: first, to offer a more philosophically rooted version of ethnography, and therefore one with a more epistemologically charged set of concepts and methods; second, and by doing so, to extend and deepen insights into literacy events which conventional qualitative approaches do not provide. The third chapter in Part I presented the background to Bourdieu and gave account of the main principles lying behind his theory of practice.

Part II of the book presented a series of researchers working, in various combinations, with language in education in a socio-culturally sensitive way, thus coming from a New Literacy Studies background and, to a greater or lesser extent drawing on angles and perspectives emerging from an engagement with the work of Pierre Bourdieu. The LETTER project in Chapter 5 highlighted distinct cultural relations between the Dalit women under discussion, those involved in 'training' them, and the UK-based researchers occupied in working with both. We saw the way that the unconscious can be made conscious, how fundamental aspects of communication were involved in the subordinate and super-ordinate positions created by the structural relations established between internal and external literacy forms, and the way these were played out in educational contexts. Here, we saw that the issue is not so much that particular literacy events are arbitrary in terms of underlying values, but that such values always need to be seen as a symbolic expression of the particular interests that generate them in the first place. We have noted Bourdieu's claim that the purpose of his brand of social philosophy was indeed to see the world in a new way – a 'new gaze' – what he termed 'metanoia'. This 'new sight' is apparent in our understanding of the literacy events of the Dalit women, but also involved both the trainers and the researchers working with them. A new way of seeing things is also evident in the creative art project described in Chapter 6. Here, the structural relations inherent in the classroom, it surrounding external context, and the policy world of power enshrined in official documents is clearly influential in what actually occurs in classroom practice. We saw the way that both this external context and the 'pedagogic habitus' of the teachers involved can be observed in terms of being 'sedimented' in literacy events embedded in the classroom discourse; in other words, actualised in practice. Creativity then arises in this 'coming together' of these sources and the (often) clash that takes place in their interaction. As a consequence, we saw how methodologically it was necessary first to 're-conceptualise' classroom language ethnography in terms of *field* relations and the structural articulation of principles of practice set up between them. Moreover, that we need to concern ourselves with the particular habitus of those involved in the actual literacy event; in other words, the generating structures of individuals which, although derived from their own socio-cultural background, predispose them to think and act in certain (creative) ways in the face of present imperatives and necessities.

Habitus was also at the centre of the Chapter 7, where individual students worked on an Odyssey theme in a series of autobiographical films. Here, the innovative nature of the project set it outside the conventional demands of official curricula; indeed, this approach was somewhat justified by the fact that the students involved were deemed as underachieving in established school practices. What emerged is a series of individual stories, themselves expressing 'slices of life' – a kind of 'fractal habitus'. We can see the process underlying the project as an externalisation of aspects of life-history – of 'fractal habitus' – and thus their re-internalisation as a form of reintegration. In Bourdieusian terms, this would be seen as an Objectivation of Subjectivity which, once objectified is re-subjectified as part of the artistic engagement. One of the features of Chapters 6 and 7 is the reflexive nature of the researchers' relationship with the object of research. In Chapter 6 we saw the distinct perspectives emerging between the teacher involved and the researcher. Chapter 7 also has the researcher reflecting on her own position within the research, and thus the different views to be found between those involved. The studies to be found in Part II are real-life empirical events. They sometimes lack uniformity of approach and they are occasionally partial or messy in their actuality. However, they do provide us with the means to objectify the main elements of our classroom language ethnography from a Bourdieusian perspective. Consequently, they demonstrate the way that Bourdieu provides us with an understanding that is both stable but dynamic, and that concepts such as *field* and *habitus* are central for exploring the relations inherent in the language classroom. These concepts are also at the core of the literacy events described in Chapter 8. Here, once again, is the issue of the relation and values at play in a classroom where the pupils and teachers do not come from the 'dominant culture'. The authors here describe a kind of 'improvisation' or play being set up between the legitimate and the illegitimate, the consecrated and the non-consecrated forms through which the values of conformity and non-conformity are expressed. Such value products amount to '*cultural capital*' in Bourdieu's terms; in other words, the medium for entry to and exclusion from what is considered acceptable in terms of literacy. As highlighted in Chapter 10, the fact that this relation implies certain dilemmas of belief and behaviour on the part of the students – what Bourdieu calls a 'double bind' necessitated by the demands for a 'double consciousness' – needs also to be understood in terms of the extra level of socio-cultural ambidexterity demanded from these students if they are to remain true to themselves and their background whilst embracing the dominant culture of the classroom; one which will eventually lead to their ultimate destiny in terms of academic success or failure.

It is evident that Parts I and II include an enormous amount of material; both principled and empirical. Indeed, we might view these in terms of a whole series of dichotomous oppositions: fact and fiction; discussion and exemplification; routine and method. However, at base, these are essentially about individuals involved within a social context: And, here, there is a new set of relations to be seen in terms of structures and the values inherent in them: researcher and teacher; teacher and student; classroom and schools; schools and government policies. Fundamentally, what all these dualities involve, however, are issues of empiricism and science; in other words, how do we capture the real world and present it in an authentic manner – in all its complexity and sophistication – and express that representation in a way that is objective, and liable to public scrutiny? This question lies at the heart of Part III.

We began this part with a chapter that concerned itself with the polyvalent nature of theory within a social context such as education. Here, we saw that it was not just a question of the character of theory, but its provenance, what could and could not be expressed in theory, and the essential characteristics of different forms of theory. Once, again, structural relations lay at the core of the discussion: between the individuals concerned, their location in time and place, their activity, and intentions. The practical chapters of Part II furnished us with further exemplification – an objectification of objectified account of empirical events – to explore such relations in a variety of terms: phenomenological, socio-cultural, pedagogic, scientific. Chapter 9 concluded this discussion by referring to the 'practice of theory' since it has become apparent in the course of the book that any practical activity does imply an underlying theoretical stance – whether explicit or implicit. Ipso facto, ethnography can never be carried out in a realm of theoretical neutrality, or whilst maintaining a position of epistemological abstention. Indeed, the whole argument of Chapter 9 was that classroom language ethnography needs to be guided not only by principles *of* theory and *of* practice but by a theory *of* practice. Of course, such a statement returns us to the sociology of Bourdieu and, exactly, the theory of practice that articulates his own methodological approach to the study of social contexts. For Bourdieu, ethnography must be shaped by a series of epistemological issues and questions which pertain to the nature of the scientific endeavour itself and the character of the resultant knowledge. We saw in Chapter 10 some of the key elements to such an approach and in the 'stages' which must be considered when undertaking ethnography from this perspective: the construction of the research object, the three-level method for field-analysis, and the reflexivity that such an approach necessitates.

We have described the book as a meeting point – of ethnography, NLS and Bourdieu – and also as a journey – from theory to practice to theory again. In conclusion, our main message must be that literacy and language in education do indeed need to be approached from the direction of ethnography. NLS has provided a good foundation for such an ethnography but Bourdieu provides a further extension to this field of study by offering a more philosophically informed theory of practice for classroom language ethnography. As stated at the outset, such a synthesis must surely offer a fresh perspective on language in classrooms, literacy events and the significance they have in the processes of pedagogic discourse.

BIBLIOGRAPHY

Adams, M. (1993) 'Beginning to read: an overview' in R. Beard (ed.) *Teaching Literacy Balancing Perspectives*. London: Hodder & Stoughton.

Agar, M. (1980) *The Professional Stranger: An Informal Introduction to Ethnography*. New York: Academic Press

Agar, M. (1995) *Language Shock: Understanding the Culture of Conversation*. New York: William Morrows.

Aikman, S. (1999) *Intercultural Education and Literacy: An Ethnographic Study of Indigenous Knowledge and Learning in the Peruvian Amazon*. Amsterdam: Benjamins.

Alvermann, D. E. and McLean, C. (2007) 'The nature of literacies' in A. Berger, L. Rush and J. Eakle (eds), *Secondary School Reading and Writing: What Literacy Reveals for Classroom Practices*. Urbana, IL: National Council of Teachers of English, pp. 11–35.

Anderson, A. B., Teale, W. H. and Estrada, E. (1980) 'Low-income children's preschool literacy experiences: some naturalistic observations', *Newsletter of the Laboratory of Comparative Human Cognition* 2, 59–65.

Anderson, G. (1989) 'Critical ethnography in education: origins, current status and new directions'. *Review of Educational Research,* 59, 3, 249–70.

Anderson, R., Hiebert, E., Scott, J. and Wilkinson, I. (1985) *Becoming a Nation of Readers*. Washington, DC: National Academy of Education.

Atkinson, P. (1990) *The Ethnographic Imagination: Textual Constructions of Reality*. New York: Routledge.

Au, K. (1980) 'Participation structures in a reading lesson with Hawaiian children'. *Anthropology and Education Quarterly*, 11, 2, 91–115.

Baker D. A., Street B. V. and Tomlin, A. (2003) 'Mathematics as social: understanding relationships between home and school numeracy practices', *For the Learning of Mathematics* 23, 3, 11–15.

Bakhtin, M. (1935/1981 trans.) *The Dialogic Imagination*. Austin, TX: University of Texas Press.

Baldwin, J. R., Faulkner, S. L., Hecht, M. L. and Lindsley, S. L. (eds) (2006) *Redefining Culture: Perspectives Across Disciplines*. Mahwah, NJ: Lawrence Erlbaum Associates.

Ball, S. (1981) *Beachside Comprehensive: A Case Study of Secondary Schooling*. Cambridge: Cambridge University Press.

Banaji, S. with Burn, A. and Buckingham, D. (2006) *Rhetorics of Creativity: A Review of the Literature*. London: Creative Partnerships.

Banks, O. (1968) *The Sociology of Education*. London: Batsford.

Banquedano-Lopez, P. , Solis, J. and Kattan, S. (2005) 'Adaptation: the language of classroom learning'. *Linguistics and Education,* 16, 1–26.

Barnes, D. (1976) *From Communication to Curriculum*. London: Penguin Books.

Barnes D. , Britton J. and Torbe, M. (1969) *Language, the Learner and the School*. London: Penguin Press.

Barnes, D. and Todd, F. (1977) *Communication and Learning in Small Groups*. London: Routledge and Kegan Paul.

Bartlett, L. and Holland, D. (2002) 'Theorizing the space of literacy practices', *Ways of Knowing,* 2, 1, 10–22.

Barton, D. and Hamilton, M. (1998) *Local Literacies: Reading and Writing in One Community*, London: Routledge.

Barton, D. , Hamilton, M. and Ivanic, R. (2000) *Situated Literacies: Reading and Writing in Context*. London: Routledge.

Barton, D. and Ivanic, R. (1991) *Writing In The Community*. Newbury Par, CA: Sage

Bassey, M. (1990) *Case Study Research in Educational Settings*. Milton Keynes: Open University Press.

Baynham, M. (1995) *Literacy Practices: Investigating Literacy in Social Contexts*. London: Longman.

Baynham, M. and Baker, D. (2002) '"Practice" in literacy and numeracy research: multiple perspectives'. Editorial to special issue of *Ways of Knowing*, 2, 1, 1–9.

Baynham, M. and Prinsloo, M. (eds) 2001 'New directions in literacy research: policy, pedagogy, practice'. Special issue of *Language and Education,* 15, 2 and 3.

Becker, H. (2000) 'The etiquette of improvisation'. *Mind, Culture and Activity,* 7, 3, 171–6.

Berger, P. L. and Luckmann, T. (1971) *The Social Construction of Reality*. Harmondsworth: Penguin.

Bernstein, B. (1971) *Class, Codes and Control, Vol. 1*. London: Routledge and Kegan Paul.

Bernstein, B. (1990) *The Structuring of Pedagogic Discourse*. London: Routledge.

Besnier, N. and Street, B. (1994) 'Aspects of literacy' in T. Ingold (ed.) *Encyclopedia of Anthropology*. London: Routledge.

Brandt, D. (2001) *Literacy in American Lives*. Cambridge: Cambridge University Press.

Brandt, D. and Clinton, K. (2002) 'Limits of the local: expanding perspectives on literacy as a social practice'. *Journal of Literacy Research,* 34, 3, 337–56.

Bloome, D. (1983) 'Reading as a social process', in B. Hutson (ed.) *Advances in Reading/ Language Research,* vol. 2. Greenwich, CT: JAI Press, pp. 165–95.

Bloome, D. (2003) 'Anthropology and research on teaching the English language arts', in J. Flood, J. Jensen, D. Lapp and J. Squire (eds) *Handbook of Research in Teaching the English Language Arts*. Mahwah, NJ: Erlbaum, pp. 53–66.

Bloome, D. and Carter, S. (2001) 'Lists in reading education reform'. *Theory Into Practice,* 40, 3, 150–7.

Bloome, D. , Carter, S. , Christian, B, Otto, S. and Shuart-Farris, N. (2005) *Discourse Analysis and The Study of Classroom Language and Literacy Events: a Micro-Ethnographic Perspective*. Mahwah, NJ: Lawrence Erlbaum Associates.

Bloome, D. , Puro, P. and Theodorou, E. (1989) 'Procedural display and classroom lessons'. *Curriculum Inquiry,* 19, 3, 265–91.

Borko, H. and Eisenhart, M. (1989) 'Reading ability groups as literacy communities', in D. Bloome (ed.) *Classrooms and Literacy*. Norwood, NJ: Ablex, pp. 107–34.

Bourdieu, P. (1958) *Sociologie de l'Algérie* (new revised and corrected edition, 1961) Paris: Que Sais-je.

Bourdieu, P. (1962a) *The Algerians* (trans. A. C. M. Ross). Boston, MA: Beacon Press.

Bourdieu, P. (1962b) 'Célibat et condition paysanne', *Études rurales*, 5–6, 32–136.

Bourdieu, P. (with Darbel, A. , Rivet, J. P. and Seibel, C.) (1963) *Travail et travailleurs en Algérie*. Paris, The Hague: Mouton.

Bourdieu, P. (with Sayad, A.) (1964) *Le Déracinement, la crise de l'agriculture tradionelle en Algérie*. Paris: Les Editions de Minuit.

Bourdieu, P. (1971a/1967) 'Systems of education and systems of thought', in M. F. D. Young (ed.) *Knowledge and Control: New Directions for the Sociology of Education*. London: Macmillan ('Systèmes d'enseignement et systèmes de pensée', *Revue Internationale des Sciences Sociales*. XIX, 3, 338–88).

Bourdieu, P. (1971c) 'Intellectual field and creative project', in M. F. D. Young (ed.) *Knowledge and Control: New Directions for the Sociology of Education*. London: Macmillan ('Champ intellectuel et projet créateur', *Les Temps Modernes*, Nov. , 865–906).

Bourdieu, P. (1972) 'Les stratégies matrimoniales dans le système de reproduction', *Annales*, 4–5, 1105–27.

Bourdieu, P. (with Passeron, J. -C.) (1977a/1970) *Reproduction in Education, Society and Culture* (trans. R. Nice) London: Sage (*La Reproduction. Eléments por une théorie du système d'enseignement*. Paris: Editions de Minuit).

Bourdieu, P. (1977b/1972) *Outline of a Theory of Practice* (trans. R. Nice) Cambridge: Cambridge University Press (*Esquisse d'une théorie de la pratique. Précédé de trois études d'ethnologie kabyle*. Geneva: Droz).

Bourdieu, P. (1977c) 'The economics of linguistic exchanges' (trans. R. Nice) *Social Science Information*, XVI, 6, 645–68.

Bourdieu, P. (with Passeron, J. -C.)(1979/1964) *The Inheritors, French Students and their Relation to Culture* (trans. R. Nice) Chicago, IL: The University of Chicago Press (*Les héritiers. Les étudiants et la culture*. Paris: Les Editions de Minuit).

Bourdieu, P. (1986b) 'The forms of capital', in J. Richardson (ed.) *Handbook of Theory and Research for the Sociology of Education*. New York: Greenwood Press.

Bourdieu, P. (1987) 'What makes a class?' *Berkeley Journal of Sociology*, 32, 1–18.

Bourdieu, P. (1988/1984) *Homo Academicus* (trans. P. Collier). Oxford: Polity (*Homo academicus*. Paris: Les Editions de Minuit).

Bourdieu, P. (with Wacquant, L.) (1989) 'Towards a reflexive sociology: a workshop with Pierre Bourdieu'. *Sociological Theory*, 7, 1, 26–63.

Bourdieu, P. (1990a/1980) *The Logic of Practice* (trans. R. Nice). Oxford: Polity (*Le sens pratique*. Paris: Les Editions de Minuit).

Bourdieu, P. (with Boltanski, L. , Castel, R. and Chamboredon, J. C.) (1990b/1965) *Photography. A Middle-brow Art* (trans. S. Whiteside) Oxford: Polity (*Un Art moyen. Essai sur les usages sociaux de la photographie*. Paris: Les Editions de Minuit).

Bourdieu, P. (with Darbel, A. and Schnapper, D.) (1990c/1966) *The Love of Art: European Art Museums and their Public* (trans. C Beattie and N Merriman). Oxford: Polity Press (*L'Amour de l'art. Les musées d'art et leurs public*. Paris: Les Editions de Minuit).

Bourdieu, P (1990d/87) *In Other Words: Essays Towards a Reflexive Sociology*. (trans. M. Adamson). Oxford: Polity Press (*Choses Dites*. Paris: Les Editions de Minuit).

Bourdieu, P. (1991) 'Introduction à la socioanalyse', *Actes de la recherché en sciences socials*, 90, 3–6.

Bourdieu, P. (1992a/1989) 'Principles for reflecting on the curriculum', *The Curriculum Journal*, 1, 3, 307–14 (*Principes pour une réflexion sur les contenus d'enseignment*).

Bourdieu, P. (with Wacquant, L.) (1992b) *An Invitation to Reflexive Sociology* (trans. L. Wacquant). Oxford: Polity Press (*Réponses. Pour une anthropologie réflexive*. Paris: Seuil).

Bourdieu, P. (1992c) *Language and Symbolic Power*. Cambridge: Polity Press.

Bourdieu, P. (1993a) *The Field of Cultural Reproduction*. New York: Columbia University Press.

Bourdieu, P. (1993b/1980) *Sociology in Question* (trans. R. Nice). London: Sage (*Questions de sociologie*. Paris: Les Editions de Minuit).

Bourdieu, P. (with Passeron, J. -C. and De Saint Martin, M.) (1994/65) *Academic Discourse*. Oxford: Polity (*Rapport Pédagogique et Communication*. The Hague: Mouton).

Bourdieu, P (1996/1992) *The Rules of Art* (trans. S. Emanuel). Oxford: Polity Press (*Les Regles de l'Art. Geneses et structure du champ litteraire*. Paris: Seuil).

Bourdieu, P. (1996/1989) *The State Nobility: Elite Schools in the Field of Power* (trans. L. C. Clough). Oxford: Polity Press (*La noblesse d'état. Grandes écoles et esprit de corps*. Paris: Les Editions de Minuit).

Bourdieu, P. (1998a) *Acts of Resistance: Against the New Myths of our Time* (trans. R. Nice) Oxford: Polity Press (*Contre-feux*. Paris: Raisons d'Agir).

Bourdieu, P. (1999/1993) *The Weight of the World: Social Suffering in Contemporary Society* (trans. P. Parkhurst Ferguson, S. Emanuel, J. Johnson, S. T. Waryn). Oxford: Polity Press.

Bourdieu, P. (2000/1997) *Pascalian Meditations*. Cambridge: Polity Press (*Méditations pascaliennes*. Paris: Seuil).

Bourdieu, P. (2001) *Firing Back: Against the Tyranny of the Market 2* (trans. L. Wacquant 2003). New York: The New Press.

Bourdieu, P. (2003) *Images d'Algérie*. Paris: Actes Sud.

Bourdieu, P (2005/2000) *The Social Structures of the Economy*. Cambridge: Polity Press (*Les structures sociales de l'economie*. Paris: Seuil).

Bourdieu, P. (2007/2004) *Sketch for a Self Analysis*. Cambridge: Polity Press (*Esquisse pour une auto-analyse*. Paris: Raisons d'Agir).

Bourdieu, P. (2008a/2002) *The Bachelors' Ball*. Oxford: Polity (*Le bal des célibataires. Cris de la société en Béarn*. Paris: Seuil).

Bourdieu, P. (eds T. Discepolo and F. Poupeau) (2008b/2002) *Interventions* (*Interventions (1961–2001)* Marseille: Agone).

Brooke, R. E. (2003) (ed.) *Rural Voices: Place-Conscious Education and the Teaching of Writing*. New York: Teachers College Press.

Boyle J. (1994) 'Styles of ethnography', in J. Morse (ed.) *Critical Issues in Qualitative Research Methods*. Thousand Oaks, CA: Sage Publications.

Brandt, D. and Clinton, K. (2002) 'Limits of the local: expanding perspectives on literacy as a social practice', *Journal of Literacy Research*, 34, 3, 337–56.

Brown, A. F. (2008) 'Constructing "race" through talk: a micro-ethnographic investigation of discussions of "race" among African American secondary students'. Unpublished doctoral dissertation, Vanderbilt University, Nashville, TN.

Brown, A. F. (2010) '"Just because I am a black male doesn't mean I am a rapper!": sociocultural dilemmas in using "rap" music as an educational tool in classrooms', in D. Alridge and J. Stewart (eds) *Hip Hop, History and Pedagogy*. Washington, DC: The Association for the Study of African American Life and History Press.

Bruner, J. (1986) *Actual Minds, Possible Worlds*. Cambridge, MA: Harvard University Press.

Burnard, P. , Craft, A. and Cremin, T. , with Duffy, B. , Hanson, R. , Keene, R. , Haynes, L. and Burns, D. (2006) 'Documenting possibility thinking: a journey of collaborative inquiry', *International Journal of Early Years Education,* 14, 3, 243–62.

Carspecken, P. F. (1996) *Critical Ethnography in Education*. New York: Routledge.

Carter, S. P. (2007) '"Inside thing": negotiating race and gender in a high school British literature classroom', in C. Clark and M. Blackburn (eds), *Research for Political Action and Social Change*. New York: Peter Lang.

Castel, R. and Passeron, J. C. (eds) (1967) *Education, développement et démocracie*. Paris, The Hague: Mouton.

Cazden, C. , John, V. and Hymes, D. (eds) (1972) *Functions of Language in the Classroom*. New York: Teachers College Press.

Champion, T. (2002) *Understanding Storytelling Among African-American Children: A Journey from Africa to America*. Mahwah, NJ: Erlbaum.

Chomsky, N. (1968) *Language and Mind*. New York: Harcourt, Brace and World.

Clifford, J. and Marcus, G. (eds) (1986) *Writing Culture: Poetics and Politics of Ethnography*. Berkeley, CA: University of California.

Coffield, F. (2000) *The Necessity of Informal Learning*. Bristol: Policy Press.

Cole, M. and Scribner, S. (1981) *The Psychology of Literacy*. Boston, MA: Harvard Educational Press.

Coles, G. (2001) 'Reading research and skills-emphasis instruction: forging "facts" to fit an explanation', in J. Larson, (ed.) *Literacy as Snake Oil: Beyond the Quick Fix*. New York: Peter Lang Publishing Inc. , pp. 27–44.

Collins, J. (1995) 'Literacy and literacies'. *Annual Review of Anthropology*, 24, 75.

Collins, J. and Blot, R. (2002) *Literacy and Literacies: Texts Power and Identity*. (Foreword by B. Street). Cambridge: Cambridge University Press.

Comaroff, J. and Comaroff, J. (1992) *Ethnography and the Historical Imagination*. Chicago, IL: University of Chicago Press.

Craft, A. (2000) *Creativity Across the Primary Curriculum: Framing and Developing Practice*. London: Routledge.

Craft, A. (2002) *Creativity and Early Years Education*. London: Continuum.

Curry, T. and Bloome, D. (1998) 'Learning to write by writing ethnography', in A. Egan-Robertson and D. Bloome (eds) *Students as Researchers of Culture and Language in Their Own Communities*. Cresskill, NJ: Hampton Press, pp. 37–58.

Darras, (1966) *Le partage des bénéfices, expansion et inégalités en France*. Paris: Editions de Minuit.

Delgado-Gaitan, C. and Trueba, H. (1985) 'Ethnographic study of participant structures in task completion: reinterpretation of "handicaps" in Mexican children'. *Learning Disability Quarterly*, 8, 1, 67–75.

DfES (1998) *National Literacy Strategy: A Framework for Teaching*. London: Department of Education and Skills.

Dewey, J. (1998/1899) *Experience and Education*. New York: Touchstone.

Dilthey, W. (1988/1923) *Introduction to the Human Sciences*. Detroit, MI: Wayne State University Press.

Dixson, A. D. (2005) 'Extending the metaphor: Notions of jazz in portraiture'. *Qualitative Inquiry*, 11, 1, 106–37.

Dixson, A. (2006) 'The fire this time: jazz, research and critical race theory', in A. D. Dixson and C. K. Rousseau (eds) *Critical Race Theory and Education: All God's Children Got a Song*. New York: Routledge.

Dixson, A. and Bloome, D. (2007) 'Jazz, critical race theories and the discourse analysis of literacy events in classrooms', in C. Clark and M. Blackburn (eds) *New Directions in Literacy Research for Political Action and Social Change*. New York: Peter Lang, pp. 29–52.

Dixson, A. D. and Rousseau, C. K. (2005) 'And we are still not saved: critical race theory in education ten years later', *Race Ethnicity and Education* 8, 1, 7–27.

Dubois, W. E. B. (1903/2000) *The Souls of Black Folk*. New York: Simon & Schuster.

Dubois, W. E. B. (2001) *The Education of Black People: Ten Critiques, 1906–1960*. New York: Monthly Review Press.

Dunkin, M. and Biddle, B. (1974) *The Study of Teaching*. Washington, DC: University Press of America.

Dyson, A. H. (1993) *Social Worlds of Children Learning to Write in an Urban Primary School*. New York: Teachers College Press.

Dyson, A. and Genishi, C. (2005) *On the Case: Approaches to Language and Literacy Research.* New York: Teachers College Press.

Eder, D. (1982) 'Differences in communicative styles across ability groups', in L. Wilkinson (ed.) *Communicating in The Classroom.* New York: Academic, pp. 245–64.

Edwards, D. and Mercer, N. (1987) *Common Knowledge.* London: Routledge.

Egan-Robertson, A. (1998) 'Learning about culture, language and power: understanding relationships among personhood, literacy practices and intertextuality'. *Journal of Literacy Research,* 30, 449–87.

Eisenhart, M. (2001) 'Changing conceptions of culture and ethnographic methodology', in V. Richardson (ed.) *Handbook of Research on Teaching,* 4th edn. Washington, DC: American Educational Research Association, pp. 209–25.

Eraut, M. (2000) 'Non-formal learning, implicit learning and tacit knowledge in professional work', in F. Coffield (ed.) *The Necessity of Informal Learning.* Bristol: Policy Press, pp. 12–31.

Erickson, F. (1982) 'Classroom discourse as improvisation: relationships between academic task structure and social participation structure in lessons', in L. Wilkinson (ed.) *Communicating in the Classroom.* New York: Academic Press, pp. 153–81.

Erickson, F. and Mohatt, G. (1982) 'Cultural organization of participation structures in two classrooms of Indian students', in G. Spindler (ed.) *Doing the Ethnography of Schooling: Educational Anthropology in Action.* Prospect Heights, IL: Waveland Press, Inc., pp. 132–75.

Erickson, F. and Shultz, J. (1977) 'When is a context?', *Newsletter of the Laboratory for Comparative Human Cognition,* 1, 2, 5–12.

Fairclough, N. (1992) *Discourse and Social Change.* Cambridge: Polity Press.

Farrell, T. J. (1977) 'Literacy, the basics, and all that jazz', *College English,* January: 443–59.

Finnegan, R. (1988) *Literacy and Orality.* Oxford: Blackwell.

Finnegan, R. (1999) 'Sociology/anthropology: theoretical issues in literacy' in D. Wagner, L. Venezky and B. Street (eds) *International Handbook of Literacy.* Boulder, CO: Westview Press.

Flanders, N. A. (1965) *Interactional Analysis in the Classroom: A Manual for Observers.* Ann Arbor, MI: University of Michigan, School of Education.

Fleming, M. (2008) *Arts in Education and Creativity: A Review of the Literature.* A Report for Creative Partnerships. London: Creativity, Culture and Education.

Flewitt, R. (2008) 'Multimodal literacies', in J. Marsh and E. Hallett (eds) *Desirable Literacies: Approaches to Language and Literacy in the Early Years.* London: Age, pp. 122–39.

Foley, D. E. (1994) *Learning Capitalist Culture Deep in the Heart of Texas.* Philadelphia, PA: University of Pennsylvania Press.

Foley, D. (2002) 'Critical ethnography: the reflexive turn'. *Qualitative Studies in Education,* 15, 5, 469–90.

Foster, M. (1995) 'Talking that talk: the language of control, curriculum and critique'. *Linguistics and Education,* 7, 2, 129–50.

Frank, C. and Bird, L. (2000) *Ethnographic Eyes: A Teacher's Guide to Classroom Observation.* Portsmouth, NH: Heinemann.

Freebody, P. (2006) 'Critical literacy' in R. Beach. J. Green, M. Kamil and T. Shanahan (eds) *Multidisciplinary Perspectives on Literacy Research.* Cresskills, NJ: Hampton Press.

Freire, P. (2000) *Pedagogy of the Oppressed,* 30th anniversary edn. New York: Continuum.

Freire, P. and Macedo, D. (1987) *Literacy: Reading the Word and the World.* South Hadley, MA: Bergin and Garvey Publishers.

Gay, G. and Banks, J. (2000) *Culturally Response Teaching.* New York: Teachers College Press.

Gebre, A. , Openjuru, G. , Rogers, A. and Street, B. (2009) *Everyday Literacies in Africa: Ethnographic Studies of Literacy and Numeracy Practices in Ethiopia.* Kampala: Fountains Press.

Gee, James P. (1990a) 'Orality and literacy: from the savage mind to ways with words', in *Social Linguistics and Literacy: Ideology in Discourses.* London: Falmer Press.

Gee, James P. (1990b) *Social Linguistics and Literacy: Ideology in Discourses*. London: Falmer Press.

Gee, James P. (2000) 'The new literacy studies: from "socially situated" to the work of the social', in D. Barton, M. Hamilton and R. Ivanic (eds) *Situated Literacies: Reading and Writing in Context*. London: Routledge, pp. 180–96.

Gee, James, P. (2001) 'Reading language abilities and semiotic resources: beyond limited perspectives on reading', in J. Larson (ed.) *Literacy as Snake Oil: Beyond the Quick Fix*. New York: Peter Lang Publishing Inc., pp. 7–26.

Geertz, C. (1973) *The Interpretation of Cultures: Selected Essays*. New York: Basic Books.

Geertz, C. (1983) *Local Knowledge: Further Essays in Interpretive Anthropology*. New York: Basic Books.

Gilmore, P. (1987) 'Sulking, stepping, and tracking: the effects of attitude assessment on access to literacy', in D. Bloome (ed.) *Literacy and Schooling*. Norwood, NJ: Ablex.

Gitlin, A., Seigel, M. and Boru, K. (1989) 'The politics of method: from leftist ethnography to educative research'. *Qualitative Studies in Education*, 2, 3, 273–353.

Goldman, S. and Bloome, D. (2005) 'Learning to construct and integrate', in A. F. Healy (ed.) *Experimental Cognitive Psychology and Its Applications*. Washington, DC: American Psychological Association, pp. 169–82.

Gonzalez, N., Moll, L. and Amanti C. (2005) (eds) *Funds of Knowledge: Theorizing Practices in Households, Communities and Classrooms*. Mahwah, NJ: Lawrence Erlbaum.

Goodenough, W. (1981) *Culture, Language, and Society*. Menlo Park, CA: Cummings.

Goodman, K. (1967) 'Reading: a psycholinguistic guessing game', *Journal of the Reading Specialist* 4: 126-135.

Goodman, K. (1996) *On Reading*. Toronto: Scholastic.

Goody, J. (ed.) (1968) *Literacy in Traditional Societies*. Cambridge: Cambridge University Press.

Goody, J. (1977) *The Domestication of the Savage Mind*. Cambridge: Cambridge University Press:

Gouldner, A. (1982) *Future of Intellectuals and the Rise of the New Class*. Oxford: Oxford University Press

Green, J. and Bloome, D. (1997) 'Ethnography and ethnographers of and in education: a situated perspective', in J. Flood, S. Heath and D. Lapp (eds) *A Handbook of Research on Teaching Literacy Through the Communicative and Visual Arts*. New York: Simon and Schuster, pp. 181–202.

Green, J. and Dixon, C. (1993) 'Talking knowledge into being: discursive and social practices in classrooms'. *Linguistics and Education*, 5, 3–4, 231–39.

Green, J. and Wallat, C. (eds) (1981) *Ethnography and Language in Educational Settings*. Norwood, NJ: Ablex Publishing Corp.

Grenfell, M. (1996) 'Bourdieu and the initial training of modern language teachers', *British Educational Research Journal*, 22, 3, 287-303.

Grenfell, M. (1999) 'Language: the construction of an object of research', in M. Grenfell and M. Kelly (eds) *Pierre Bourdieu: Language, Culture and Society*. Bern: Peter Lang.

Grenfell, M. (2004) *Pierre Bourdieu: Agent Provocateur*. London: Continuum.

Grenfell, M. (2006) 'Bourdieu in the field: from the Béarn to Algeria – a timely response', *French Cultural Studies*, 17, 2, 223–40.

Grenfell, M (2007) *Pierre Bourdieu: Education and Training*. London: Continuum.

Grenfell, M. (ed.) (2008) *Pierre Bourdieu: Key Concepts*. Stocksfield: Acumen.

Grenfell, M. (2009) 'Bourdieu, language and literacy'. *Reading Research Quarterly*, 44, 4, 438–48.

Grenfell, M. (2010) *Pierre Bourdieu: Language and Linguistics*. London: Continuum.

Grenfell, M. and Hardy, C. (2007) *Art Rules: Bourdieu and the Visual Arts*. London: Berg.

Grenfell, M. and James, D. (1998) *Bourdieu and Education: Acts of Practical Theory*. London: Falmer Press.

Guilmet, G. M. (1979) 'Instructor reaction to verbal and nonverbal-visual styles: an example of Navajo and Caucasian children'. *Anthropology and Education Quarterly,* 10, 4, 254–66.

Gumperz, J. (1986) *Discourse Strategies*. New York: Cambridge University Press.

Gumperz, J. and Hymes, D. (eds) (1972) *Directions in Sociolinguistics: The Ethnography of Communication*. New York: Holt, Rinehart & Winston.

Gutiérrez, K. (2008) 'Developing a sociocritical literacy in the third space'. *Reading Research Quarterly,* 43, 2, 148–64.

Gutiérrez, K. D. , Rymes, B. and Larson, J. (1995) 'Script, counterscript, and underlife in the classroom: James Brown versus Brown v. Board of Education'. *Harvard Educational Review,* 65, 445–71.

Habermas, Jürgen (1987) *Lifeworld and System: A Critique of Functionalist Reason,* vol. 2 of *Theory of Communicative Action* (trans. Thomas McCarthy). Boston: Beacon Press (originally published in German in 1981).

Habermas, Jürgen (1989) *The Structural Transformation of the Public Sphere: An Inquiry into a Category of Bourgeois Society* (trans. Thomas Burger with the assistance of Frederick Lawrence). Cambridge, MA: MIT Press (originally published in German in 1962).

Hager, P. (2001) 'Lifelong learning and the contribution of informal learning', in D. Aspin, J. Chapman, M. Hatton and Y. Sawano (eds), *International Handbook of Lifelong Learning*. Dordrecht: Kluwer Academic Publishers, pp. 79–92.

Hagood, M. (2009) *New Literacies: Learning from Youth in Out-of-school Contexts*. New York: Peter Lang.

Hammersley, M. (1990) *Classroom Ethnography: Empirical and Methodological Essays*. Milton Keynes: Open University Press.

Hammersley, M. and Atkinson, P. (1983) *Ethnography: Principles and Practices*. London: Tavistock.

Hardy, C. (2010) 'Bourdieu and the art of education', Unpublished doctoral dissertation, University of Southampton.

Hardy, C. (2011) 'Language and education', in M. Grenfell (ed.) *Bourdieu, Language and Linguistics*. London: Continuum International Publishing Group.

Hargreaves, D (1967) *Social Relations in the Secondary School*. London: Routledge and Kegan Paul.

Hargreaves, D. (1993) 'Whatever happened to symbolic interactionism?' in M. Hammersley (ed.) *Controversies in Classroom Research*. Milton Keynes: Open University Press.

Harrison, C. (2002) *The National Strategy for English at Key Stage 3: Roots and Research*. London: DfES.

Heath, S. (1982a) 'Ethnography in education: defining the essential', in P. Gilmore and A. Glatthorn (eds) *Children In and Out of School*. Washington, DC: Center for Applied Linguistics, pp. 33–58.

Heath, S. (1982b) 'What no bedtime story means: narrative skills at home and at school'. *Language in Society,* 11, 1, 49–76.

Heath, S. (1983) *Ways with Words: Language, Life, and Work in Communities and Classrooms*. Cambridge: Cambridge University Press.

Heath, S. and Street, B. (2008) *On Ethnography*. New York: Teachers College Press.

Heath, S. B and Wolf, S. (2004) *Visual Learning in the Community School*. London: Creative Partnerships.

Heller, M. (2008) 'Bourdieu and literacy education', in J. Albright and A. Luke (eds) *Pierre Bourdieu and Literacy Education*. New York: Routledge.

Heras, A. I. (1993) 'The construction of understanding in a sixth grade bilingual classroom'. *Linguistics and Education,* 5, 3 and 4, 275–300.

Hilliard, A. G., III (1978) 'Equal educational opportunity and quality education'. *Anthropology and Education Quarterly*, 9, 2, 110–26.

Hilliard, A. G., III (1999/2000) '"Race", identity, hegemony, and education: what do we need to know now?' *Rethinking Schools*, Winter, 4–6.

Hinton, S. E. (1967) *The Outsiders*. New York: Puffin Books.

Hirsch, E. D. (2006) *The Knowledge Deficit: Closing the Shocking Education Gap for American Children*. New York: Houghton Mifflin.

Hirsch, E. D, Kett, J. and Trefil, J. (2002) *Cultural Literacy: What Every American Needs to Know*. New York: Houghton Mifflin.

Hirst, P. H. (1967) 'Educational theory', in J. W Tibble (ed.) *The Study of Education*. London: Routledge and Kegan Paul.

Holland, D., Lachicotte, W., Jr., Skinner, D. and Cain, C. (1998) *Identity and Agency in Cultural Worlds*. Cambridge, MA: Harvard University Press.

Homer (1996) *The Odyssey* (trans. Robert Fagles). New York: Penguin Books.

hooks, b. (1994) *Teaching to Transgress: Education as the Practice of Freedom*. London: Routledge.

Hornberger, N. (ed.) (2002) *The Continua of Biliteracy: A Framework for Educational policy, Research and Practice in Multiple Setting* (Afterword by B. Street). Bristol: Multilingual Matters.

Hughes, C. (1992) 'Ethnography'. Word-process? Product? Promise?', *Qualitative Health Research*, 4, 439–50.

Hull, G. and Schultz, K. (2002) *School's Out: Bridging Out-of-School Literacies with Classroom Practice*. New York: Teachers College Press.

Hunt, I. (1976) *The Lottery Rose*. New York: Berkley Jam Books.

Hurdley, R. (2006) 'Dismantling mantelpieces: narrating identities and materializing culture in the home'. *Sociology*, 40, 4, 707–13.

Hymes, D. (1967) 'On communicative competence', in J. B. Pride and J. Holmes (eds) *Sociolinguistics*. Harmondsworth: Penguin.

Hymes, D. (1974) *The Foundations of Sociolinguistics: Sociolinguistic Ethnography*. Philadelphia, PA: University of Pennsylvania Press.

Hymes, D. (1982) 'What is ethnography?' in P. Gilmore and A. Glatthorn (eds) *Children In and Out of School*. Washington, DC: Center for Applied Linguistics, pp. 21–32.

Janks, H. (2000) 'Domination, access, diversity and design: a synthesis for critical literacy education'. *Educational Review*, 52, 2, 175–86.

Jeffrey, B. and Craft, A. (2006) 'Creative learning and possibility thinking' in B. Jeffrey (ed.) (2006) *Creative Learning Practices: European Experiences*. London: Tufnell Press pp. 47-62.

Jeffrey, B. and Craft. A. (2004) 'Creative teaching and teaching for creativity: Distinctions and relationships'. *Educational Studies*, 30, 1, 77–87.

Johnson, N. B. (1980) 'The material culture of public school classrooms: the symbolic integration of local schools and national culture'. *Anthropology and Education Quarterly*, 9, 3, 173–90.

Jones, K. (2009) *Culture and Creative Learning: A Literature Review*. London: Creativity, Culture and Education.

Jordan, C. (1985) 'Translating culture: From ethnographic information to educational program'. *Anthropology and Education Quarterly*, 16, 2, 105–23.

Kalman, J. (1999) *Writing on the Plaza: Mediated Literacy Practices Among Scribes and Clients in Mexico City*. Cresskill, NJ: Hampton Press.

Kantor, R., Elgas, P. and Fernie, D. (1993) 'Cultural knowledge and social competence within a preschool peer culture group'. *Early Childhood Research Quarterly*, 8, 125–47.

Kantor, R., Green, J., Bradley, M. and Lin, L. (1992) 'The construction of schooled discourse repertoires: an interaction sociolinguistic perspective on learning to talk in preschool'. *Linguistics and Education*, 4, 131–72.

Keddie, N. (1971) 'Classroom knowledge' in M.Young (ed.) *Knowledge and Control*. London: Collier-Macmillan.

Kinloch, V. (2009) *Harlem on Our Minds: Place, Race, and the Literacies of Urban Youth*. New York: Teachers College Press.

Kintsch, W. (1994) 'Text comprehension, memory, and learning', *American Psychologist, 49*, 294–303.

Kress, G. (1993) 'Against arbitrariness: the social production of the sign as a foundational issue in critical discourse analysis', *Discourse and Society, 4*, 2, 169–91.

Kress, G. (1997) *Before Writing: Rethinking the paths to literacy*. London: Routledge.

Kress, G. (2010) *Multimodality: A Social Semiotic Approach to Contemporary Communications*. London: Routledge.

Kress, G. and Leeuwen, T. van (1996) *Reading Images: The Grammar of Visual Design*. London: Routledge.

Kroeber, A. L. and Kluckhorn, C. (1952) *Culture: A Critical Review of Concepts and Definitions*. New York: Random House.

Kulick, D. and Stroud, C. 1993 'Conceptions and uses of literacy in a Papua New Guinean village' in B. Street (ed.) *Cross Cultural Approaches to Literacy*. Cambridge: Cambridge University Press, pp. 30–61.

Lacey, C. (1970) *Hightown Grammar: The School as a Social System*. Manchester: Manchester University Press.

Ladson-Billings, G. (1994) *The Dreamkeepers: Successful Teachers of African American children*. San Francisco, CA: Jossey-Bass.

Ladson-Billings, G. (1999) 'Just what is critical race theory and what's it doing in a *nice* field like education?', in L. Parker, D. Deyhle and S. Villenas (eds), *Race Is . . . Race Isn't: Critical Race Theory and Qualitative Studies in Education*. Boulder, CO: Westview, pp. 7–30.

Laing, R. D. (1971) *The Politics of the Family and Other Essays*. London: Tavistock Publications.

Laing, R. D., Phillipson, H. and Lee, A. R. (1966) *Interpersonal Perception: A Theory and a Method of Research*. London: Tavistock.

Larson, J. (ed.) (2001) *Literacy as Snake Oil: Beyond the Quick Fix*. New York: Peter Lang Publishing Inc.

Lee, C. (2001) '"Is October brown Chinese?" A cultural modeling activity system for underachieving students', *American Educational Research Journal, 38*, 1, 97–141.

Lee, C., Spencer, M. and Harpalani, V. (2003) '"Every shut eye ain't sleep": studying how people live culturally', *Educational Researcher, 32*, 5, 6–13.

Leeuwen, T. van (2008) *Discourse and Practice: New Tools for Critical Discourse Analysis*. New York: Oxford University Press.

Lefstein, A. (2003) 'Teaching and reading between technical rationality and practical Reason in the National Literacy Strategy' Paper for discussion in RWLL, King's College London.

Lefstein, A. (2008) 'Changing classroom practice through the English National Literacy Strategy: a micro-interactional perspective', *American Educational Research Journal, 45*, 3, 701–37.

Le Roux, B. and Rouanet, H (2010) *Geometric Data Analysis: From Correspondence Analysis to Structured Data Analysis*. Dordrecht: Kluwer Academic Publishers.

Lévi-Strauss, C. (1961) *The Savage Mind*. London: Weidenfeld and Nicholson.

Lévi-Strauss, C. (1963) *Structural Anthropology*. New York: Basic Books.

Lomotey, K. (1990) *Going to School: The African-American Experience*. Albany, NY: State University of New York Press.

Lomotey, K. (1992) 'Independent Black institutions'. *Journal of Negro Education, 61*, 4, 455–62.

Luke, A. and Carrington, V. (2002) 'Globalisation, literacy, curriculum practice', in R. Fisher, M. Lewis and G. Brooks (eds) *Language and Literacy in Action*. London: Routledge/Falmer.

Luke, A. and Freebody, P. (2002) 'Reading as a social practice' in S. Muspratt, A. Luke and P. Freebody (eds) *Constructing Critical Literacies*. New York: Hampton Press.

Maddox, B. (2001) 'Literacy and the market: the economic uses of literacy among the peasantry in northwest Bangladesh' in B. Street (ed.) *Literacy and Development: Ethnographic Perspectives* London: Routledge.

Martin-Jones, M. and Jones, K. (2000) (eds) *Multilingual Literacies: Comparative Perspectives on Research and Practice*. Amsterdam: John Benjamins.

Maybin, J. (1993) *Language and Literacy in Social Practice*. Milton Keynes: Open University Press.

Maybin, J. (2000) 'The New Literacy Studies: context, intertextuality and discourse' in D. Barton, M. Hamilton and R. Ivanic (eds) *Situated Literacies: Reading and Writing in Context*. London: Routledge.

Maybin, J. (2007) 'Literacy under and over the desk: oppositions and heterogeneity'. *Language and Education*, 21, 6, 515–30.

McCarty, T. L., Wallace, S., Lynch, R. H. and Benally, A. (1991) 'Classroom inquiry and Navajo learning styles: a call for reassessment'. *Anthropology and Educational Quarterly*, 22, 1, 42–59.

McCollum, P. (1989) 'Turn-allocation in lessons with North American and Puerto Rican students: a comparative study'. *Anthropology and Education Quarterly*, 20, 2, 133–58.

McDermott, R. (1977) 'Social relations as contexts for learning in school'. *Harvard Educational Review*, 47, 2, 198–213.

McDermott, R. P., Gospodinoff, K. and Aron, J. (1978) 'Criteria for an ethnographically adequate description of concerted activities and their contexts'. *Semiotics*, 24, 246–75.

McDermott, R. and Varenne, H. (2006) 'Reconstructing culture in educational research', in G. Spindler and L. Hammond (eds) *Innovations in Educational Ethnography: Theory, methods and Results*. Mahwah, NJ: Erlbaum Associates, pp. 3–32.

Meacham, S. J. (2001) 'Vygotsky and the blues: re-reading cultural connections and conceptual development'. *Theory into Practice*, 40, 3, 190–97.

Mead, M. (2001/1930) *Growing Up in New Guinea: A Comparative Study of Primitive Education*. New York: Harper Perennial Classics.

Mehan, H. (1980) 'The competent student'. *Anthropology and Education Quarterly*, 11, 3, 131–52.

Mercado, C. (1998) 'When young people from marginalized communities enter the world of ethnographic research – scribing, planning. reflecting and sharing', in A. Egan-Robertson and D. Bloome (eds) *Students as Researchers of Culture and Language in Their Own Communities*. Cresskill, NJ: Hampton.

Mercer, N. (1981) *Language in School and Community*. London: Edward Arnold.

Mercer, N. (1995) *The Guided Construction of Knowledge: Talk amongst Teachers and Learners*. Clevedon: Multilingual Matters

Michaels, S. (1981) '"Sharing time": children's narrative styles and differential access to literacy'. *Language in Society*, 10, 3, 423–42.

Michaels, S. (1986) 'Narrative presentations: an oral preparation for literacy with first graders', in J. Gumperz (ed.) *The Social Construction of Literacy*. Cambridge: Cambridge University Press.

Mitchell, C. (1984) 'Case studies', in R. Ellen (ed.) *Ethnographic Research: A Guide to General Conduct*. New York: Academic Press, pp. 237–41.

Moll, L., Amanti, C., Neff, D. and Gonzalez N. (1992) 'Funds of knowledge for teaching: using a qualitative approach to connect homes and classrooms'. *Theory into practice*, 31, 2, 131–41.

Moll, L. and Diaz, R. (1987) 'Teaching writing as communication: the use of ethnographic findings in classroom practice', in D. Bloome (ed.) *Literacy and Schooling*. Norwood, NJ: Ablex Publishing Corporation.

Morris, J. E. (2003) What does Africa have to do with being African-American? A micro-ethnographic analysis of a middle school inquiry unit on Africa. *Anthropology and Education Quarterly*, 34, 3, 255–76.

Mukherjee, A. and Vasanta, D. (eds) (2003) *Practice and Research in Literacy*. London and Delhi: Sage Publications.

Musgrave, P. (1966) *The Sociology of Education*. London: Methuen.

Nabi, R., Rogers, A. and Street, B. (2009) *Hidden Literacies: Ethnographic Case Studies of Literacy and Numeracy from Pakistan*. Uppingham: Uppingham Press.

National Advisory Committee on Creative and Cultural Education (NACCCE) (1999) *All Our Futures: Creativity, Culture and Education*. London: Department for Education and Employment.

National Commission on Excellence in Education (1983) *A Nation at Risk: The Imperative for Educational Reform*. Washington, DC: Department of Education.

NRP (National Reading Panel Report) (2000) *Teaching Children to Read: An Evidence Based Assessment of the Scientific Research Literature on Reading and its Implications for Reading Instruction*. Bethesda, MA: National Institute of Health.

Nelson, M., Hull, G. and Roche-Smith, J. (2008) 'Challenges of multimedia self-presentation'. *Written Communication*, 25, 4, 415–44.

Neuman, S. & Celano, D. (2001) Access to print in low-income and middle-income communities: An ecological study of four neighbourhoods. *Reading Research Quarterly*. 36(1), 8-26.

Nichols, S. Nixon, H. and Rowsell, J. (2009) Shaping the identities and practices in relation to early years literacy', *Literacy*, 43, 2, 65–74.

Nirantar (2007) *Exploring the Everyday: Ethnographic Approaches to Literacy and numeracy*. Delhi: Nirantar. Available www.nirantar.org

No Child Left Behind (2002) Available www2.ed.gov/policy/elsec/leg.html.

O'Connor, D. J. (1958) 'An introduction to the philosophy of education', *The Journal of Philosophy*, 56, 19, 766–70.

Olson, D. (1977) From utterance to text: the bias of language in speech and writing. *Harvard Educational Review*, 47, 257–81.

Olson, D. (1994) *The World on Paper*. Cambridge: Cambridge University Press.

Pahl, K. (2002a) 'Ephemera, mess and miscellaneous piles: texts and practices in families'. *Journal of Early Childhood Literacy*, 2, 145–66.

Pahl, K. (2002b) 'Habitus and the home: texts and practices in families'. *Ways of Knowing Journal*, 2, 1, May, 45–53.

Pahl, K. (2003) 'Children's text making at home: transforming meaning across modes', in C. Jewitt and G. Kress (eds) *Multimodal Literacy*. New York: Peter Lang Publishers, pp. 139–54.

Pahl, K. (2004) 'Narratives, artifacts and cultural identities: an ethnographic study of communicative practices in homes', *Linguistics and Education*, 15, 4, 339–58.

Pahl, K. (2007) 'Creativity in events and practices: a lens for understanding children's multimodal texts'. *Literacy*, 41, 2, 86–9.

Pahl, K. (2009) 'Interactions, intersections and improvisations: Studying the multimodal texts and classroom talk of six to seven year olds', *Journal of Early Childhood Literacy*, 9, 2, 188–210.

Pahl, K. (2010) 'Improvisations and transformations across modes: the case of a classroom multimodal box project', in J. Swann, R. Pope and R. Carter (eds) *Creativity, Language, Literature: The State of the Art*. London: Palgrave Macmillan.

Pahl, K. and Rowsell, J. (2010) *Artifactual Literacy: Every Object Tells A Story*. New York: Teachers College Press.

Panowsky, E. (1957) *Gothic Architecture and Scholasticism*. New York: Meridan.

Papen, U. (2005) *Adult Literacy as Social Practice*. London: Routledge.

Pelto, P. and Pelto, G. (1978) *Anthropological Research: The Structure of Inquiry*. New York: Cambridge University Press.

Phillips, S. (1972) 'Participant structures and communicative competence: Warm Springs children in classroom and community', in C. Cazden, V. John and D. Hymes (eds) *Functions of Language in the Classroom*. New York: Teachers College Press, pp. 370–94.

Phillips, S. (1983) *Invisible Culture: Communication in Classroom and Community on the Warm Springs Indian Reservation*. New York: Longman.

Polyani, M. (1998/58) *Personal Knowledge: Towards a Post Critical Philosophy*. London: Routledge.

Popper, K. R. (1967) *The Logic of Scientific Discovery*. London: Hutchinson.

Prinsloo, M. and Breier, M. (1996) *The Social Uses of Literacy*. Amsterdam: Benjamins/Sacched.

Quinn, N. (2005) *Finding Culture in Talk*. New York: Palgrave Macmillan.

Rampton, B. (2007) 'Neo-Hymesian linguistic ethnography in the UK', *Journal of Sociolinguistics*, 11, 5, 584–608.

Reay, D. and Lucey, H. (2000) '"I don't really like it here but I don't want to be anywhere else": children and inner city council estates', *Antipode*. 32, 4, 410–28.

Robinson, J. L. (1987) 'Literacy in society: readers and writers in the worlds of discourse', in D. Bloome (ed.) *Literacy and Schooling*. Norwood, NJ: Ablex, pp. 327–53.

Robinson-Pant, A. (1997) 'Why eat green cucumbers at the time of dying?', *The Link between Women's Literacy and Development*, Hamburg: Unesco.

Rogers, A. (1992) *Adults Learning for Development*. London: Cassell Educational Ltd.

Rogers, A. (1994) *Using Literacy: A New Approach to Post Literacy Materials*. London: DFID.

Rogers, A. (2002) *Teaching Adults* Buckingham: Open University Press.

Rogers, A. (2003) *What is the Difference? A New Critique of Adult Learning and Teaching*. Leicester: NIACE.

Rogers, A. (2004) *Non-formal Education: Flexible Schooling or Participatory Education?* Dordrecht and Hong Kong: Kluwer and Hong Kong University Press.

Rogers, A. (2008) 'Informal learning and literacy', in B. Street and N. Hornberger (eds) *Encyclopedia of Language and Education*, 2nd edn. New York: Springer Press, pp. 133–144.

Rogers, T. (2010) *Theorizing Media Productions as Complex Literacy Performances Among Youth in and Out of School*.

Rosenfeld-Halverson, E., Lowenhaupt, R., Gibbons, D. and Bass, M. (2009) 'Conceptualizing identity in youth media arts organizations: a comparative case study', *E-Learning*, 6, 1, 23–41.

Rowsell, J. (2009) 'Artifactual literacy', in M. Hagood (ed.) *New Literacies: Learning from Youth in Out-of-School and In-School Contexts*. New York: Routledge, pp. 65–80.

Rowsell, J and Burke, A. (2008) 'Reading by design: two case studies of digital reading practices', *Journal of Adolescent and Adult Literacy*, 53, 2, 106–18.

Rowsell, J. and Pahl, K. (2007) 'Sedimented identities in texts: instances of practice'. *Reading Research Quarterly*, 42, 3, 388–401.

Safford, K. and Barrs, M. (2005) *Creativity and Literacy – Many Routes to Meaning: Children's Language and Literacy Learning In Creative Arts Projects*. London: CLPE.

Saussure, F. de (1966/1916) *Course in General Linguistics*, trans. W. Baskin. New York: McGraw-Hill.

Schoenhals, M. (1994) 'Encouraging talk in Chinese classrooms'. *Anthropology and Education Quarterly*, 25, 4, 399–412.

Schon, D. (1983) *Reflective Practitioner.* New York: Basic Books.

Scott, J. , Straker, D. and Katz, L. (eds) (2008) *Affirming Students' Right to Their Own Language.* New York: Routledge.

Scribner, S. and Cole, M. (1978) 'Unpackaging literacy'. *Social Science Information*, 17, 1, 19–39.

Scribner, S. and Cole, M. (1981) *The Psychology of Literacy.* Cambridge, MA: Harvard University Press.

Sefton-Green, J. (2007) 'Evaluating creative partnerships: the challenge of defining impact', in *This Much we Know…Thinkpiece: The Challenge of Defining Impact.* London: Creative Partnerships.

Sennet, R. (2008) *The Craftsman.* London: Penguin.

Sheridan M. P. and Rowsell, J. (2010) *Design Literacies: Learning and Innovation in Digital Environments.* London: Routledge.

Sinclair, J. and Coulthard, R. (1975) *Towards an Analysis of Discourse: The Language Used by Teachers and Pupils.* Oxford: Oxford University Press.

Slavin, R. (2002) 'Evidence-based education policies: transforming educational practice and research'. *Educational Researcher*, 31, 7, 15–21.

Smith, F. (1971) *Understanding Reading.* New York: Holt, Rinehart & Winston.

Snow, C. E. , Burns, S. M. and Griffin, P. ,(eds) (1998) *Preventing Reading Difficulties in Young Children.* Committee on the Prevention of Reading Difficulties in Young Children. Washington, DC: National Academy Press.

Solorzano, D. and Yasso, T. (2001) 'From racial stereotyping and deficit discourse toward a critical race theory in teacher education', *Multicultural Education*, 9, 1, 2–8.

Spindler, G. and Spindler, L. (1987a) 'Issues and applications in ethnographic methods', in G. Spindler and L. Spindler (eds) *Interpretive Ethnography of Education at Home and Abroad.* Hillsdale, NJ: Lawrence Erlbaum Associates, pp. 1–10.

Spindler, G. and Spindler, L. (eds) (1987b) *Interpretive Ethnography of Education: At Home and Abroad.* Hillsdale, NJ: Lawrence Erlbaum Associates.

Steadman, A. (1983) *The Tidy House: Little Girls' Writing.* London: Virago.

Street, B. (1984) *Literacy in Theory and Practice.* New York: Cambridge University Press.

Street, B. (1985) *Literacy in Theory and Practice.* Cambridge: Cambridge University Press.

Street, B. (1988) 'Literacy practices and literacy myths', in R. Saljo (ed.) *The Written Word: Studies in Literate Thought and Action,* Language and Communication Series, vol. 23. Heidelberg: Springer-Verlag, pp. 59–72.

Street, B. (1993) 'Culture is a verb', in D. Graddol (ed.) *Language and Culture.* Clevedon: Multilingual Matters/British Association of Applied Linguists.

Street, B. (1995) *Social Literacies.* London: Longman.

Street, B. (1996) 'Preface', in M. Prinsloo and M. Breier (1996) *The Social Uses of Literacy.* Amsterdam: Benjamins/Sacched.

Street, B. (1997) 'The implications of the New Literacy Studies for literacy education'. *English in Education*, 31, 3, 26-39.

Street, B. (2000) 'Literacy events and literacy practices' in M. Martin-Jones and K. Jones (eds) *Multilingual Literacies: Comparative Perspectives on Research and Practice.* Amsterdam: John Benjamins, pp. 17–29.

Street, B. (ed.) (2001) *Literacy and Development: Ethnographic Perspectives.* London: Routledge.

Street, B. (2003) 'What's "new" in New Literacy Studies? Critical approaches to literacy in theory and practice'. *Current Issues in Comparative Education*, 5, 3, 1–14.

Street, B. (ed.) (2005) *Literacies Across Educational Contexts.* Philadelphia, PA: Caslon Publishing.

Street, B. (2009) 'Multiple literacies and multi-literacies', in R. Beard, J. Riley, D. Myhill and M. Nystrand (eds) *The Sage Handbook of Writing Development.* London: Sage.

Street, B. and Street, J. (1991) 'The schooling of literacy', in D. Barton and R. Ivanic (eds) *Writing in the Community*. London: Sage, pp. 143-66.

Street, B. , Baker, D. and Rogers, A. (2006) 'Adult teachers as researchers: ethnographic approaches to numeracy and literacy as social practices in South Asia' *Convergence*, 39, 1, 31–44.

Street, B. and Lefstein, A. (2007) *Literacy: An Advanced Resource Book* London: Routledge.

Street, B. , Lefstein, A. and Pahl, K. (2007) 'The National Literacy Strategy, England: contradictions of control and creativity' in J. Larson (ed.) *Literacy as Snake Oil 2*. Portsmouth, NH: Peter Lang.

Street, J. and Street, B. (1991) 'The schooling of literacy', in D. Barton and R. Ivanic (eds) *Writing in the Community*. Thousand Oaks, CA: Sage.

Street, B.V. (2008) 'New lLiteracies, new times: developments in literacy studies', in B.V. Street and N. Hornberger (eds) *Encyclopedia of Language and Education*, Volume 2: Literacy. New York: Springer, pp. 3-14.

Sutton-Smith, B. (1997) *The Ambiguity of Play*. Cambridge, MA: Harvard University Press.

Thomson, P. and Hall, C. (2008) '"Opportunities missed and/or thwarted?" "Funds of knowledge" meet the English National Curriculum'. *Curriculum Journal*, 19, 2, 87–103.

Todorov, T. (1988) *Literature and its Theorists: A Personal View of Twentieth Century Criticism*. London: Taylor and Francis.

Torres, M. (1998) 'Celebrations and letters home: research as an ongoing conversation among students, parents, and teacher', in A. Egan-Robertson and D. Bloome (eds) *Students as Researchers of Culture and Language in Their Own Communities*. Cresskill, NJ: Hampton Press, pp. 59–68.

Trueba, H. (1994) 'Reflections on alternative visions of schooling'. *Anthropology and Education Quarterly*, 25, 3, 376–93.

Trueba, H. , Guthrie, G. P. and Au, K. (eds) (1981) *Culture and the Bilingual classroom: Studies in Classroom Ethnography*. Rowley, MA: Newbury House Publisher.

Unesco (2006) 'Defining and conceptualising literacy' in *EFA Global Monitoring Report*. Paris: Unesco, pp. 148–59.

Valencia, R. (ed.) (1997) *The Evolution of Deficit Thinking: Educational Thought and Practice*. London: Falmer.

Vandenberg, D. (1974) 'Phenomenology and educational research', in D. E. Denton (ed.) *Existentialism and Phenomenology in Education*. New York: Teachers College Press.

Vasudevan, L. (2009) 'Performing new geographies of teaching and learning'. *English Education*, 41, 4, 356–74.

Veblen, T. (1915) *The Theory of the Leisure Class: A Theory of Institutions*. New York: Macmillan.

Volosinov, V. (1929/1973 trans.) *Marxism and the Philosophy of Language*, trans. L. Matejka and I. Titunik. Cambridge, MA: Harvard University Press.

Vygotsky, L. (1962) *Thought and Language*. Cambridge, MA: MIT Press.

Vygotsky, L. (1978) *Mind in Society: The Development of Higher Psychological Processes*. London: Harvard University Press.

Vygotsky, L. (1987) *The Collected Works of L. S. Vygotsky, Volume 1: The Problems of General Psychology* (eds R. Rieber and A. Carton; trans. N. Minick). New York: Plenum Press.

Warwick, D. and Littlejohn, G. (1992) *Coal, Capital and Culture: A Sociological Analysis of Mining Communities in West Yorkshire*. London: Routledge.

Werner, O. and Schoepfle, G. M. (1987) *Systematic Fieldwork: Ethnographic Analysis and Data Management*. London: Sage Publications.

Wilkinson, L. (ed.) (1982) *Communicating in the Classroom*. New York: Academic Press.

Willams, C. H. (2006) 'You gotta reach "Em": an African-American teacher's multiple literacies Approach'. *Theory into Practice,* 45, 4, 346–51.

Williams, R. (1989) *Resources of Hope: Culture, Democracy, Socialism.* London:Verso.

Willis, P. (1998) 'Notes on common culture: towards a cultural policy for grounded aesthetics'. *Cultural Policy,* 4, 2, 413–30.

Wolcott, H. F. (1994*) Transforming Qualitative Data: Description, Analysis and Interpretation.* London: Sage.

Woodson, C. G. (1933/2000) *The Mis-education of the Negro.* Trenton, NJ: First Africa World Press.

Yeager, B. , Floriani, A. and Green, J. (1998) 'Learning to see learning in the classroom', in A. Egan-Robertson and D. Bloome (eds) *Students as Researchers of Culture and Language in Their Own Communities.* Cresskill, NJ: Hampton Press.

Yin, R. K. (ed.) (1984) *Case Study Research: Design and Methods* (Applied Social Research Methods) London: Sage Publications.

Young, M. F. D. (ed.) 1971 *Knowledge and Control: New Directions for the Sociology of Education.* London: Collier Macmillan.

Zaharlick, A. and Green, J. (1991) 'Ethnographic research' in J. Flood, D. Lapp and J. Squire (eds) *Handbook of Research on Teaching the English Language Arts.* New York: Macmillan, pp. 205–25.

INDEX

Bold page numbers indicate figures, *italic* numbers indicate tables.

academic discourse 56–63
Adams, M. 33
adult literacy programmes 34–5
African-Americans: and the dominant narrative 139–41; language of, use of 141–3, 170; relationship with Africa 16
agency, learner 96–7, 107–8
Althusser, Louis 51
analytic induction 39
artefactual English: LETTER project 87. *See also* digital story production, study of
assumptions about literacy 32–3
Atkinson, P. 25
Au, K. 23
autonomous model of literacy 28–9, 41–2, 138, 158

Baker, D.A. 47
Banajai, S. 92
Barnes, Douglas 61
Bartlett, L. 44, 86
Bassey, M. 186
batch production of students 137–8
Bean, Sally. *See* infant school study, North England
behaviourism/structuralism collision in research 154–5
Bernstein, Basil 61
biliteracy 45
Black Church 147

Bloome, D. 19, 22, 39, 115, 138–9, 142, 169, 180–1
Blot, R. 43
Borko, H. 21
Bourdieu, Pierre: breaks from empirical knowledge 65, 178–9, **179**; construction of the research object 183–5, 187; and culture, traditions in understanding of 64–5; and data collection 187–9; elusive nature of language 187–8; *field:* 3 step approach 190–2; defined 66; and forms of knowledge 163–4; LETTER project 84–5, **86,** 164–6; on globalization 130; *habitus (See also* fractal *habitus);* adjustment of with life changes 112; conversion to scientific 195; defined 66; and forms of knowledge 163–4; as fuzzy 182–3; improvising on 118, **119**; LETTER project 84–5, **86,** 164–6; linguistic 66–7; modes as fractures of 121; researcher's, impact on research 176; shifts in 111; *homo academicus,* characterisation of 57–8; infant school study, North England 107–8; invisible structures, analysis of 189; and language and education: academic discourse 56–63; antecedents 51–2; critical position on 62–3; culture as form of 58–9; early work on education/culture 52–3; formative experiences 52; inequality in education 53–6; influences on 51–2; provenance of language 62–3; reconceptualisation of language 68; sociology of 52; and the

LETTER project 84–7, **85, 86**; linguistic market 67; master patterns, culture as providing 59; and multimodality 117–21; participant objectification 194–5; personal issues and research 176; relational thinking 69, 109; scholastic fallacy 166, 193; social, economic and cultural capital 56–7; spiritual exercise, research as 189; structural relations focus 156; and study of literacy 86; as suggesting conspiracy 173; theory of practice 65–6, 161, 171, 172, 173, 177–82, 185–6; use of terms developed by 69; view of literacy 68; words, warning about 183–4. *See also* synthesis of Bourdieu, ethnography and NLS
Brandt, D. 41–3
Breier, M. 37
Brian's film **127, 128,** *129*
Brown, A.F. 169, 180–1
Burnard, P. 93

capital: individuals/groups using to define selves 181; linguistic 67; social, economic and cultural 56–7, 67, 87, 130–1
Carter, S.P. 15
cases studies, Bourdieusian approach to 186–7
Caspian's film 122–3, **124,** *129*
Celano, D. 115–16
chairs, desks and 17
Chomskyan revolution 154
classroom ethnography: as alternative to process-product studies 8; classrooms: broader context to 10–11; defining 12, 13–14; desks and chairs 17; language and culture in 20–1; meanings of for teachers and students 18; students in 14–16; what happens in? 18–20; what is in? 17–18; who is in? 14–16; competent students 21–2; contextualized knowledge base of 25; and cultural (mis)communication 22–5; culture, definition of 10; as distinct from qualitative methods 9–10; distinguished from Critical Ethnography 19; ethnography: defined 9; as distinct from ethnographic 11; focus on in book 8; and fractured *habitus* 129–30; goal of 12; and individuals's perspectives and locations 7–8; and links with outside structures 172; as political stance 88–9; reflexive component of 25; as research practice 7
classroom language ethnography: 3 step approach 190–2; characteristics of as

Bourdieusian 195–6; meaning of 174–5; reflexivity 193–5
classrooms: broader context to 10–11; defining 12, 13–14; desks and chairs 17; language and culture in 20–1; meanings of for teachers and students 18; naturalized absences 16; online 15; procedural display 22; race in 15; rules of 21; as separate from everyday life 13–14; students in 14–16; what happens in? 18–20; what is in? 17–18; who is in? 14–16
Clifford, J. 153
Clinton, K. 41–3
cognition and literacy 30–3
Cole, Michael 30–1
Collard, Paul 94
Collins, J. 43
Common Knowledge (Edwards and Mercer) 155
communication and culture 22–5
community experiences, use of in education 45–8
competent students 21–2
construction of the research object 183–5, 187
Coulthard, R. 61
Craft, Anna 92–3, 108
Creative Partnerships 91–4. *See also* infant school study, North England
creativity, versions of 106–8
Critical Ethnography, distinguished from classroom ethnography 19
cultural capital 56–7, 67, 87, 130–1
cultural production agents, students and teacher as 142–3
culture: and Bourdieu's work on education 53; definition 10; as form of language and education 58–9; and inequality in education 55–6; and language in classrooms 20–1; (mis)communication due to 22–5; paradox concerned with differences in 170; and structure 64–5; traditions in understanding of 64–5
curriculum: cultural miscommunication as spur to 22–5; science as authority for 138

data collection 187–9
desks and chairs 17
Dewey, J. 45–6
different eye, seeing through. *See* infant school study, North England
differentiation-polarisation theory 177
digital story production, study of: active participation of researchers 116–17;

background to project 112–13; Bourdieu
and multimodality 117–21; Brian's
film 126–7, **127**, **128**, *129*; Caspian's
film 122–3, **124**, *129*; critique, teaching
students to 131; ecological ethnographic
perspective 115–16; Esme's film 123–4,
129; ethnographic perspective 169; fractal
habitus 119–21, 168–9; case studies of
122, 122–8, **123**, **125**, **127**, **128**, *129*;
images, types of 121; improvising on
habitus 118, **119**; inequality in access to
multimodality 130–1; Manuel's film
125–6, *129*; methodology 113–15;
modes as fractures of *habitus* 121;
multimodality, use of in students' films
111; participants 112–13; Patsy's film
124–5, **125**, *129*; repositioning of
students 111; and theory 167–9
Dilthey, W. 186
discourse, academic 56–63
discourse genres: 'a good effect' 99; 'we
decided that' 97
distance and proximity 40–1
distant literacies 42–3
Dixson, A. 142
Dyson, A. 122

ecological ethnographic perspective 115–16
economic capital 56
education: application of New Literacy
Studies to 45–8; defining 13–14;
history and development of research in
1–2; inequality in 53–6; as knowledge
accumulation 13–14; language of 56–63;
research and ethnography 152–4; as
separate from everyday life 13–14. *See
also* Bourdieu, Pierre
Edwards, D. 62, 155
Eisenhart, M. 21
emic/etic approach 9, 16, 41
empirical knowledge, Bourdieu's breaks from
65, 178–9, **179**
empirical research 187–9
enumerative induction 39
environment of the classroom 17–18
Esme's film 123–4, *129*
ethnographic perspective: adoption of in
LETTER project 75–8; digital story
production, study of 169; as distinct from
ethnographic tools 11, 39; as distinct
from ethnography 11; ecological 115–
16; LETTER project 164; on literacy
research 37–41
ethnography: defined 9; difficulties defining
152, 185; as distinct from ethnographic

11, 39; and educational research 152–4;
meaning of 174–5. *See also* synthesis of
Bourdieu, ethnography and NLS
ethnology 185
events, literacy 36–7, 37–41

Farrell, T.J. 30
field: 3 step approach 190–2; defined 66; and
forms of knowledge 163–4; LETTER
project 84–5, **86**, 164–6; and linguistic
habitus 67
field analysis 185–92
figured worlds 44–5, 86
film-making. *See* digital story production,
study of
Firing Back: Against the Tyranny of the Market
(Bourdieu) 130
Flanders, N.A. 61
Flewitt, R. 91
Foley, D.E. 10
Foucault, Michel 51
fractal *habitus:* case studies of digital story
production **122**, 122–8, **123**, **125**, **127**,
128, *129*; example of 110–11; theory of
119–21
fractured *habitus* and classroom ethnography
129–30
Freebody, P. 44
furniture in the classroom 17

Gebre, A. 35, 78, 356
Gee, J.P. 44
Geertz, C. 18
Genishi, C. 122
globalization, Bourdieu on 130
Goodman, K. 34
Goody, J. 30
Greene, Judith 39, 115
Grenfell, M. 50, 65, 66, 89, 90, 93, 132, 190,
192, 195
Gutierrez, K.D. 23–4

Habermas, Jürgen 158–9
habitus: adjustment of with life changes 112;
conversion to scientific 195; defined
66; and forms of knowledge 163–4; as
fuzzy 182–3; improvising on 118, **119**;
LETTER project 84–5, **86**, 164–6;
linguistic 66–7; modes as fractures of
121; researcher's, impact on research 176;
shifts in 111. *See also* fractal *habitus*
Hall, C. 93
Hammersley, M. 8–9, 177
Hardy, C. 93, 156, 172, 190
Heath, S. 15

Heath, Shirley Brice 36
Heller, M. 156
Hirst, Paul 153
Hirst, P.H. 157
Holland, D. 44, 86
home experiences, use of in education 45–8
homo academicus, Bourdieu's characterisation
of 57–8
Hornberger, N. 45
Hull, G. 45–6, 111
Hurdley, Rachel 117
hybrid literacy practices 43
Hymes, D. 154, 175
Hymes, Del 153

identity, sedimented 120
ideological model of literacy 29, 34
illiterate people, danger of studying only 77
images, types of 121
inequality in education 53–6
infant school study, North England:
Bourdieusian analysis 107–8; box
creation 96; context for 91–4; creativity,
versions of 106–8; discourse genres: 'a
good effect' 99; 'we decided that' 97;
image of researcher **99**; methodology
94–6; New Literacy Studies 91; and
theory 166–7; Year 1 themes: 'A good
effect' 97–9; contrasting definitions of
creativity 101; 'Funds of knowledge'
100–1, 107; 'Unexpected outcome'
100, 101; 'We decided on' 96–7; Year 2
themes: material and narrative problem
solving 106; narrative connected to the
boxes 102–5; 'Unexpected outcome'
101–2
inference, positivistic and logical 186
Intellectual Field and Creative Project
(Bourdieu) 61
intertextual reading. *See* reading as
intertextual practice, study of
invisible structures, analysis of 189

Janks, H. 44
jazz conversational style 141–3, 170
Jeffery, Bob 92–3, 108
Johnson, N.B. 17
Jones, K. 92, 108

Keddie, N. 155
Keddie, Nell 61
knowledge: accumulation of, education as
13–14; empirical, Bourdieu's breaks from
65, 178–9, **179**; forms of 159–64, **161,**
170, 178–9, **179**

Knowledge and Control (Young) 61, 62, 156
Kress, G. 91, 121
Kulick, D. 43

Ladson-Billings, G. 23
language: African-American, use of in
classroom 141–3, 170; and culture in
classrooms 20–1; of education 56–63;
elusive nature of 187–8; history and
development of research in 1–2; meaning
of 175; structuralism/behaviourism
collision 154–5. *See also* Bourdieu, Pierre
langue 51
Larson, Joanne 48
Le déracinement (Bourdieu) 52–3
learning: creative 93–4; and literacy 33–5
Learning for Empowerment Through
Training in Ethnographic Research
(LETTER) project: abandonment of
own position, need for 76–7; adoption
of ethnographic perspective 75–8; aim
of 78; and Bourdieu 84–7, **85, 86**;
and *habitus* 164–6; identifying existing
practices, difficulty of 74–5; measuring
crops **79**; motive for 73–4; origins of
73–4; Part 1 78–81; Part 2 81–4, **82, 83,**
turtle and fish story 76–7
Leeuwen, T. van 121
Lefstein, A. 97
Les héritiers (Bourdieu) 54–5, 62
LETTER. *See* Learning for Empowerment
Through Training in Ethnographic-style
Research (LETTER) project
Lévi-Strauss, C. 32, 51, 64
linguistic ethnography 94, 167
linguistic *habitus* 66–7
linguistic market 67
literacy: autonomous model of 28–9,
41–2; Bourdieusian view of 68; and
cognition 30–3; contested nature of 184;
ethnographic perspective on research
37–41; events and practices 36–7, 36–41;
hybrid practices: 43; ideological model
of 29, 34; and learning 33–5; multiple
literacies 35–6; myths of 32–3; policy in
UK and US 48; scientific approach 48;
shifts in perception of 2–3; study of and
Bourdieu 86
Literacy as Snake Oil (Larson) 48
Literacy in Theory and Practice (Street) 29
local focus of NLS, criticism of 39, 41–4
Logic of Practice, The (Bourdieu) 118
logical inference 186
Lucey, H. 108

Manuel's film 125–6, *129*
Marcus, G. 153
master patterns, culture as providing 59
material culture of the classroom 17–18
material objects, use of in LETTER project 87
Maybin, J. 43–4
McDermott, R.P. 21, 25
Mehan, H. 21
Mercer, N. 62, 155
miscommunication, cultural 22–5
Mitchell, Clyde 39, 122, 186
modes as fractures of *habitus* 121
Morris, J.E. 16
multimodality: and Bourdieu 117–21; case studies of fractal *habitus* **122,** 122–8, **123, 125, 127, 128,** *129*; inequality in access to 130–1; modes as fractures of *habitus* 121; use of in students' films 111
multiple literacies 35–6, 40
myths of literacy 32–3

naturalized absences 16
Nelson, M. 111
Neuman, S. 115–16
New Literacy Studies: and broader social theory 44–5; cognition and literacy 30–3; dichotomy between social and cognitive 172; educational applications 45–8; ethnographic approach of 28; ethnographic perspectives on literacy research 37–41; future for 49; ideological model of literacy 29, 34; infant school study, North England 91; international context 47; as leading to better research 173; learning and literacy 33–5; literacy as contextually defined 160; literacy as social practice 27; local focus, criticism of 39, 41–4, 46; meaning of 'new' in 27–8; multiple literacies 35–6; numeracy practices 47; policy in UK and US 48; reflexivity 40; as suggesting conspiracy 173; theoretical concerns 41–5. *See also* Learning for Empowerment Through Training in Ethnographic Research project (LETTER); synthesis of Bourdieu, ethnography and NLS
Nichols, S. 115
Nirantar: motive for LETTER project 73–4; training provided by 80–1
numeracy practices 47

objectification of the objectifying subject 194–5

O'Connor, D.J. 153
Olson, David 13, 32–3
online classrooms 15
Openjuru, George 77
Outline to a Theory of Practice (Bourdieu) 178

Pahl, K. 44, 107
Panowsky, Erwin 58
Parker, David 92
parole 51
participant objectification 194–5
participation structures 22, 23
participatory competency 21–2
Patsy's film 124–5, **125,** *129*
personal issues in research 176
Phillips, S. 22
Philosophical Investigations (Wittgenstein) 51–2
photography, Bourdieu on 117
policy in UK and US 48
political stance, classroom ethnography as 88–9
Polyani, M. 159
Popper, Karl 153, 157
positivistic inference 186
post-modernism 51, 185
practice of theory 170–3
practices, literacy 36–7, 37–41
Prinsloo, M. 37
procedural display 22
process-product studies, classroom ethnography as alternative to 8
professorial language 59
provenance of language 62–3
proximity and distance 40–1
Puro, P. 22

qualitative methods as distinct from classroom ethnography 9–10

race: in classrooms 15; and the dominant narrative 139–41
reading as intertextual practice, study of: African-American language, use of 141–3; batch production of students 137–8; challenge to school reading practice 141–2; context for study 133–4; conversation excerpts 134–7; jazz conversational style 141–3; methodology, theory and ideology 133; race and the dominant narrative 139–41; redemption and change discourse 147; school reading practice 138–9; science as curriculum authority 138; as space for self-reflection and ownership 143–7; teacher/students

as cultural production agents
142–3; theory 169–70
Reay, D. 108
redemption and change discourse 147
reflexivity: as component of classroom
ethnography 25; different
eye, seeing with 166–7; and
identification of existing practices
74–5; implication for classroom
language ethnography 193–5; of
postmodernism 185; proximity and
distance 40–1
relational thinking 69, 109, 184, 186
research in language and education,
history and development of 1–2
research object, construction of the
183–5, 187
Rhetorics of Creativity (Banajai) 92
Robinson, J.L. 12
Rogers, A. 34, 74–5
Rogers, Theresa 111
Rowsell, J. 84–5, 87, 107, 167–8
rules of the classrooms 21

Saussure, Ferdinand de 51, 154
scaffolding 155
scholastic fallacy 166, 193
school study. *See* infant school study,
North England
Schultz, K. 45–6
science: -based approach to literacy 48;
as curriculum authority 138, 169
Scribner, Sylvia 30–1
sedimented identity 120
Sefton-Green, Julian 92, 94
self-reflection and ownership, reading as
space for 143–7
signifier/signified 51
Sinclair, J. 61
Smith-Roche, J. 111
social capital 56
social class 180
social constructivism 155
social context as broader context to
classrooms 10–11
social structure in classrooms 18–19
Social Uses of Literacy, The (Prinsloo and
Breier) 37
socialization to classroom rules 21–2
Spindler, G. 13
Spindler, L. 13
spiritual exercise, research as 189
Steadman, A. 108
story time 18–19
Street, B. 2, 10, 19, 29, 47, 91, 141, 155

Stroud, C. 43
structural knowledge 178
structuralism 51
structuralism/behaviourism collision in
research 154–5
structure and culture 64–5
student language 59
students: African-American, and the
dominant narrative 139–41; batch
production of 137–8; in classrooms
14–16; competent 21–2; as
ethnographers 24; and teacher as
cultural production agents 142–3
synthesis of Bourdieu, ethnography and
NLS: classroom language ethnography
174–5, 182–3; construction of the
research object 183–5; conversion to
scientific *habitus* 195; differentiation-
polarisation theory 177; field analysis
185–92; need for 175–6; participant
objectification 194–5; personal issues
in research 176; reflexivity 193–5;
theory and practice 176; theory of
practice 177–82
Systems of Education and Systems of Thought
(Bourdieu) 61

tables and chairs 17
tacit knowledge 159–60, 161–2, 170
Teaching Literacy Balancing Perspectives
(Adams) 33
themes from infant school study, North
England: 'A good effect' 97–9;
contrasting definitions of creativity
101; 'Funds of knowledge' 100–1;
material and narrative problem
solving 106; narrative connected
to the boxes 102–5; 'Unexpected
outcome' 100, 101–2; 'We decided
on' 96–7. *See also* infant school study,
North England
Theodorou, E. 22
theory: digital story production, study
of 167–9; infant school study, North
England 166–7; LETTER project
164–6; and practice 176; practice of
170–3; reading as intertextual practice,
study of 169–70; types of 157–64,
158, 159, 161, 162
theory of practice 161, 171, 172, 173,
177–82, 185–6
thick description 18–19
third space construct 23–4
Thompson, P. 93
Todorov, T. 40

Tomlin, A. 47
tools, ethnographic 11, 39
turtle and fish story 76–7

United States, development of classroom
    ethnography in 7–8

Varenne, H. 25
Vygotsky, Lev 62, 155

Waquant, L. 182, 190
Weight of the World, The (Bourdieu) 189
Wittgenstein, Ludwig 51–2
words, Bourdieu's warning about 183–4

Young, Michael 62

Zone of Proximal Development 62, 155